I0901079

IMAGES
of America

LIBERAL AND SEWARD COUNTY

ON THE COVER: Photographer F.M. Steele caught this drama being played out in the Rock Island Railroad cut west of Kismet. Lee Larrabee, a well-known prankster, is searching through the pockets of one of his "victims." (Courtesy Seward County Historical Society.)

IMAGES
of America

LIBERAL AND SEWARD COUNTY

Lidia Hook-Gray

ARCADIA
PUBLISHING

Copyright © 2011 by Lidia Hook-Gray
ISBN 978-0-7385-8279-5

Published by Arcadia Publishing
Charleston, South Carolina

Printed in the United States of America

Library of Congress Control Number: 2011931576

For all general information, please contact Arcadia Publishing:
Telephone 843-853-2070
Fax 843-853-0044
E-mail sales@arcadiapublishing.com
For customer service and orders:
Toll-Free 1-888-313-2665

Visit us on the Internet at www.arcadiapublishing.com

This book is dedicated to the hardy men and women pioneers who braved the early days.

CONTENTS

Acknowledgments

Seward County families had the generous thought to donate their family photographs to the Seward County Historical Society. A giant thank you to the Bangs, Hayes, Feather, Peacock, Tomacelli, Vance, Larrabee, Baughman, and Chance families and others for giving a glimpse into our history. Many images from these families were loaned to this project by the Seward County Historical Society, so a special thanks to director JoAnne Mansell for her trust. Also, nothing would have been accomplished without the help of Dr. Jack Jacobs and Gary Classen for their talented technical assistance. Thank you also to Ted Gerstle at Arcadia Publishing, Harriet Glick and Jim Bert of the Mid-America Air Museum, Debbie King and her grandmother Mary Brewington, Bob Killingsworth, Marlin and Dorothy Meisenheimer, Ellen Pelton, Mary Brooks, Jim Andrews, Gary Krueger, Bruce Jackson, Nancy Sherbert at the Kansas State Historical Society, Kathy Immell, Bob Immell, Dessie Jenkins, Ken Thompson for his pancake expertise, and my mom, Maria Hook. Also, thank you to my husband, Wayne, who never complained about the dining room being commandeered by photographs and who gives me encouragement no matter what I do. Lastly, a thank you to my dad, George Hook, who made me listen to all those great old stories.

INTRODUCTION

From towns by the name of Beer City to Liberal and from county seat wars to pancake races, Seward County, Kansas, has a diversified history of unusual happenings accented by tough, dedicated people. In 1820, anything west of the 100th meridian was considered uninhabitable. This publicity, written so many years ago, is an image the high plains still fights today. However, to the Kiowa, Comanche, and Cheyenne following the massive bison herds, the area was a paradise.

The Kansas Nebraska Act of 1854 opened western Kansas and neighboring states for settlement, but it was not until railroad access into Dodge City and Garden City 90 miles to the north did anyone venture south across the sand hills. In the late 1870s, cattlemen driving their herds up from the Texas Panhandle to the railroad discovered the nutritious buffalo grass along the Cimarron River and its intermittent tributaries. Thomas Price, a successful rancher from Emporia, Kansas, decided the Cimarron River range would make perfect headquarters. Working for Price, Robert Davies established his own ranch, which is still operated by the Davies family today. He was not alone. The Lemerts, Larrabees, Adams, Lights, and Smiths were among those families with early ranching interests that still live in Seward County today.

Meanwhile, to the south, S.S. Rogers dug a 90-foot-deep well by hand to supply water for his homestead. Word of mouth from thirsty travelers soon had a trail beat into the prairie past Rogers's home. When asked what was owed for the water, Rogers would always reply, "Nuthin'." To that, the thankful visitors would say, "That's mighty liberal!" By 1885, Rogers added a general store and post office. Of course, it was called Liberal.

Back to the north along the Cimarron River, a new burg by the name of Fargo Springs was formed. Springfield came into being three miles north of Fargo. Each town vied to become the county seat, which typically ensured a town's survival. Both towns were inhabited by passionate, loyal folks. The townspeople became embroiled in an insult-tossing, gun-wielding fuss that changed the county seat from one town to the other. During this time, the Rock Island Railroad decided to build towards the southern portion of the county. The railroad installed track across the Cimarron to Liberal where it deadheaded for 13 years. Now, with the railroad advantage, Liberal competed to become the county seat. An election was held, and Springfield (at the time the county seat) got 13 votes, Liberal, 132. With nothing more to argue about, Springfield and Fargo Springs faded away within a few years.

The boom was on in Liberal. Within a few years, the population had grown to 8,000 folks. Not every one of those residents was of sterling character. Adjacent to the county line in No Man's Land, what is now the Oklahoma Panhandle, a town was formed entirely of bars, gaming houses, and brothels. Beer City was the name, and fun was the game. Characters such as Pussy Cat Nell and self-appointed Sheriff Lew "Brushy" Bush were known inhabitants who made the place rock. Beer City had brawls, several murders, and plenty of drinking, all of which raised the hackles of the decent ladies of Liberal. By 1901, Beer City was nothing but foam on the prairie after the Women's Christian Temperance Union started holding church services there, and the Rock Island Railroad built farther southwest.

Several other burgs sprang up during this period of growth. Tyrone was actually located at the state line between Liberal and No Man's Land. This small town served the Rock Island by having wide wing chutes that would capture the longhorn cattle being driven up from the Texas Panhandle to the railhead. Loading day was special, as the girls from Liberal would ride on top of the boxcars to Tyrone to watch the cowboys load 'em up. Arkalon came into being in 1886 as the crossing point of the Cimarron River for the Rock Island Railroad. After many bridge washouts and a horrible train wreck in 1938, Arkalon was abandoned by the railroad and almost everyone else when the colossal Sampson of the Cimarron River Bridge was constructed downstream. Kismet was also a railroad baby, first founded in 1886. The origin of the name has always been questioned, but the town has survived nicely throughout the years.

Liberal and Seward County have weathered booms and busts with a spirit borne of those first pioneers. Agriculture has been key for the area economy, but when the depression and droughts of the 1930s hit, the county was right in the middle of the Dust Bowl. Contrary to thought, the area lost few people. Residents who survived that era have always said they did not leave simply because they could not afford to. After the dust quit blowing and World War II began, Liberal was chosen as a site for the training of B-24 bomber pilots. A construction crew began the Liberal Army Air Base in 1943, and within two years, over 4,400 officer pilots were ready to defend our country. By the time the pilots, commanders, trainers, maintenance people, and their families came, Liberal's population almost doubled. Oil and gas had been discovered earlier, but during the 1950s and 1960s, this industry took hold, causing Liberal and the county to grow even more.

From 1886 to 1960, Seward County has been home to Glenn L. Martin, Minnie Grinstead, Earnest Boles, John Baughman, Alice Nichols, Rod and Virginia Leete, Jack Vickers, and many other pioneers who have given Liberal and Seward County its unique personality. The images in this book are a cross section of well-known and not-so-well-known people and happenings, collected to give the reader an idea of their very own place and time.

One

We Pioneers

1886–1900

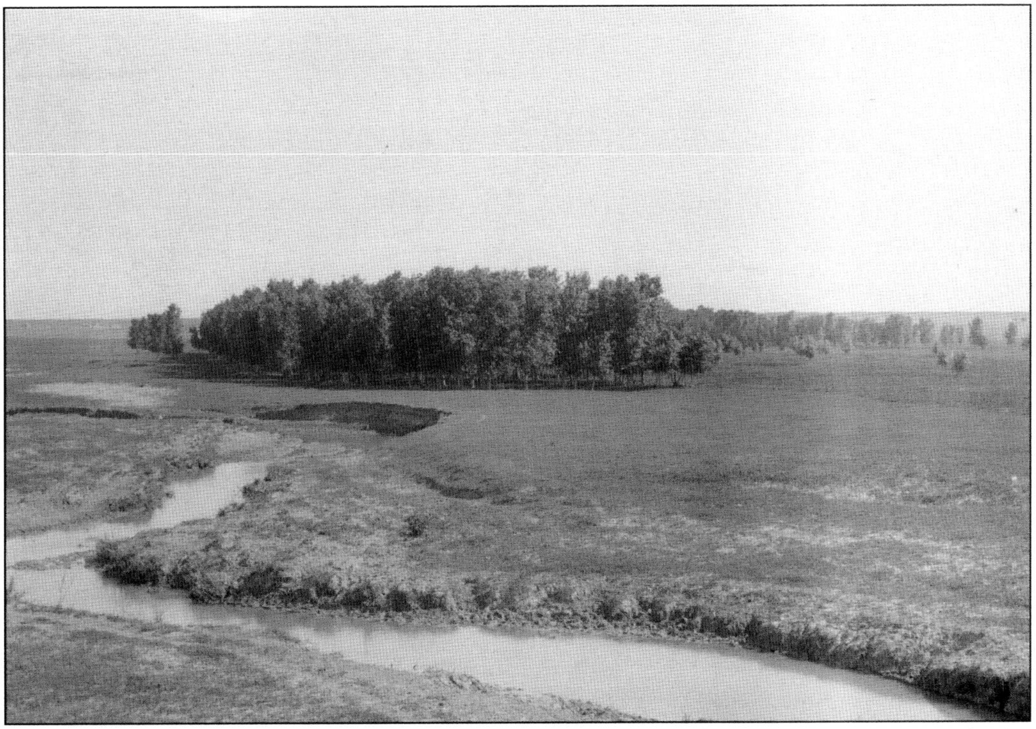

According to Bob Davies, whose father, Robert, came to Seward County in 1881 to ranch, the Cimarron was a deep, narrow stream with little timber, except for the occasional cottonwood grove. Cattlemen favored the Cimarron River valley and its free range. A devastating blizzard in 1886 killed most of the ranchers' free-range cattle. (Courtesy of Seward County Historical Society.)

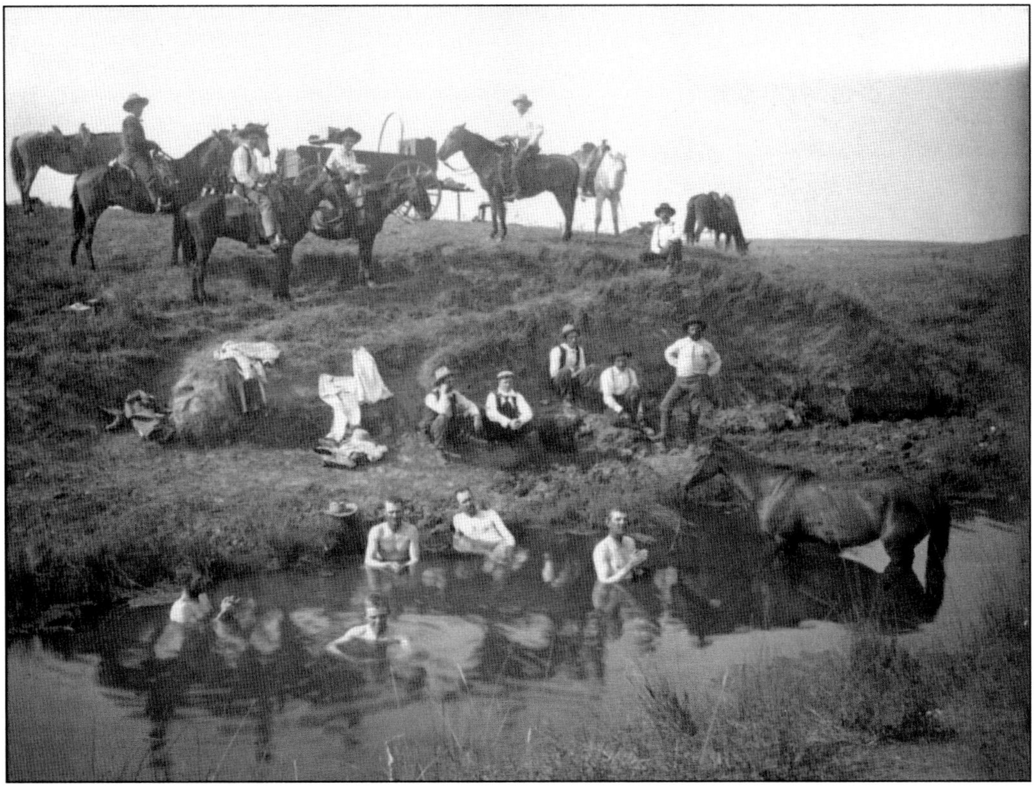

Freighters, buffalo hunters, and cattlemen followed the old trails blazed first by the Kiowa, Cheyenne, Apache, and Comanche tribes, who had followed trails worn by the bison and other plains animals that knew where reliable water sources could be found. These cowboys and a horse not only found enough water for drinking, but also enough for a Saturday night bath. (F.M. Steele photograph; courtesy Seward County Historical Society.)

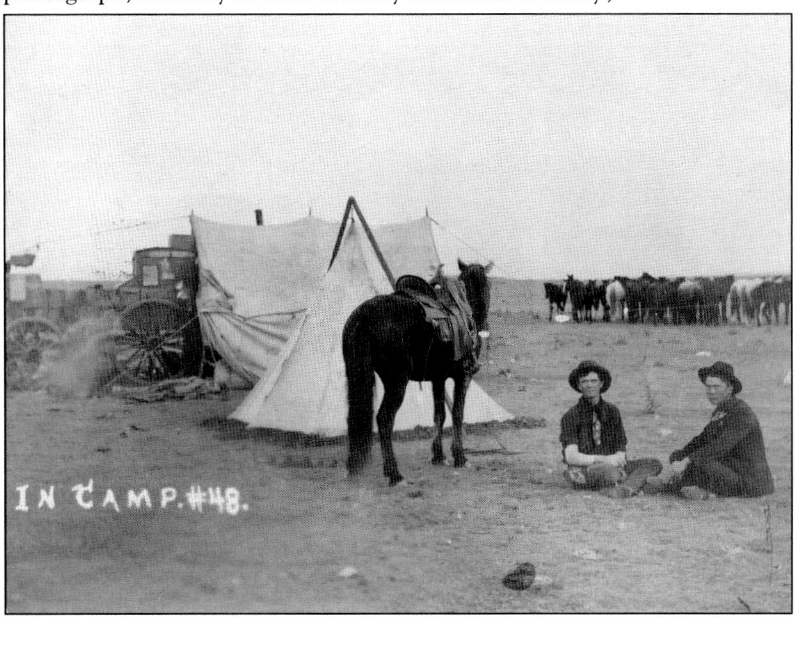

Cowboys were vital to the first ranches that settled in early Seward County. Available grass, live water, and a good camp of cowboys were essential for the success of the cattlemen. These two ranch hands, identified only as Jess (left) and George, have joined the chuck wagon and horse remuda near present-day Liberal.

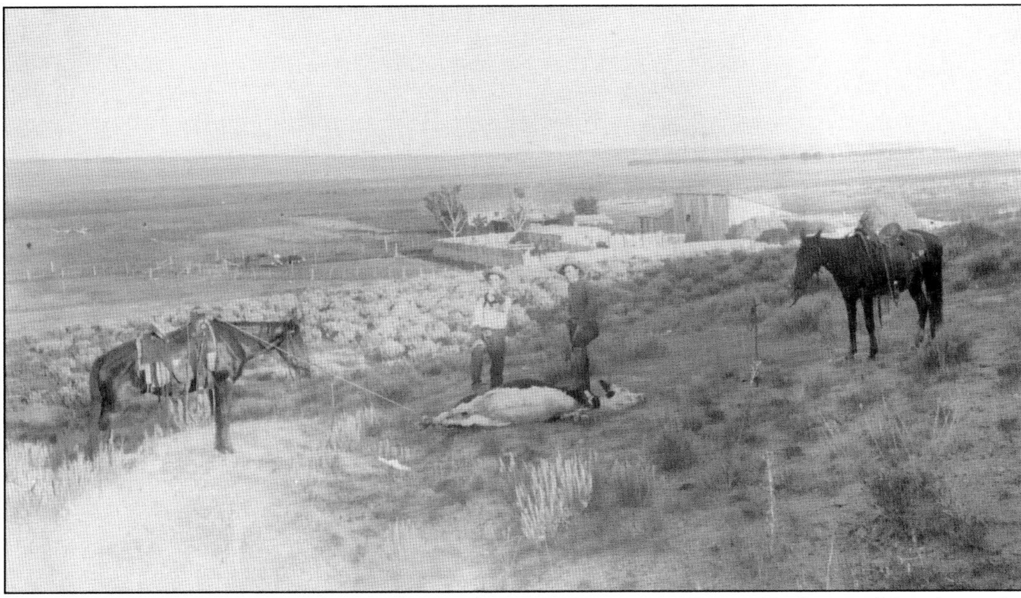

Cattle were not the only stock raised in early Seward County. Hervey Forbes and family settled in 1879 on the north bank of the Cimarron River, one mile from the future town of Arkalon. Here, the Forbes raised sheep until 1887, when they converted to cattle. In 1881, Forbes built the first wood frame home in Seward County. This image, taken in 1897, shows the Forbes ranch house and outbuildings in the background and neighbors Lee Larrabee (in white shirt) and Con Jackson. (F.M. Steele photograph; courtesy Seward County Historical Society.)

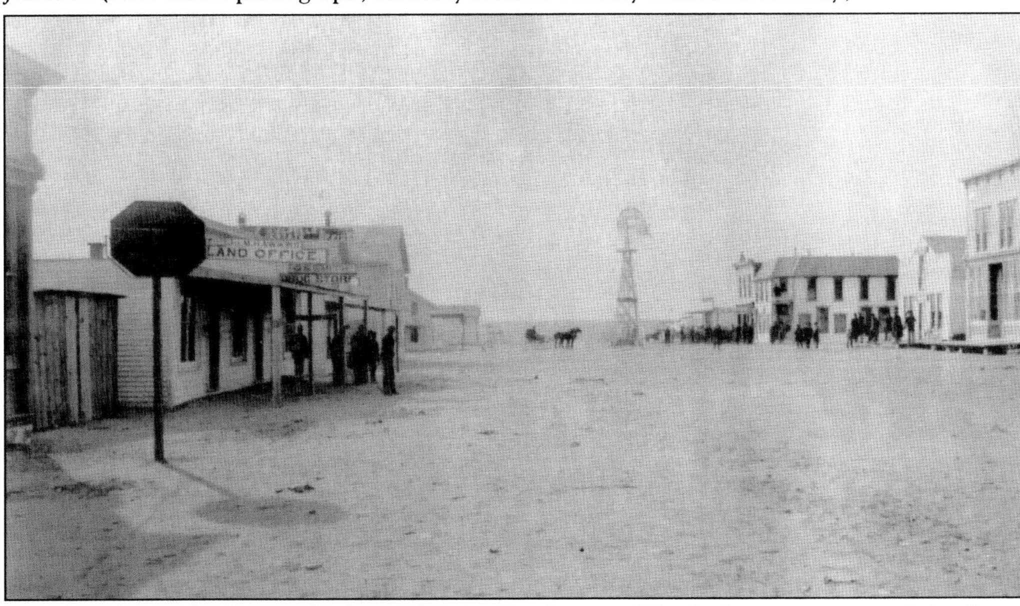

After the blizzard of 1886, the high plains turned green. The lush prairie tempted the future homesteaders and town developers with its natural abundance, there for the taking. Behind the old trading stop of Adobe and the fledgling Eureka Springs and Seward Center, the town of Fargo Springs was surveyed in May 1885. Established on the north side of the Cimarron River, Fargo Springs was named the second county seat in August 1886. The town boomed and quickly reached a population of 500. (Courtesy of Gary Krueger.)

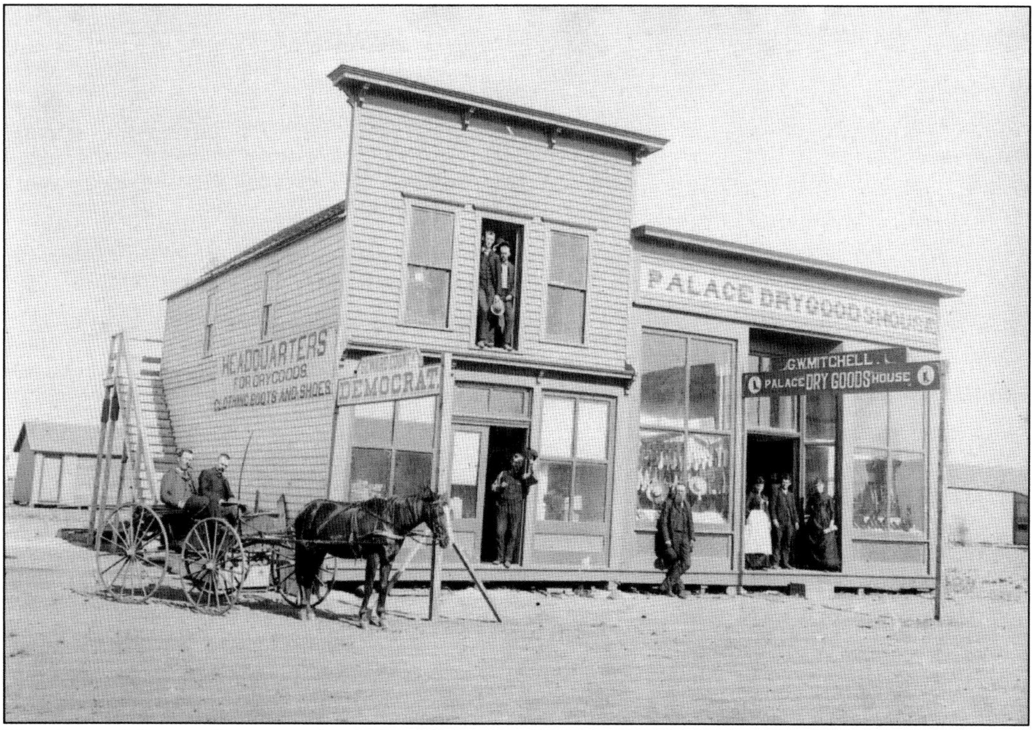

The *Seward County Democrat* began publishing in Fargo Springs on April 30, 1886. W.C. Rankin was the first editor. Shortly after the issue appeared, Lisle Lane became editor, assisted by her sister Kate Lane. Their brother Had Lane came to Seward County in 1879 with the US 7th Cavalry. The *Seward County Democrat* published until 1888. The adjacent Palace Dry Goods House had a nice display of shoes, hats, and socks. (Courtesy of Gary Krueger.)

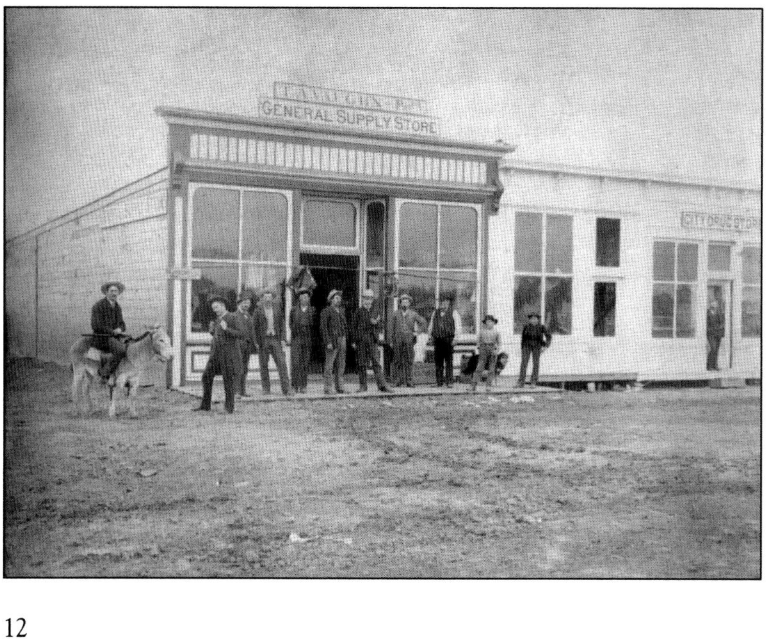

In the 1880s, Kansas's drugstores sold liquor to be used only for medicinal purposes. The fellow beside the donkey looks to have had too much "medicine." This image, taken in Fargo Springs in 1887, shows a growing town with established businesses and even a boardwalk. The T.A. Vaughn Store was co-owned by C.C. Hood. (Courtesy of Gary Krueger.)

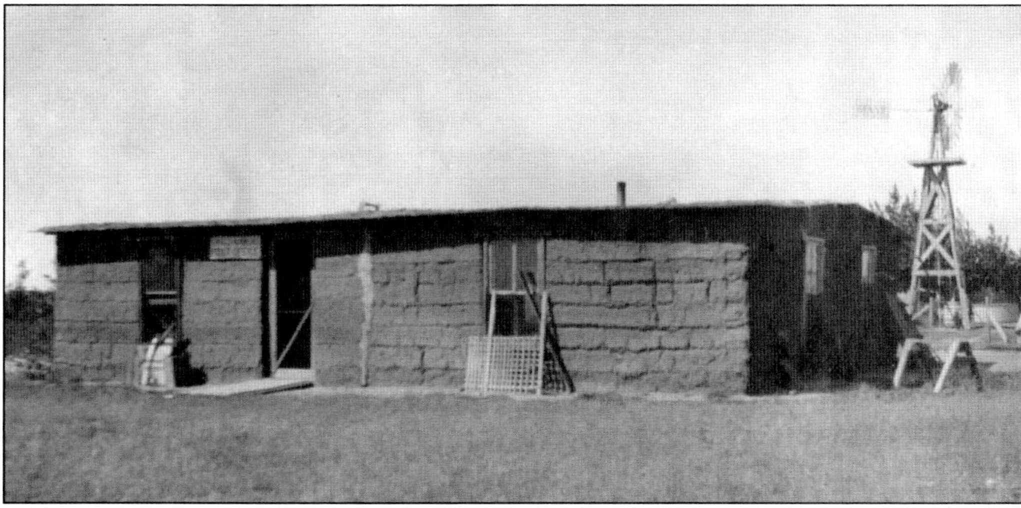

The Fargo Springs Post Office began as Hardwoodville in January 1885 and changed to Fargo Springs in December 1885. William Gillum was the first postmaster. Fargo Springs ebbed and flowed, and within three years, the post office was discontinued in June 1888. The sod house shown in this photograph was reestablished nine miles northeast of the original Fargo Springs. This time, the post office was known as just Fargo and lasted from March 1906 to December 1912. Ida Burchard and N.B. Swink were two of the postmasters. (Courtesy of Seward County Historical Society.)

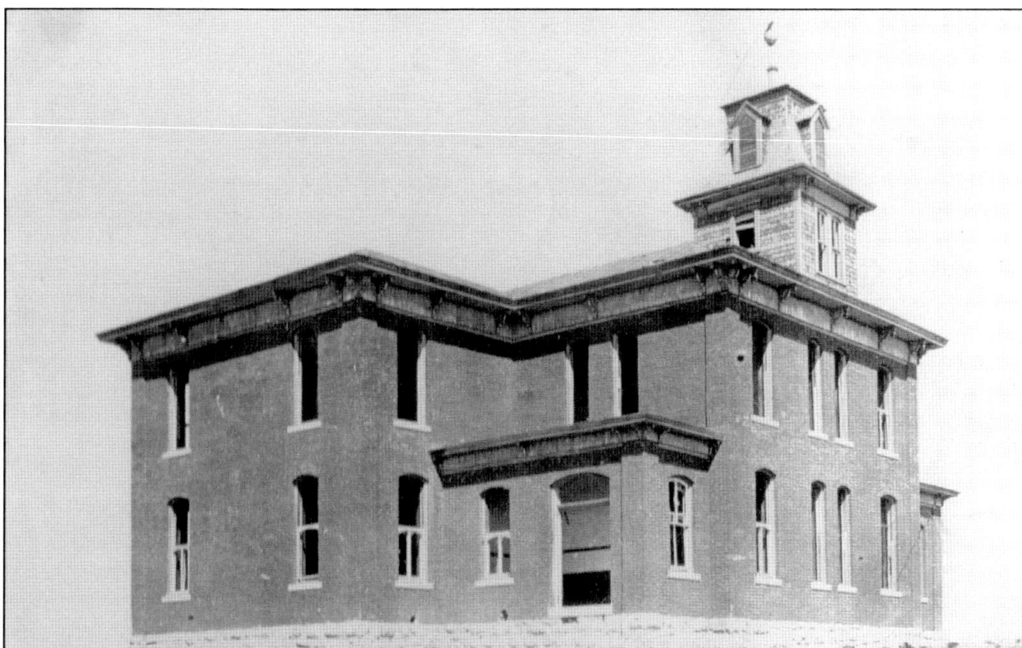

The people of Fargo Springs were looking toward the future with the solid-brick schoolhouse built in 1886. Fargorites assumed they would soon be the county seat, simply because of its early establishment and central riverside location. Neighboring Springfield had other ideas. Town promoters campaigned to Kansas governor John Martin and were able to convince him to designate Springfield the county seat in June 1886. (Courtesy of Seward County Historical Society.)

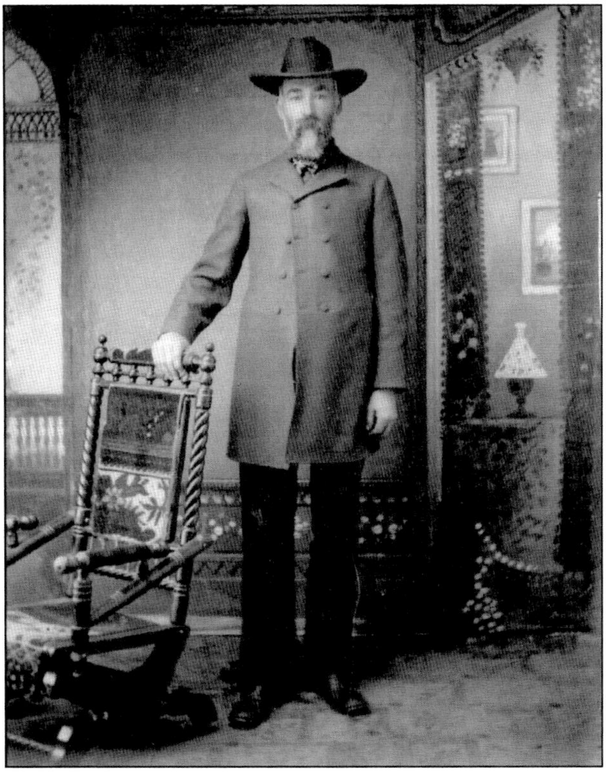

Adam T. Ragland helped found Springfield. He had previously served in the Kentucky Volunteer Infantry during the Civil War. He moved to Kentucky after the war and in 1884 moved to Kansas, ending up in Springfield, where he served as the first county treasurer in 1886. In 1890, he left Springfield to make the land rush into Oklahoma. He died in Oklahoma City in 1930. (Courtesy of Gary Krueger.)

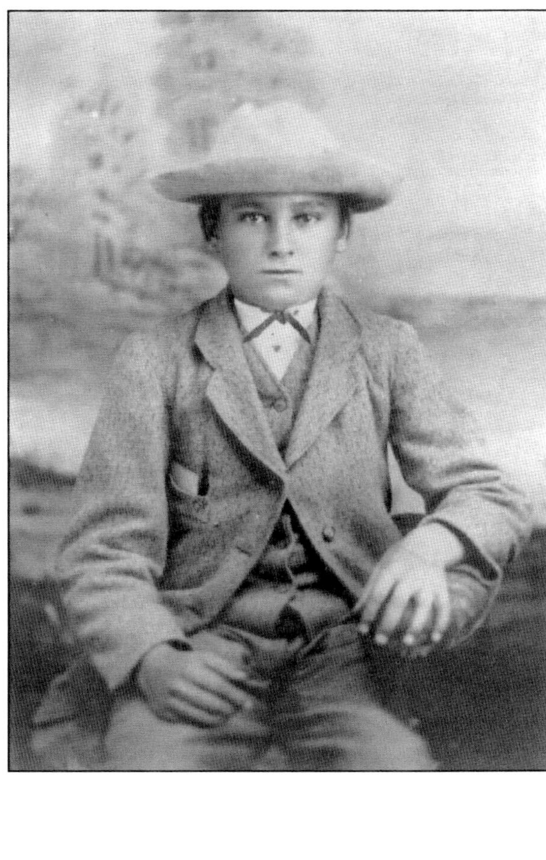

Walter Ragland, son of Adam and Bethlehem Ragland, was born in Barren County, Kentucky, in 1872 and moved to Springfield with his parents. On April 23, 1890, Walter suffered congestion of the brain and died several days later. The popular young man's funeral was held the next day, attended by the entire town and countryside. He was laid to rest in the Springfield Cemetery. (Courtesy of Gary Krueger.)

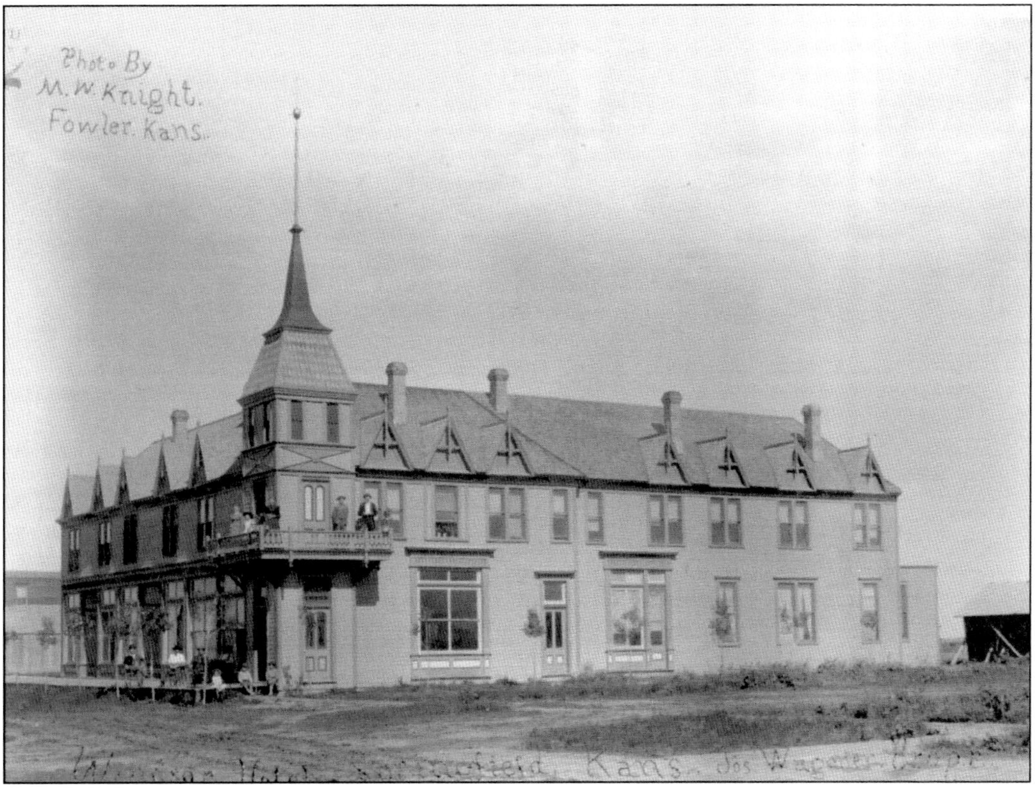

Springfield was a well-planned town. There were six newspapers, two drugstores, an underground water system, a two-story schoolhouse, and this beautiful hotel. The Windsor Hotel, located on high-table land and just three miles north of Fargo Springs, could be seen for miles. After Springfield lost the county seat and most of its population in 1892, the remaining Springfieldites did everything possible to keep the hotel and its elegant furnishings from falling into ruin. Efforts eventually fizzled, and the hotel was razed. (Courtesy of Kansas State Historical Society.)

The public schoolhouse was another attractive Springfield building. With its two-story style, it also was easily seen for miles. The land surrounding Springfield was so level that parents who lived miles away could see their children to and from school and never accompany them. (Courtesy of Seward County Historical Society.)

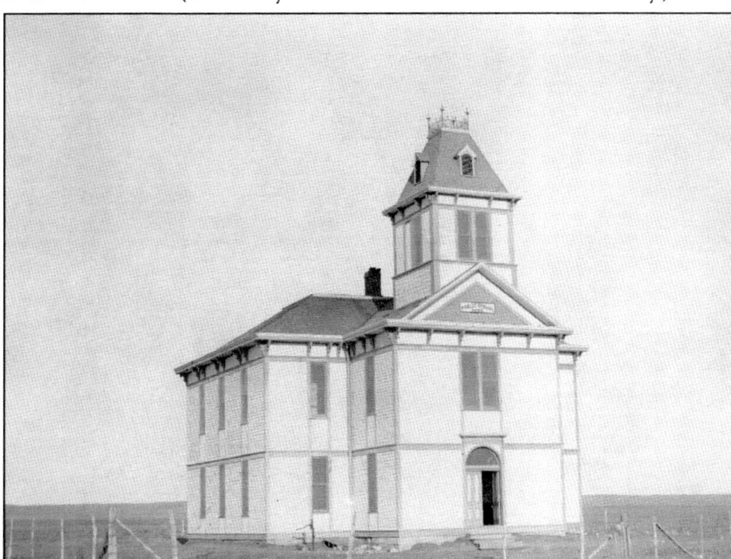

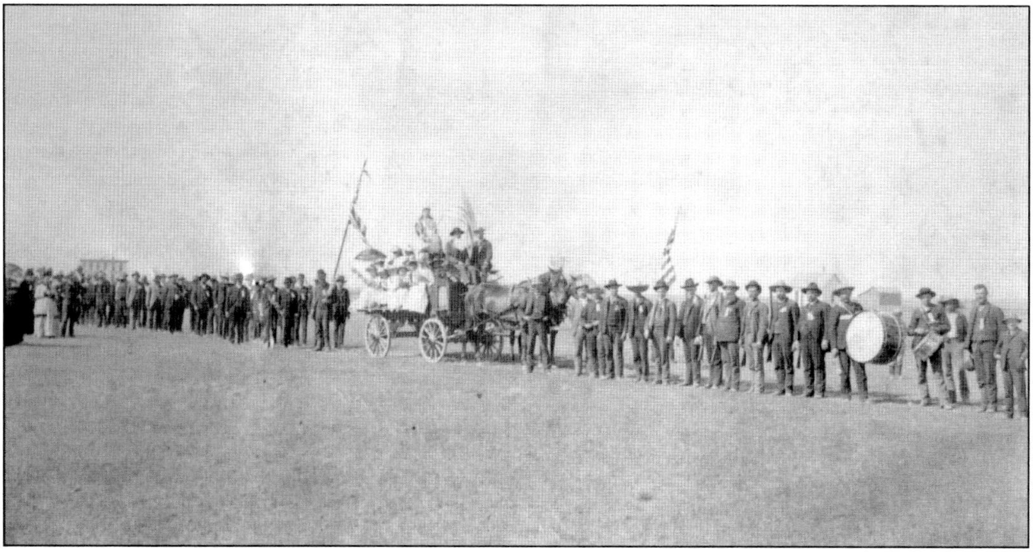

Decoration Day in 1889 was a day to honor fallen Civil War soldiers. This image shows a large contingent of townspeople ready for a parade and celebration. All the men have badges, perhaps designating them as members of the Grand Army of the Republic (GAR). (Courtesy of Seward County Historical Society.)

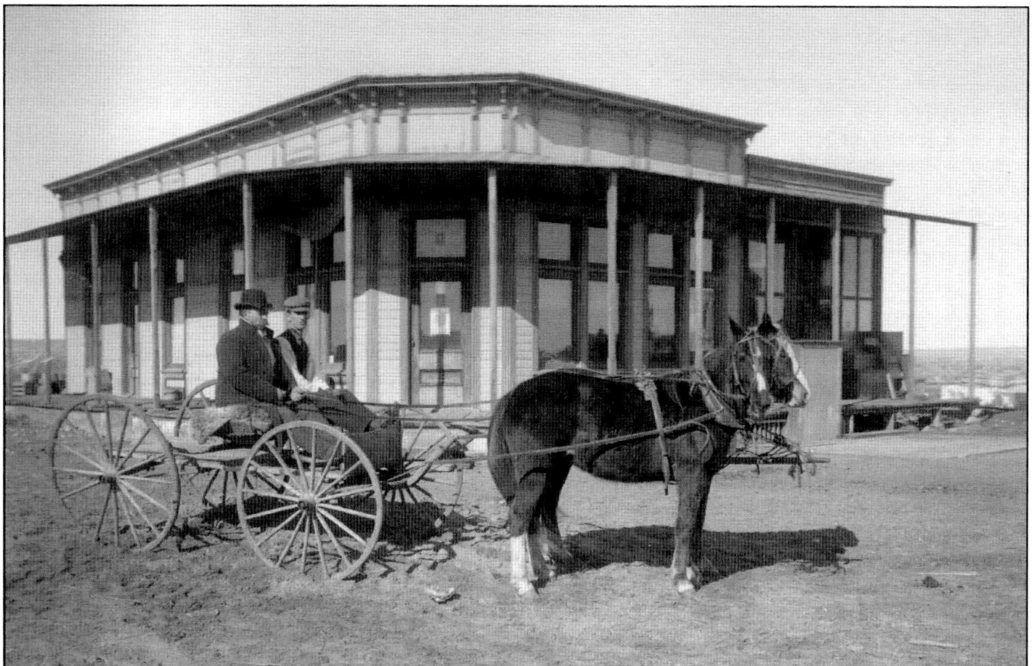

The impressive Custer Store was built in Arkalon soon after the post office was established on May 7, 1888. The first postmaster was a Mr. Tenny, who named the fledgling town after his father. Here, the Rock Island Railroad crossed the Cimarron River with several low, easily washed out slough bridges that plagued the railroad for years. Lee Larrabee is in the cap, and Bill Custer is wearing the derby. Custer moonlighted as a bodyguard for district judge Theodosius Botkin. (Courtesy of Seward County Historical Society.)

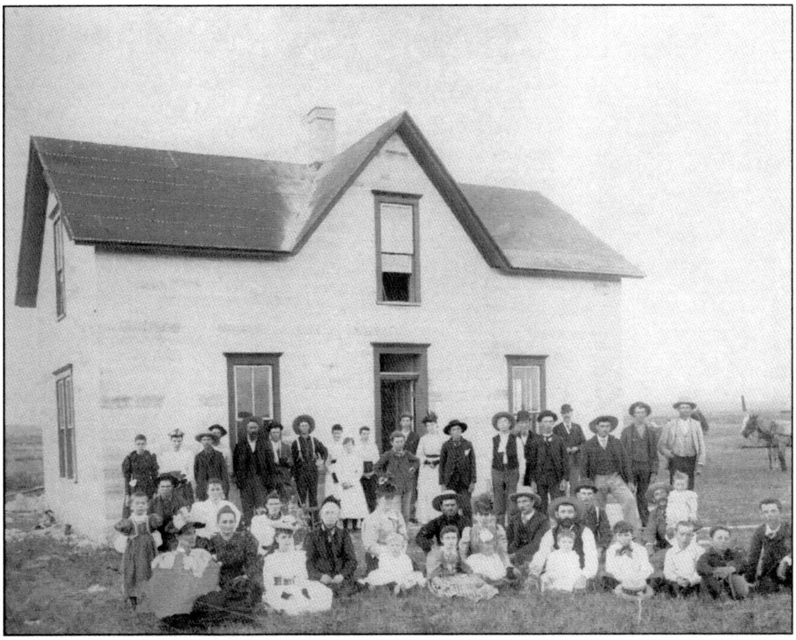

Friends and neighbors have gathered at the home of William and Cora (Larrabee) Stout's home located east of Arkalon. William Stout came to Seward County in 1886 by way of West Virginia. This home measured 32 by 38 feet and was considered a showplace. (Courtesy of Seward County Historical Society.)

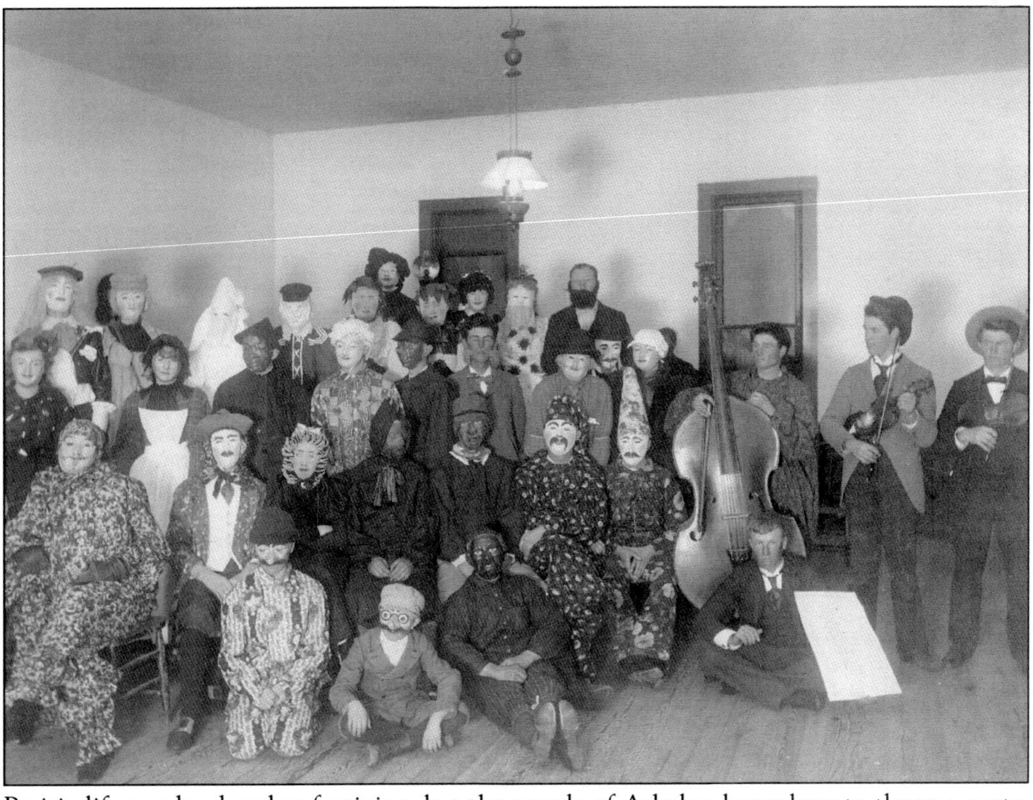

Prairie life was hard and unforgiving, but the people of Arkalon knew how to throw a party. Homemade costumes and imagination coupled with a small band made this the place to be on January 29, 1897. Notice the bass, which was an instrument that rarely made it to the high plains. (Courtesy of Seward County Historical Society.)

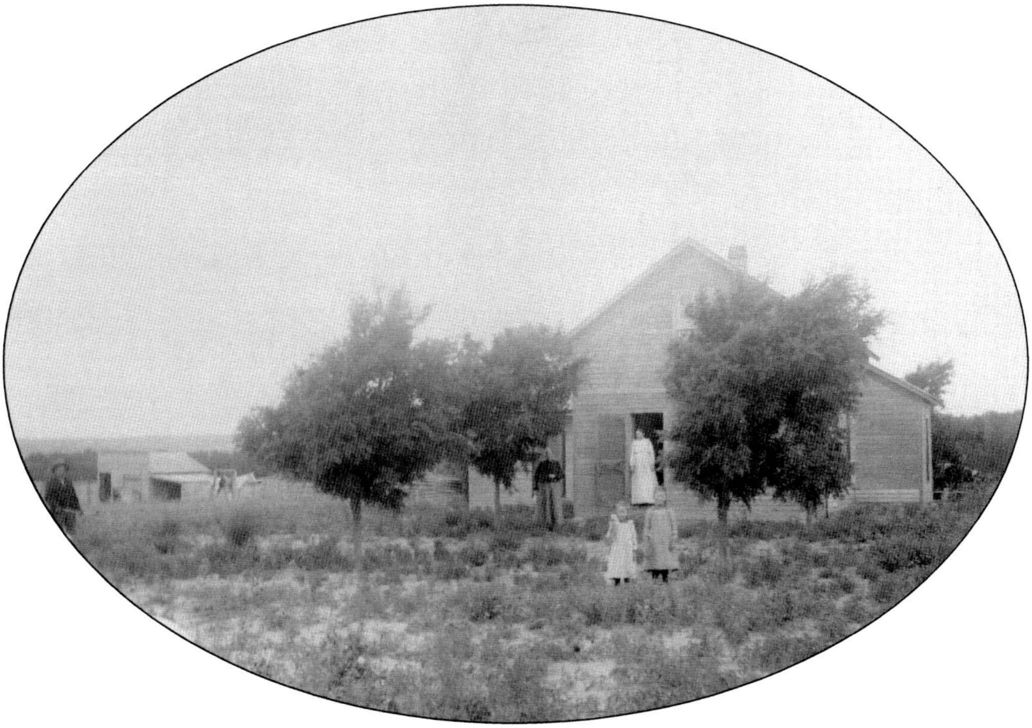

William H. Feather, mother Pearl Feather, grandmother Elmira Brown, and daughters Mildred and Rita Feather stand outside of the Feather ranch home located five miles south of Fargo Springs along the Cimarron River. William Feather married Pearl Brown on July 2, 1893. The couple lived on the ranch until 1900 when they moved to Liberal. At the time, Feather had been elected county treasurer. (Courtesy of Seward County Historical Society.)

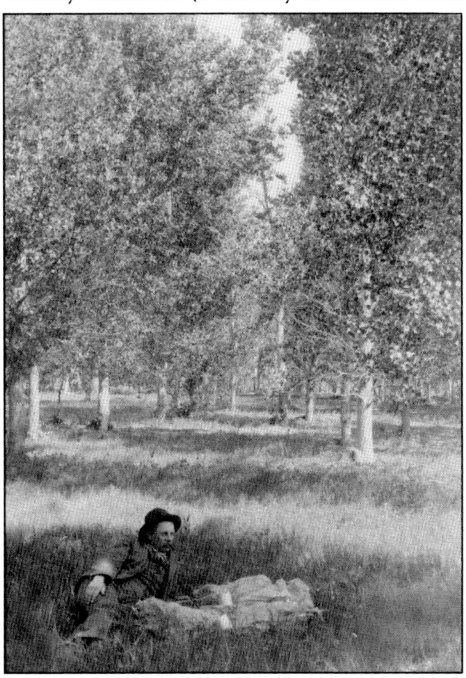

William H. Feather (left) loved to plant trees. His grove of trees became known as Feathers Grove, which became a favorite picnic spot, enjoyed for many generations. The grove, which consists mainly of cottonwoods, still exists but now provides shade for grazing cattle. (Courtesy of Seward County Historical Society.)

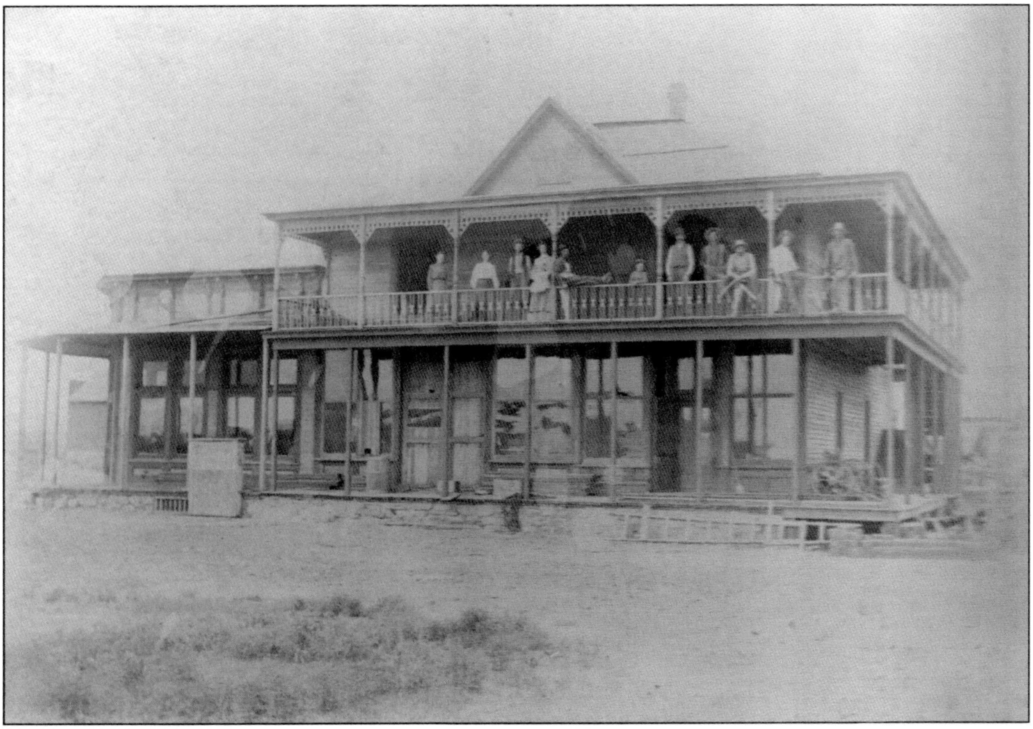

The Custer Store was purchased by William and Cora Stout shortly after their marriage in 1896. The Stouts kept the store stocked with fresh merchandise, and it was popular with area stockmen. The Stouts built this addition for more retail space and convenient living area. (Courtesy of Seward County Historical Society.)

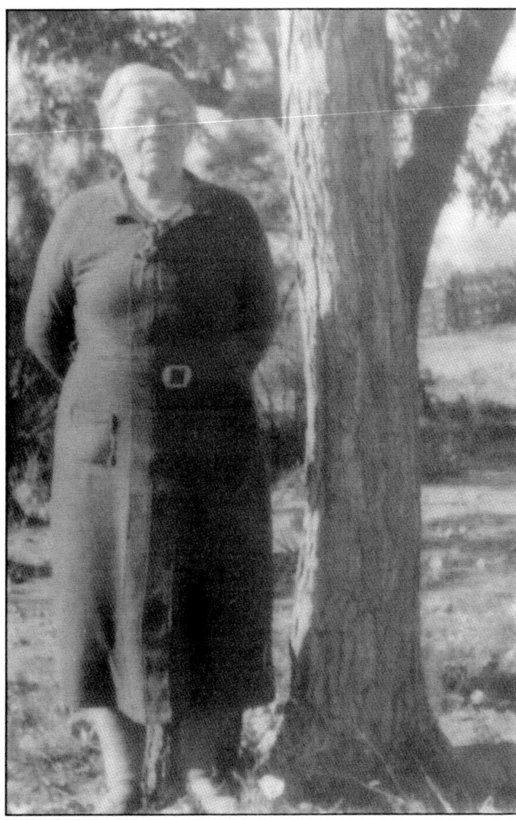

Alma Edmonds came to Seward County in 1883 as the bride of A.O. Edmonds. Arthur and Alma had married in New York and moved to their ranch located 20 miles north of Liberal alongside the Cimarron River. Even from her remote home, Alma loved literature and was the nucleus of the Liberal Memorial Library. She was also instrumental in forming the Liberal Women's Club in the early 1900s. (Courtesy of Seward County Historical Society.)

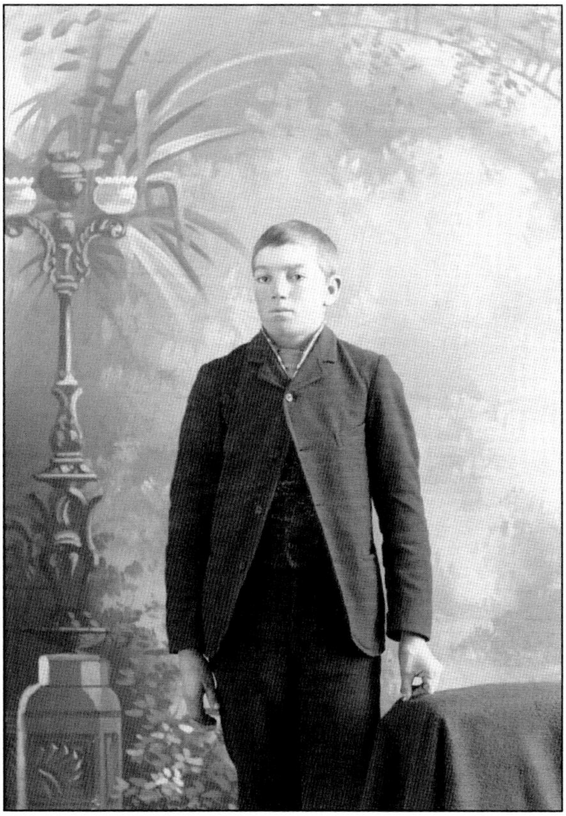

Con Jackson grew up in the Arkalon vicinity. At a young age, he was said to be a top hand, no matter what the chore, as long as it was on horseback. In the late 1890s and early 1900s, Walt Naylor, a fellow cowboy, and Con would always walk away from rodeos with "pockets full of jingle." This photograph was taken February 16, 1893. (Courtesy of Seward County Historical Society.)

The whole county of early Seward pioneers came to this Fourth of July gathering in 1896. Young and old alike wore their best, groomed their favorite horse, and baked their tastiest pie in this patriotic picnic at Feathers Grove. (Courtesy of Seward County Historical Society.)

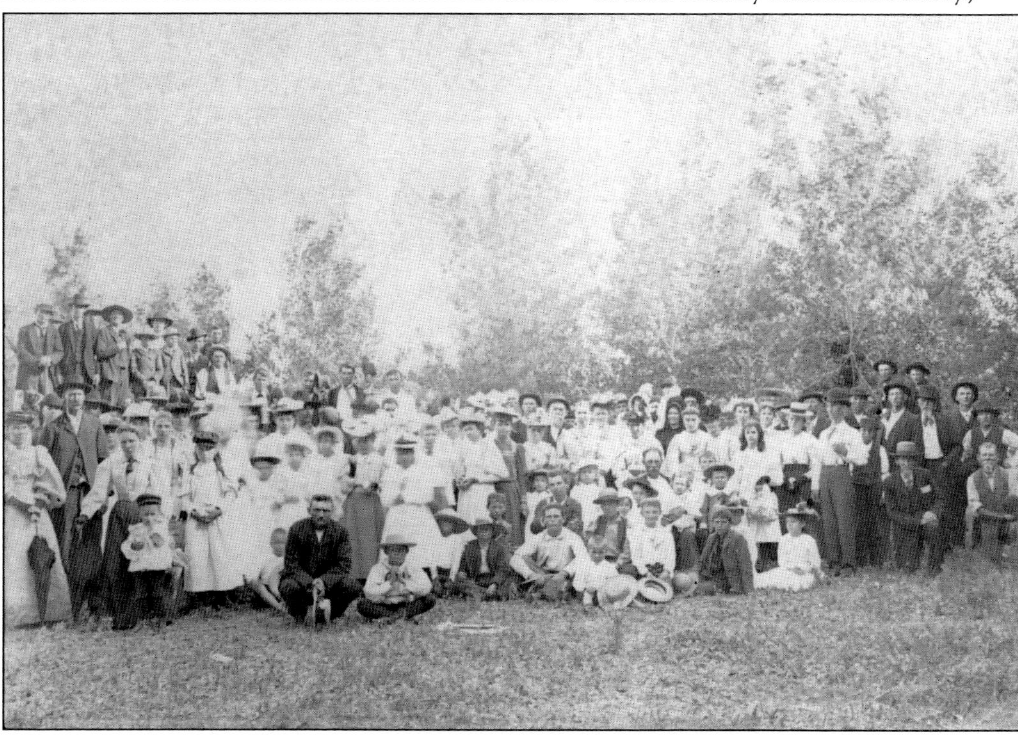

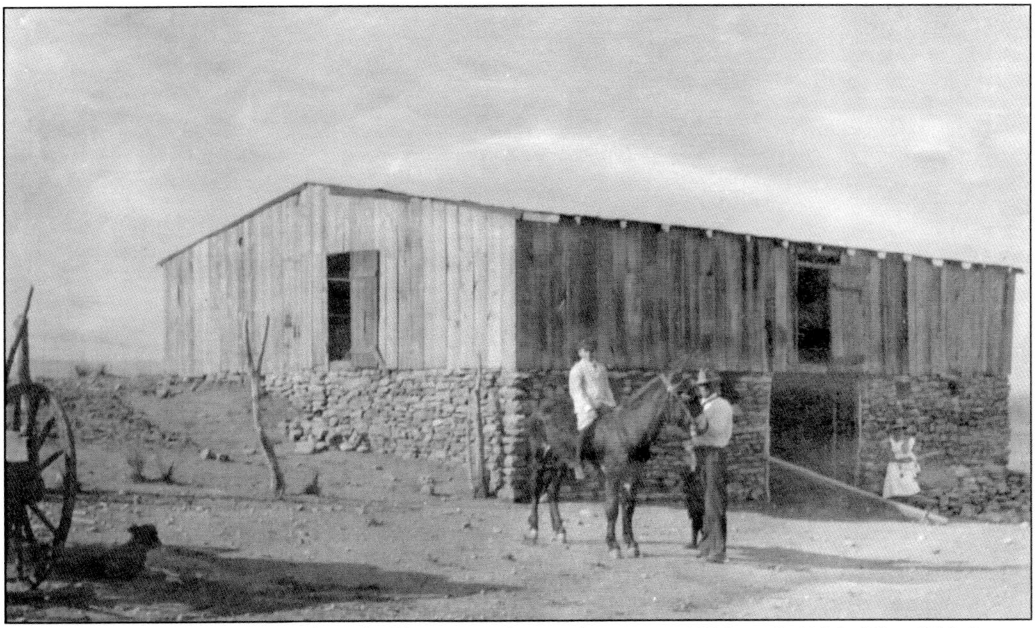

Seward County lost more than half its population between 1890 and 1900. The Oklahoma Land Rush, a national depression, and lingering drought drove early settlers to greener pastures. This unidentified family has bucked that trend by building a substantial barn. Mother and baby are in the shade, while the two family dogs have joined the men. (Courtesy of Seward County Historical Society.)

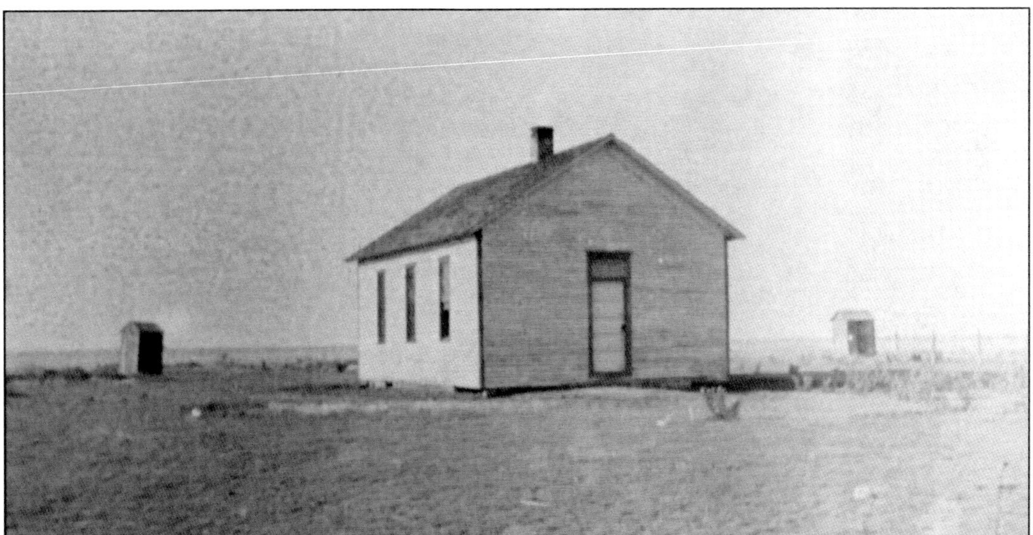

Education was important to early Seward County residents. Built in 1891, the Riverside School, District 17, was located a half mile from the Davies Ranch home. As the name implies, the school was on the north bank of the Cimarron River. Children at Riverside who were unable to cross the river at flood stage were not counted as absent, only tardy. The Davies, Whites, Penningtons, and other area children received their first through eighth grade education from teachers who were typically not much older than their students.

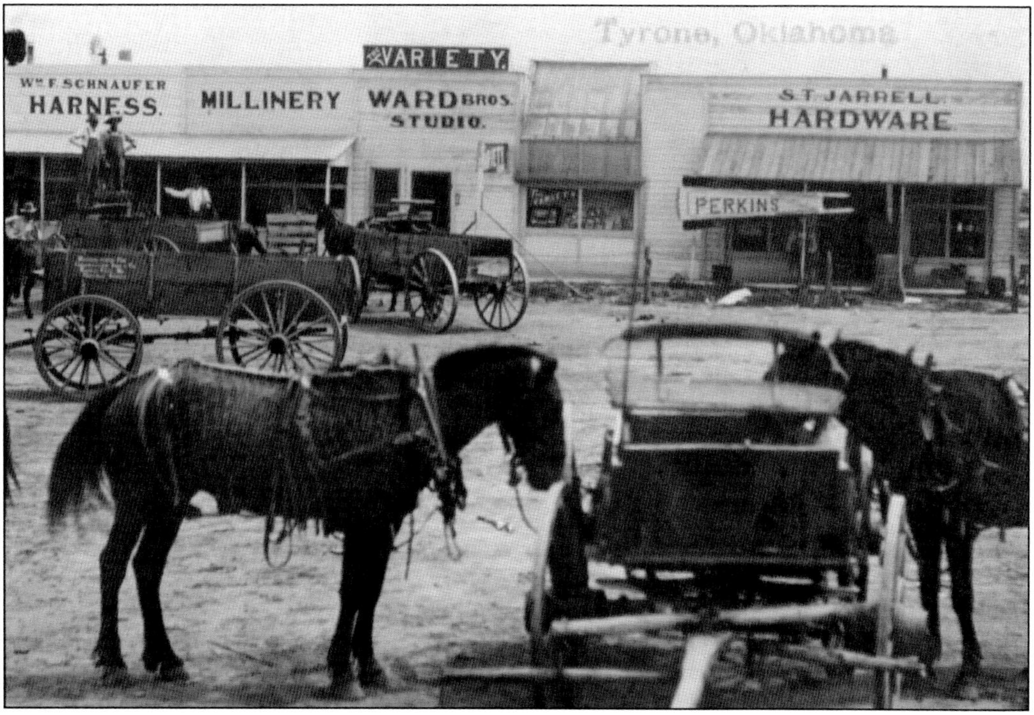

"Half of the cowboys in the world were at Shade's Well (No Man's Land) and half the good looking girls in the world were at Old Tyrone," wrote Charlie Hitch. Old Tyrone was originally located in Kansas. For 13 years, Tyrone was the end of the tracks for the Rock Island Railroad. Cattle driven up from the Texas and Oklahoma Panhandles were loaded into railcars from the pens and huge wing chutes set up on the edge of town. Tyrone was platted in May 1888. The post office was later moved into Oklahoma in May 1892.

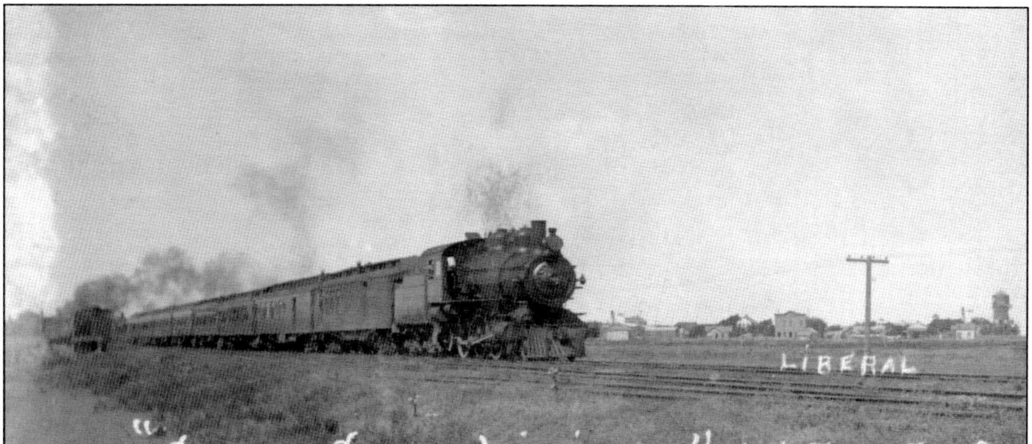

If not for the Chicago, Rock Island & Pacific Railroads' decision to build southwest across Seward County, Liberal would not have obtained the county seat or, possibly, even exist. Hoping to catch the Texas and Oklahoma Panhandle's cattle shipping business and avoid the Kansas law preventing shipping of Texas cattle because of the quarantine of Texas ticks, the railroad terminated its tracks just beyond Liberal at the state line. The Rock Island eventually pushed on into the Oklahoma Panhandle and into Texas in 1901.

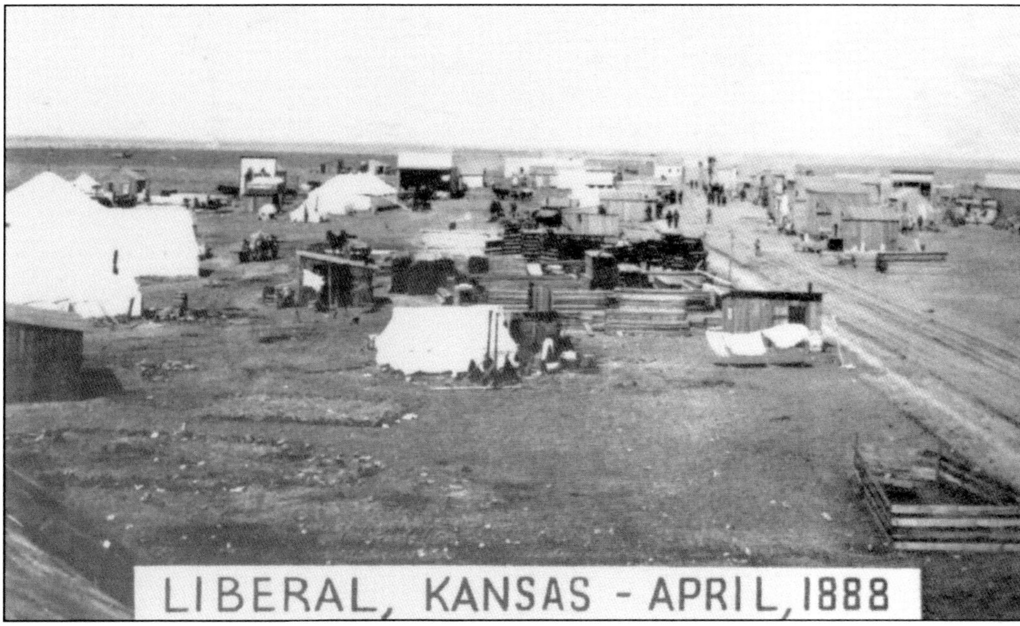

On April 13, 1888, a sale of lots was opened for the new town of Liberal. Within 24 hours, sales totaled $180,000. Three shanties appeared the next day, and by April 21, there were 83 buildings and houses. Within a year, population continued to soar, and Liberal was incorporated into a third-class city. (Courtesy of Seward County Historical Society.)

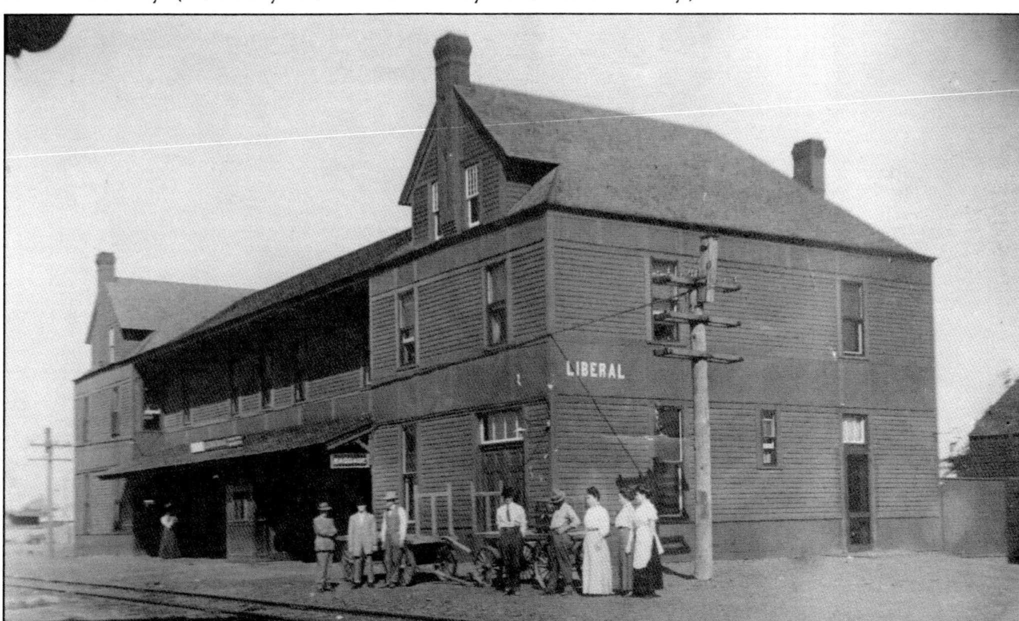

The railroad constructed two substantial buildings in 1888—a brick roundhouse and the depot and hotel. The hotel consisted of guest rooms, a telegraph and ticket office, and Liberal's first restaurant. T.J. McDermott and family actually followed and fed the tracklayers as they came to Liberal, then managed the depot and restaurant until 1907 when John Grier took over management and changed the name to the Grier House.

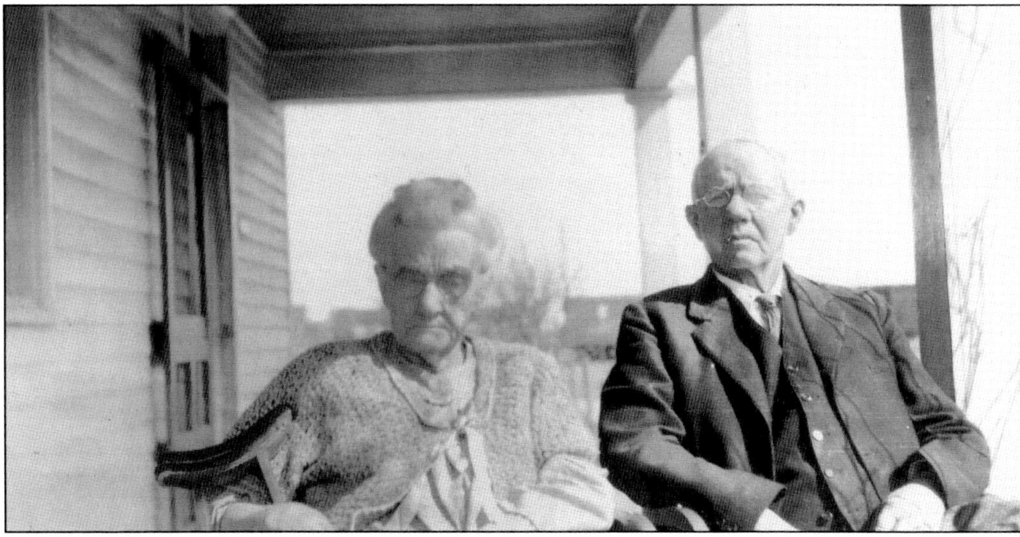

T.J. and Mary Parker McDermott arrived in Liberal on the first work train. Accompanying them was their daughter Myra Electra. The McDermotts excelled at running a first-rate hotel and eating establishment. During the first year, the McDermotts insisted all gentlemen wear coats while dining. Typically, cowboys would dine in their shirtsleeves, and when a group of the fellows came in without coats, the McDermotts gently reminded the cowpunchers of the coats-at-dinner rule. The group would all file out and promptly return wearing their gaudy yellow fishtailed slickers. The McDermotts soon accepted defeat and relaxed the dining room dress code. (Courtesy of Seward County Historical Society.)

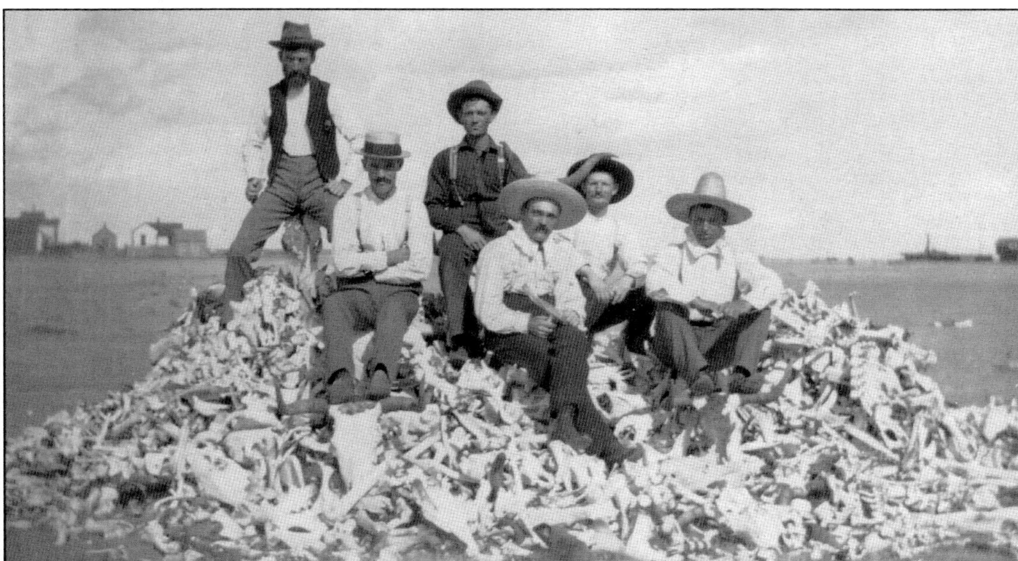

Industry in Liberal was limited. However, railroad business and lumber, grocery, and dry good sales were enough to keep the town lively. In addition, bone hauling became a way for homesteaders to make extra money. After the blizzard of 1886, the plains were covered with the bones of perished cattle. Tons of their gathered bones were sold and shipped out of Liberal to eastern fertilizer markets. These gentlemen posed for the camera with their stack of bones next to the rail yard. (Courtesy of Mary Brewington.)

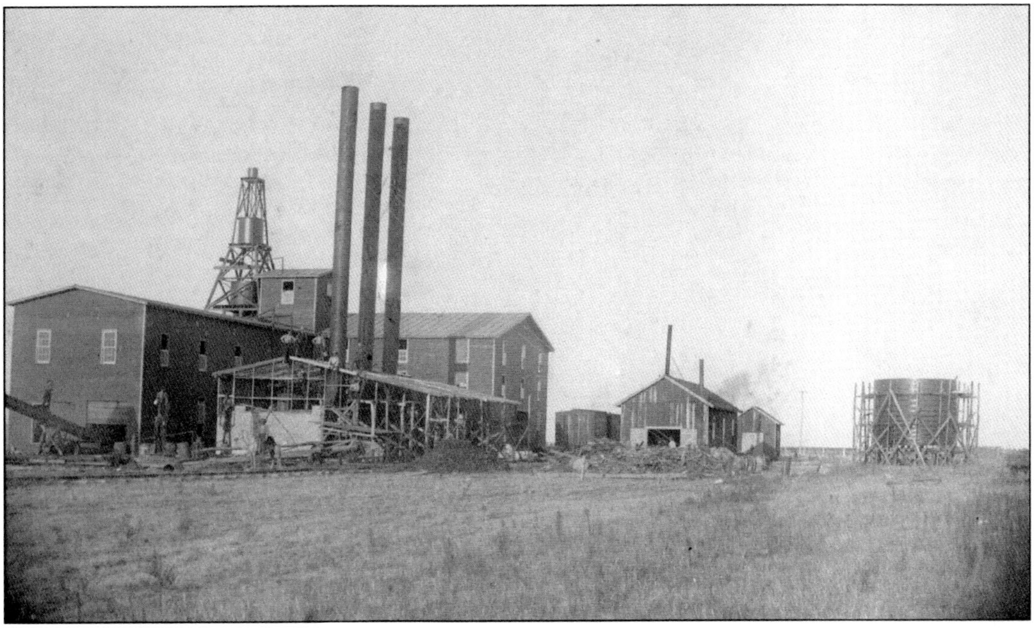

This impressive structure, built in 1889, was located in the 1500 block of East Eighth Street. The mill, which cost $100,000 to build, converted sorghum bought from local farmers to crystal sugar. Unfortunately, the promoters were scam artists. Very little crude sugar was produced. After the first season, the mill was closed and the buildings torn down. The farmers and townspeople lost what they had invested in stock and grain, and the sugar mill promoters were nowhere to be found.

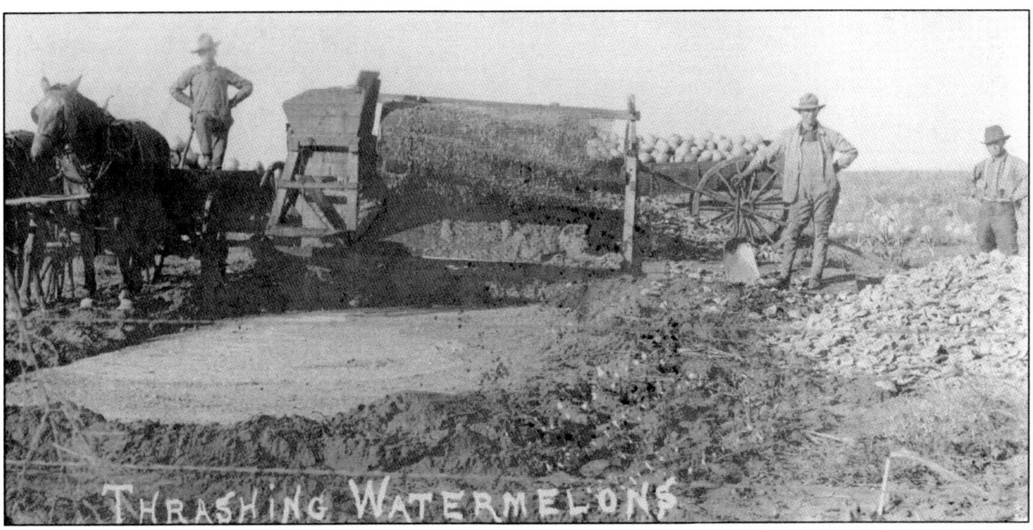

The pristine prairie of Seward County produced an unlikely cash crop for the new homesteaders. Watermelon did exceptionally well on the land surrounding Liberal. D.M. Ferry Seed Company sent out their salesmen to contract with local farmers. Seed was provided to the farmers, who in turn planted hundreds of acres to watermelon.

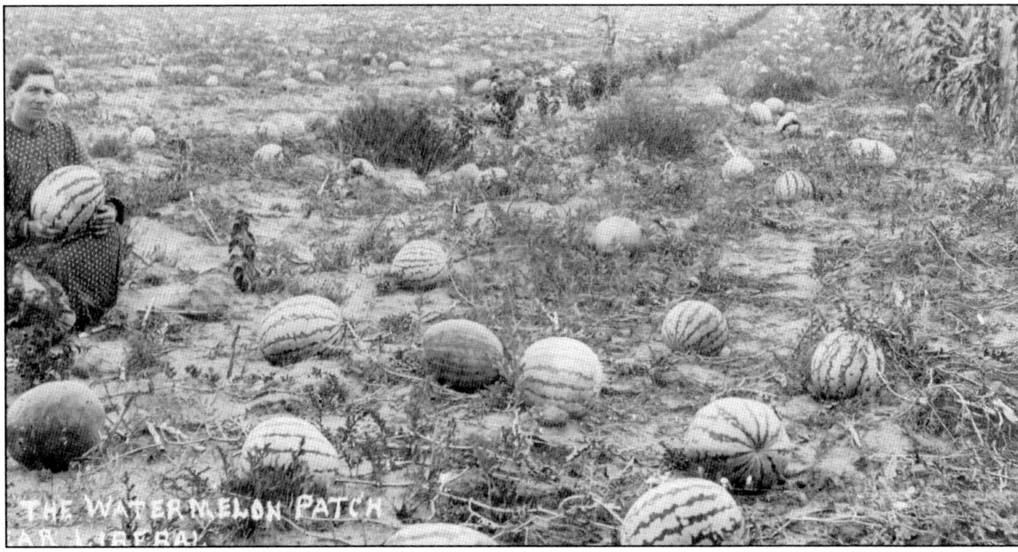

In the early fall, farmers delivered their melons to the crusher, which smashed the melons to extract the seed from the fruit. The seed was then spread out on large trays to be dried in the sun and wind. The seed was then sacked and freighted back to the D.M. Ferry Company. Over 48,000 pounds of watermelon seed was delivered to the company from the Liberal-area growers.

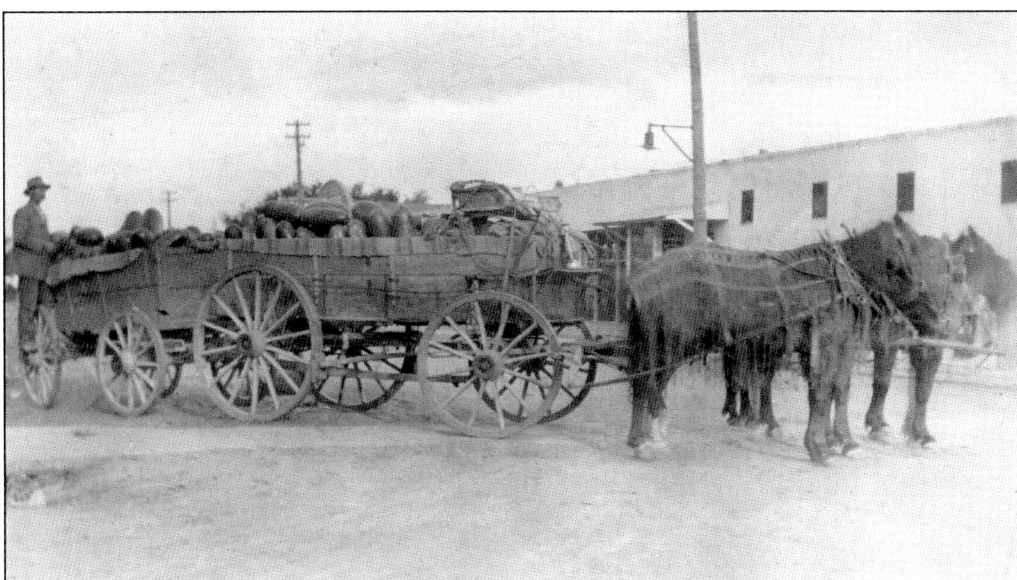

On occasion, farmers would simply bring whole watermelons to town merchants for resale. In the photograph, a local farmer is delivering his melons to the Enterprise Store. Purchasers were often encouraged to save the seed after consuming the melons to be given back to the grower. (Courtesy of Seward County Historical Society.)

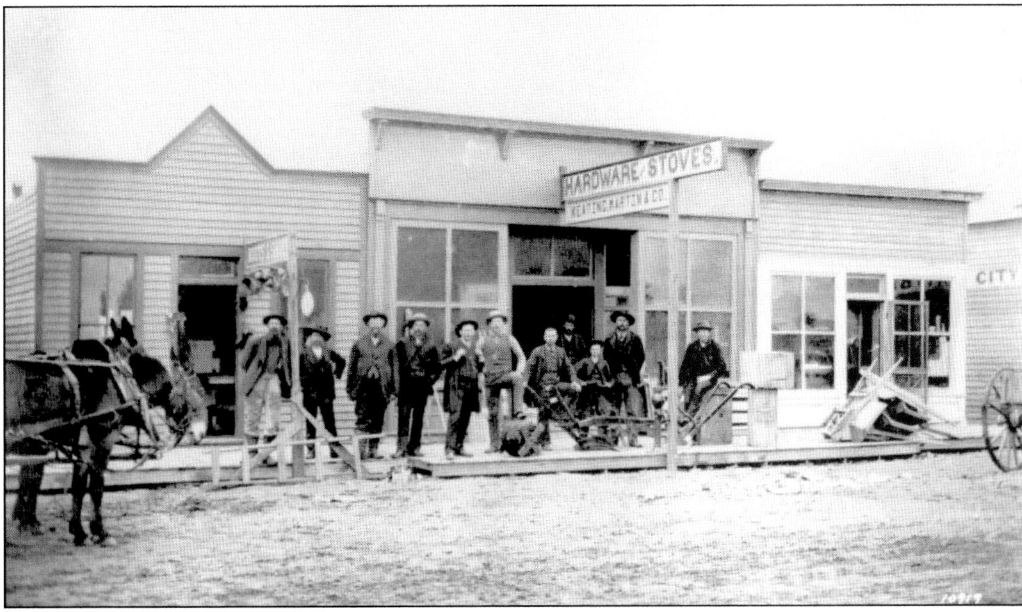

Standing in front of the Keating, Martin & Company hardware store, located at 4 South Kansas Avenue, are the proprietors and some of their customers. Clarence Y. Martin moved to Liberal from Iowa to partner with Brice Keating in 1888. Accompanying him was wife Araminta and son Glenn Luther. Glenn made kites on his mother's kitchen table and often sold them to neighborhood boys. In later years, Glenn became an aviation pioneer and builder, establishing Martin Aviation, eventually evolving to Martin Marietta and Martin Lockheed.

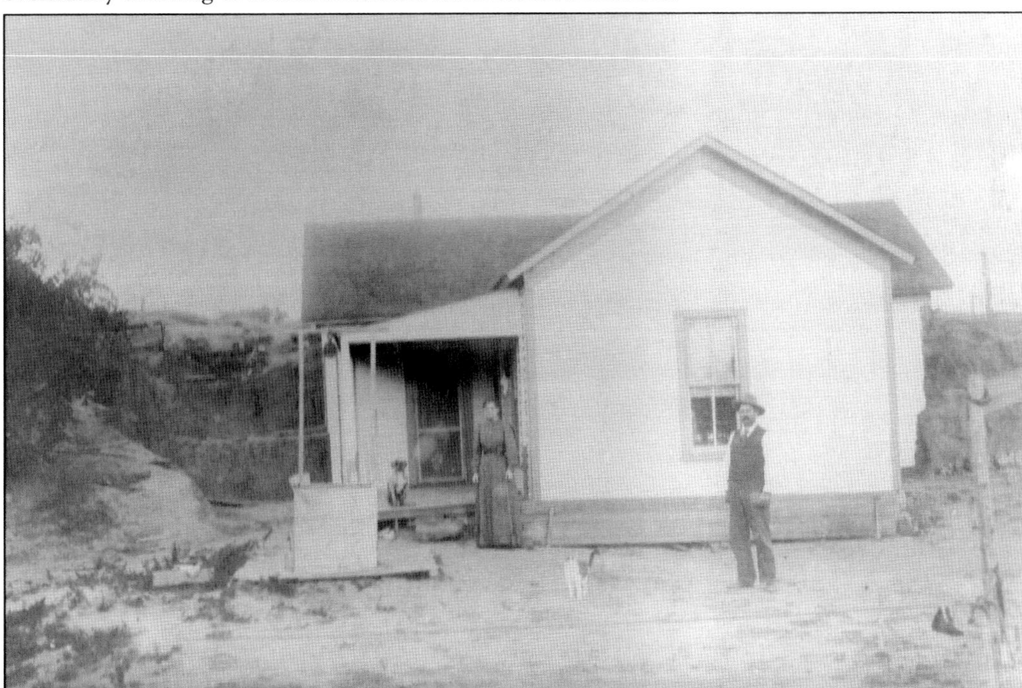

This image was taken by L. Ward, a professional photographer who had studios in Liberal and Old Tyrone. The rancher and his wife have a convenient hand-dug well right out the front door.

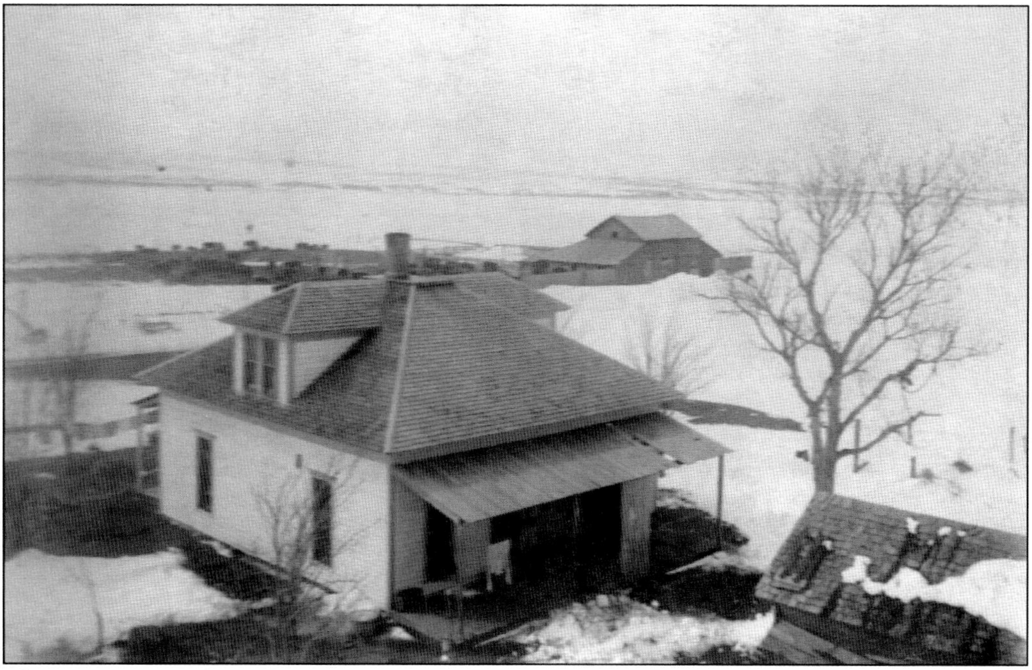

This 1880s image shows the G.H. and Mary Evans ranch on the Cimarron. The Evans had come by lumber wagon from Tiderite, Pennsylvania, in 1887 and built this so-called aboveground house. Robert Evans, a well-known Liberal merchant, was born here in 1888. (Courtesy of Seward County Historical Society.)

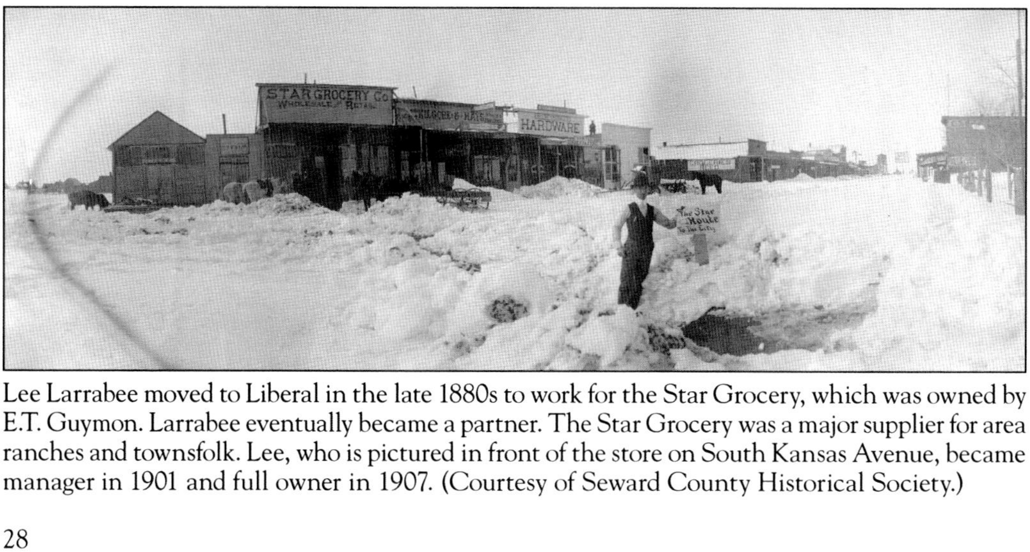

Lee Larrabee moved to Liberal in the late 1880s to work for the Star Grocery, which was owned by E.T. Guymon. Larrabee eventually became a partner. The Star Grocery was a major supplier for area ranches and townsfolk. Lee, who is pictured in front of the store on South Kansas Avenue, became manager in 1901 and full owner in 1907. (Courtesy of Seward County Historical Society.)

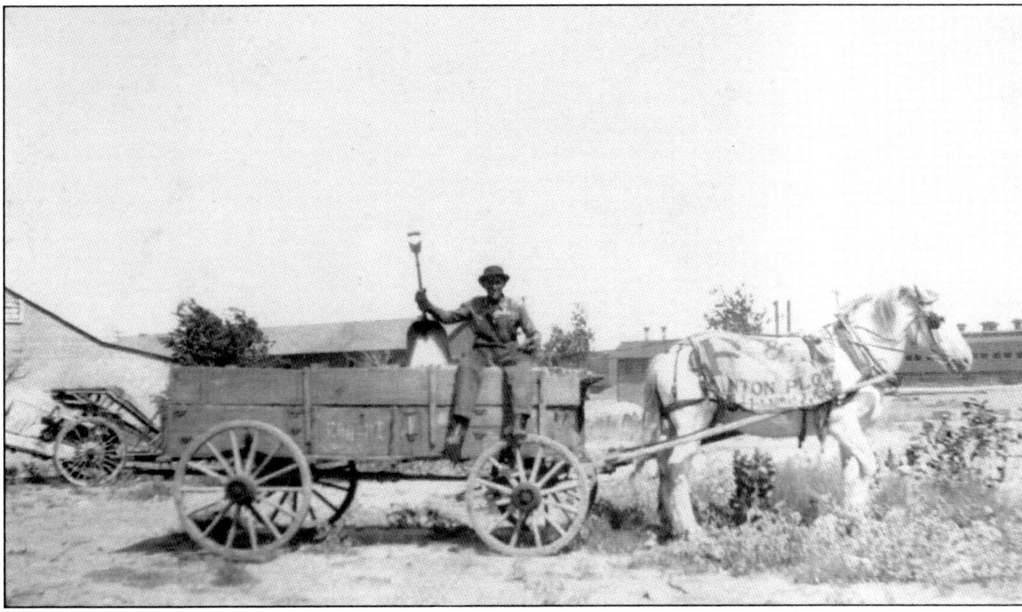

R.B. (Bert) Holloway poses with his shovel and a load of coal to be delivered to local households in Liberal. Holloway worked for the Star Lumber Company. In Bert's spare time, he played baritone for the Liberal Woodmen Band. (Courtesy of Seward County Historical Society.)

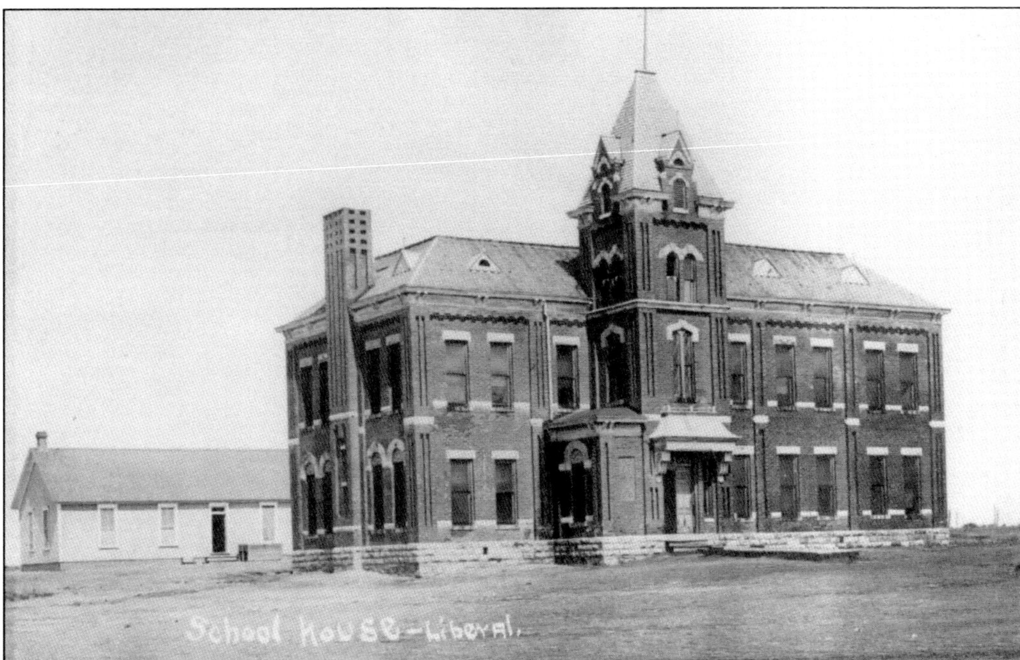

This grand building was the Liberal School, built in 1890. The bricks were made locally, and the stone accents were quarried from the Oklahoma Panhandle. Each floor had three classrooms. The first high school graduation was held in 1904 with four graduates. They were Ethel Gelhousen, Lydia Wood, Nettie Summer, and Bedia Richardson. (Courtesy of Seward County Historical Society.)

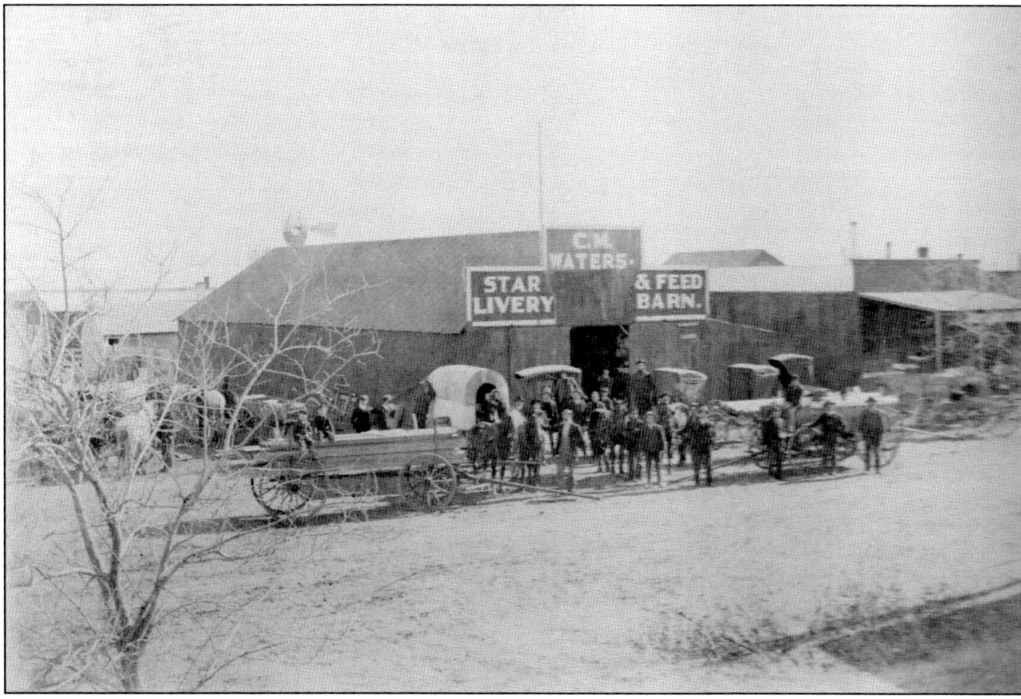

Horses and mules were important in early Liberal days, and a good livery barn was vital. Cash Waters owned this popular livery barn located at 223 North Kansas Avenue. Waters always sported a full mustache and was the bass drum player for the Liberal Woodman Band.

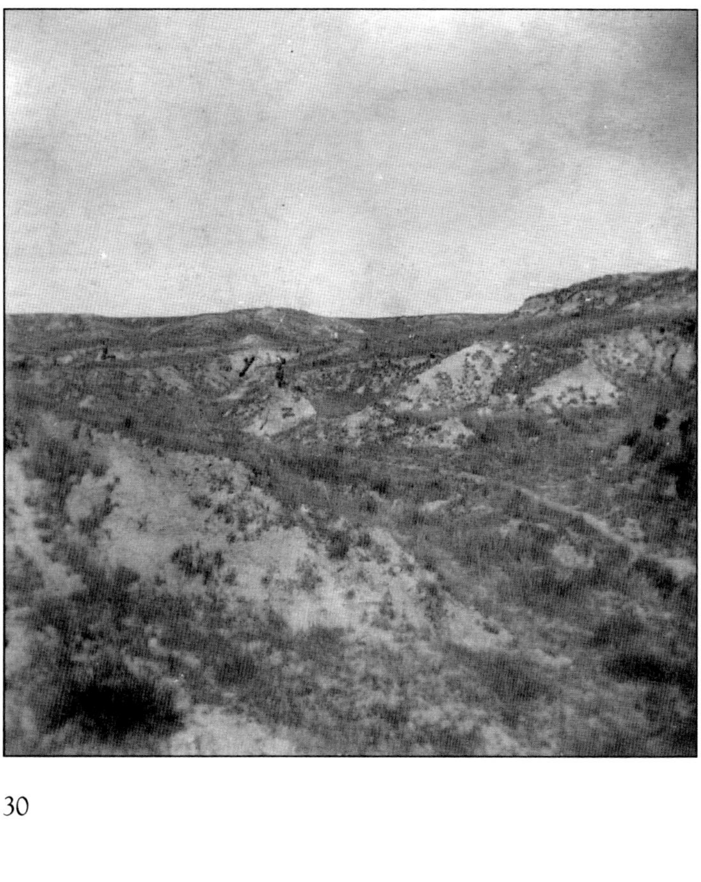

Trouble had been brewing between the town of Springfield and Fargo Springs since 1886. The two burgs had been vying for the county seat until 1892, when Liberal obtained the honor instead. In neighboring Stevens County, problems were still at the surface and emotions and opinions floated over the county borders. This image shows the canyon where Seward County sheriff Sam Dunn was ambushed and killed the morning of January 4, 1892. The original plan was to take the life of district judge Theodosius Botkin, a major character in the Stevens County Seat War. (Courtesy of Seward County Historical Society.)

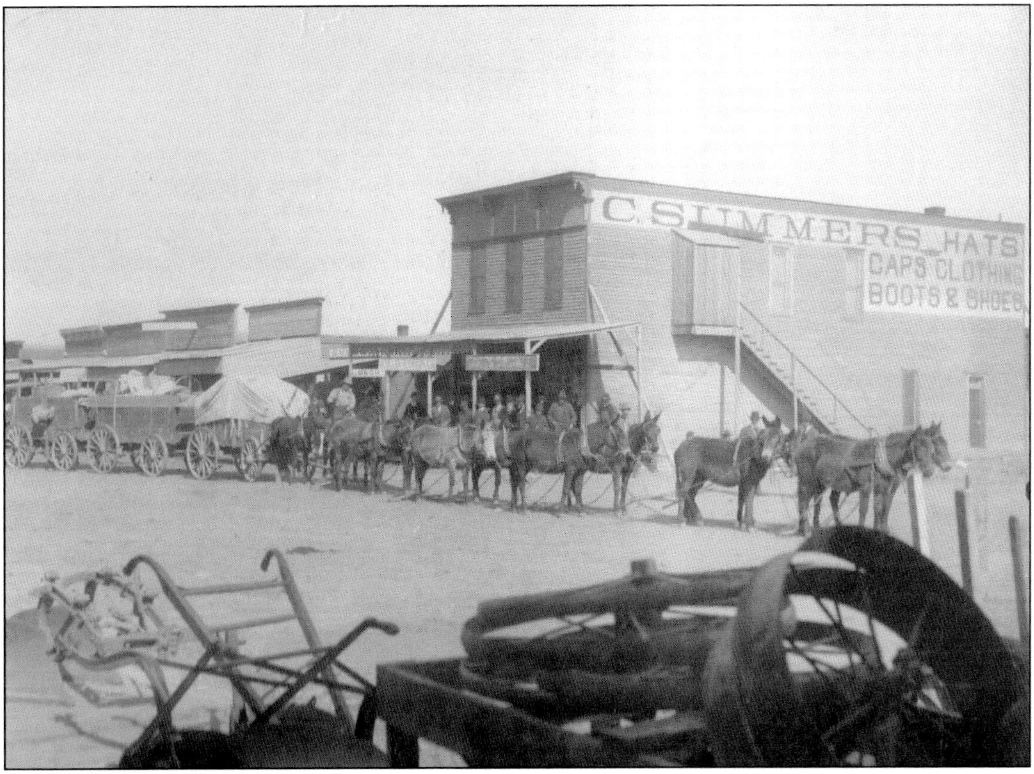

Taken from the southwest corner of Second Street and Kansas Avenue on March 15, 1893, this image shows the Charles Summers Store, an important supplier for surrounding ranches. This 12-mule team has a full load and was headed for the Texas Panhandle. The Charles Summers Store was first established in Fargo Springs in 1886 and moved to Liberal in the early 1890s. The wooden store became one of Liberal's leading dry goods stores.

Theodosius Botkin served as district judge for the 32nd Court District, with legal jurisdiction over Seward and Stevens Counties. Judge Botkin was a Fargo Springs sympathizer. Ultimately, Judge Botkin's feud with Samuel Wood, of Stevens County, led to the killing of Sheriff Dunn and Wood himself. In 1890, Wood brought impeachment proceedings against Botkin for holding court while drunk and armed and for authorizing illegal arrests. Botkin was able to hold on to his judgeship, but Wood was shot and killed at the Stevens County Courthouse on June 23, 1891. Botkin was implicated in the murder, but the case never went to trial. (Courtesy of Kansas State Historical Society.)

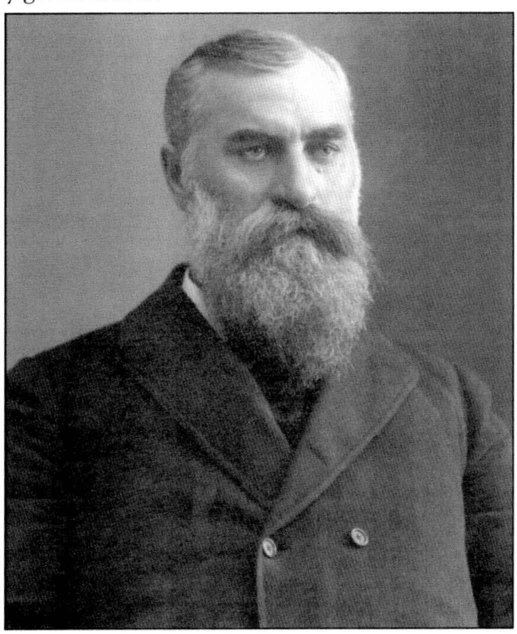

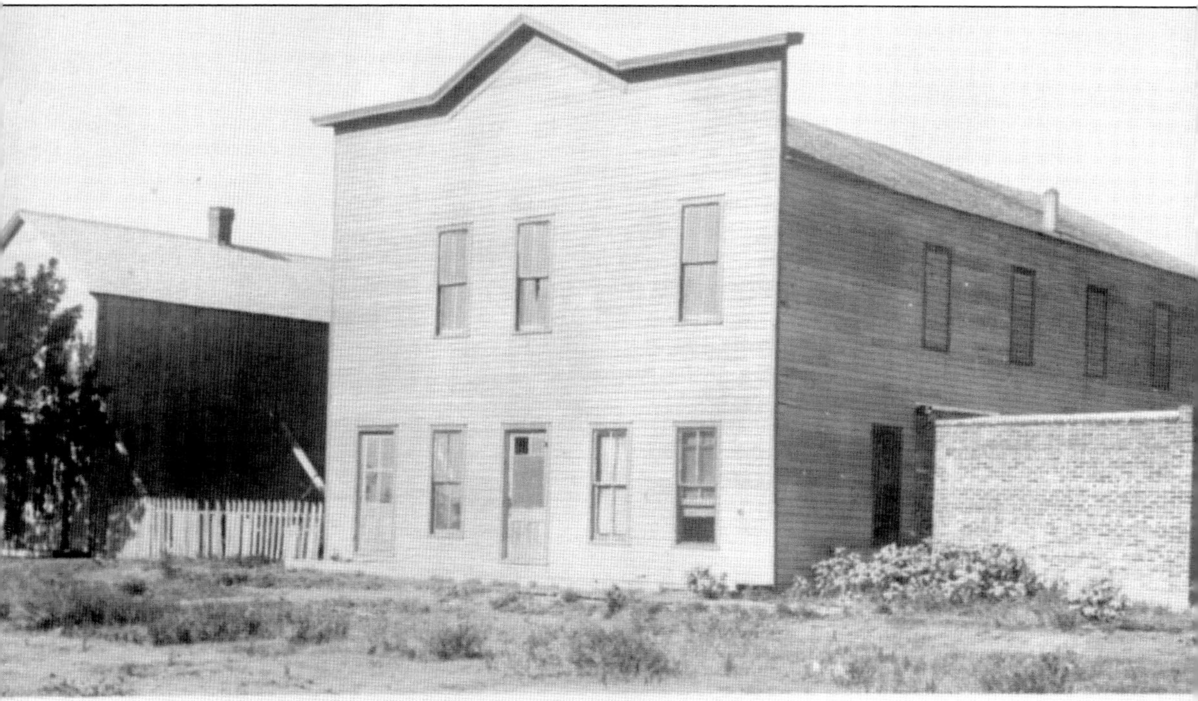

1894 Seward County Courthouse

After Fargo Springs and Springfield lost their bids for the county seat to Liberal in 1892, county records were moved to the abandoned Washington Hotel in the 300 block of North Washington Avenue. The building was at first rented and then purchased by the county in 1896 for $650. The building was no bargain, though. The floors were so weak that when three people walked across the floor at the same time, the creaking noises could be heard across the street. The old building was relieved of duty in 1908. (Courtesy of Seward County Historical Society.)

Two

CIVILIZATION ON THE PLAINS 1900–1920

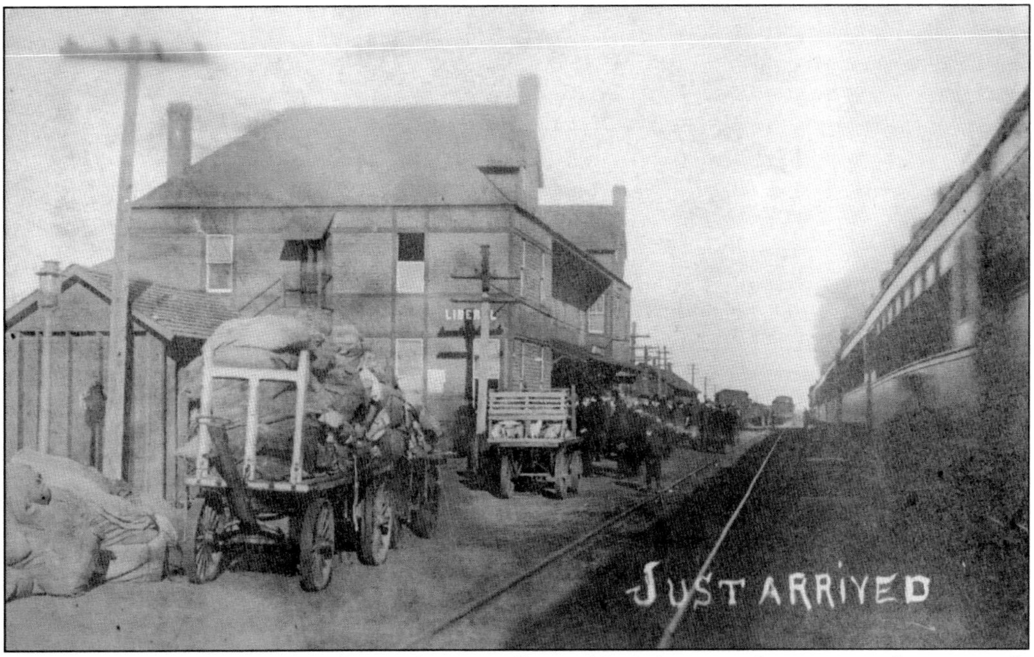

Liberal began as a humble post office and water well. It suddenly became a boom town, then promptly lost two-thirds its population, only to gain it right back. Successful farms, determined retailers, and the railroad kept the town alive and kicking. (Courtesy of Seward County Historical Society.)

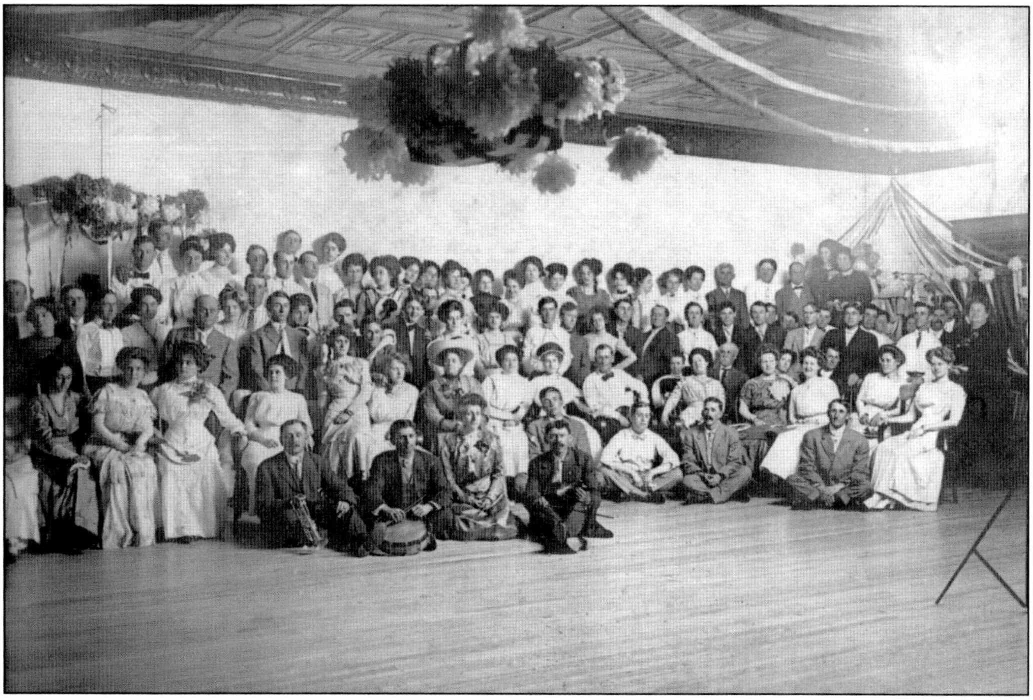

The years between 1900 and 1920 were a period of amazing growth for the town. Population in Seward County increased from 822 in 1900 to 6,082 in 1920. Rains had returned, bringing new homesteaders and townspeople. This group celebrated in a festive style at the Craig Hall, which was located at 18½ West Second Street. Warren Zimmerman, Frank Summers, Osa Nichols, Lee and Nettie Larrabee, Earl and Pearl Cooper, and John and Ella Baughman were among the partygoers. (Courtesy of Seward County Historical Society.)

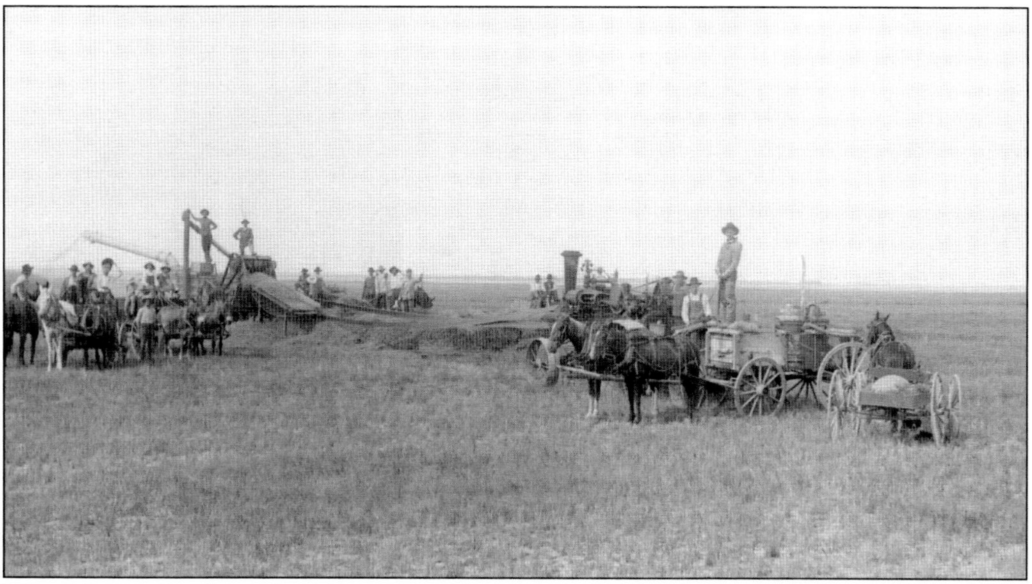

Wheat harvest in the early 1900s required large groups of men to bring in the crop. This scene in central Seward County shows a crew of 21 men. Crews typically had the engineer (the "boss"), the separator man, the feeders, the stackers, and the water hauler (the "monkey").

To obtain 160 acres, a family had to work hard, face harsh conditions, and most importantly, stay. The only happy one in this unidentified Seward County family seems to be the dog.

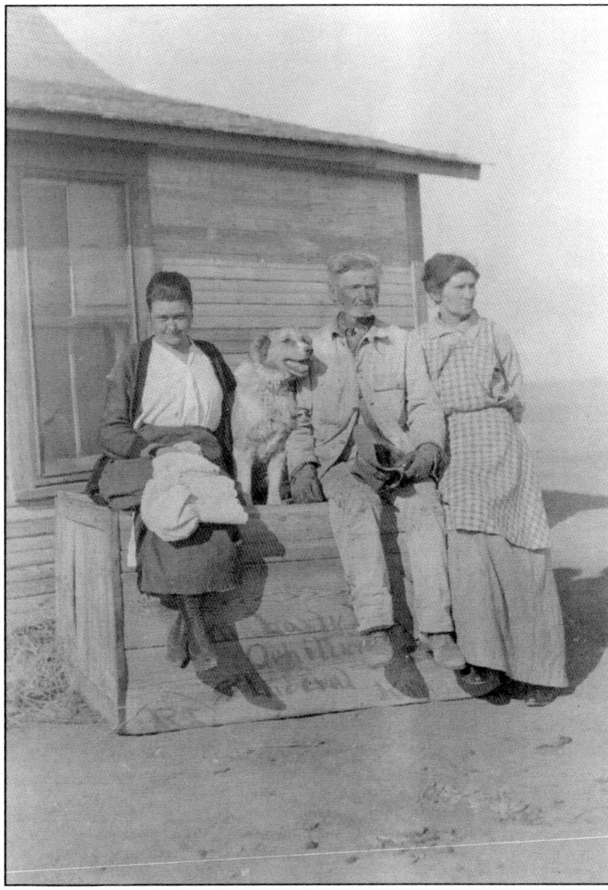

Given the right conditions, almost anything could be grown on the Kansas high plains. These farmers have attracted a crowd with their wagon loads of potatoes. Over 1,000 bushels of potatoes were reported grown and harvested in Seward County in 1918.

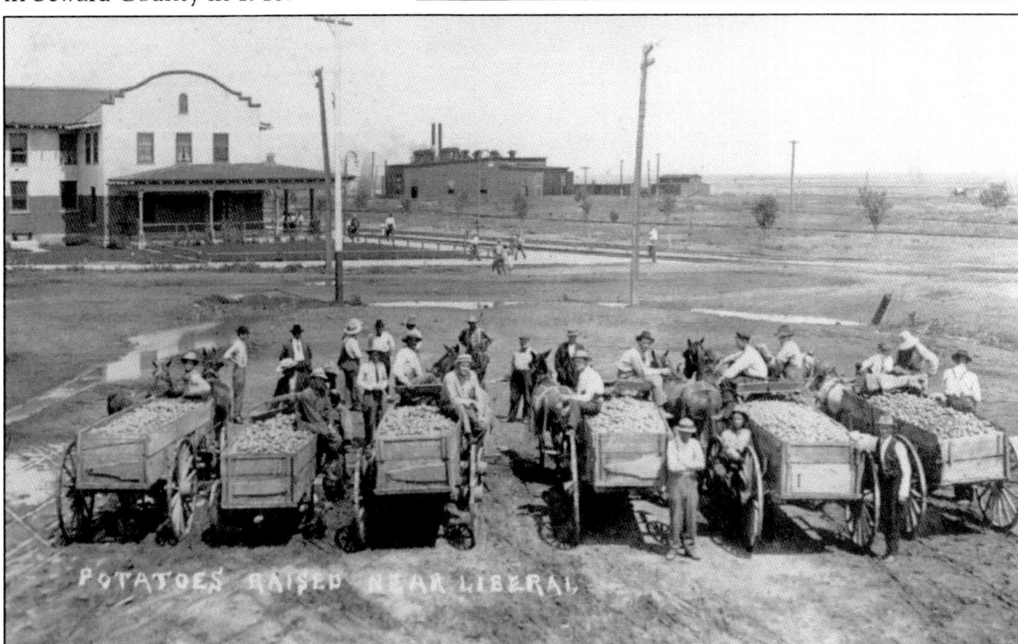

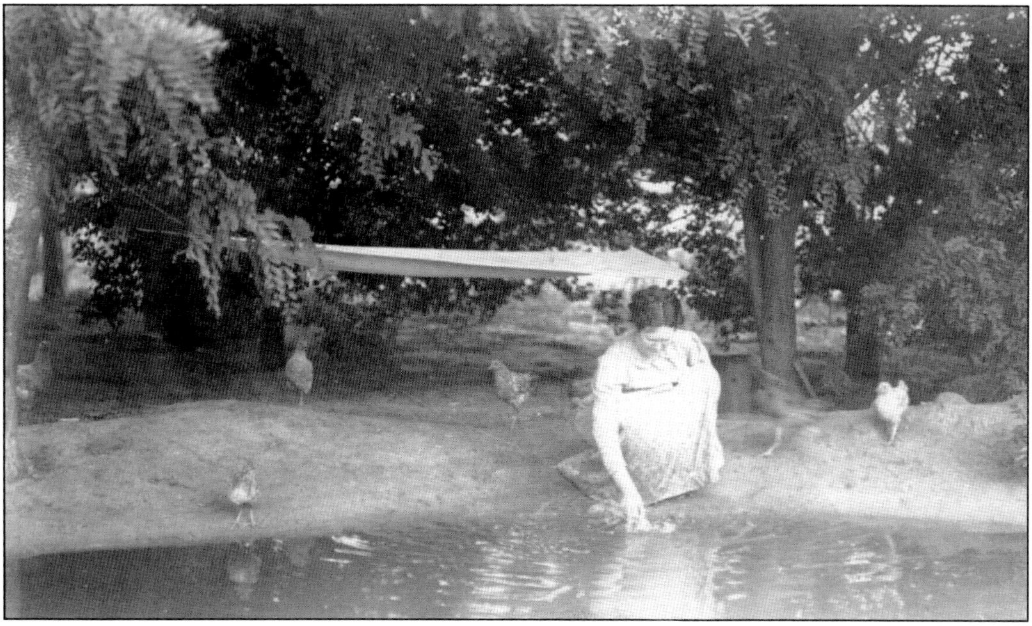

Ida and William Dobson homesteaded four miles northwest of Liberal in 1902. In a short seven years, Ida had created a shady haven complete with mature trees, a pond, a hammock, and a flock of chickens. (Courtesy of Seward County Historical Society.)

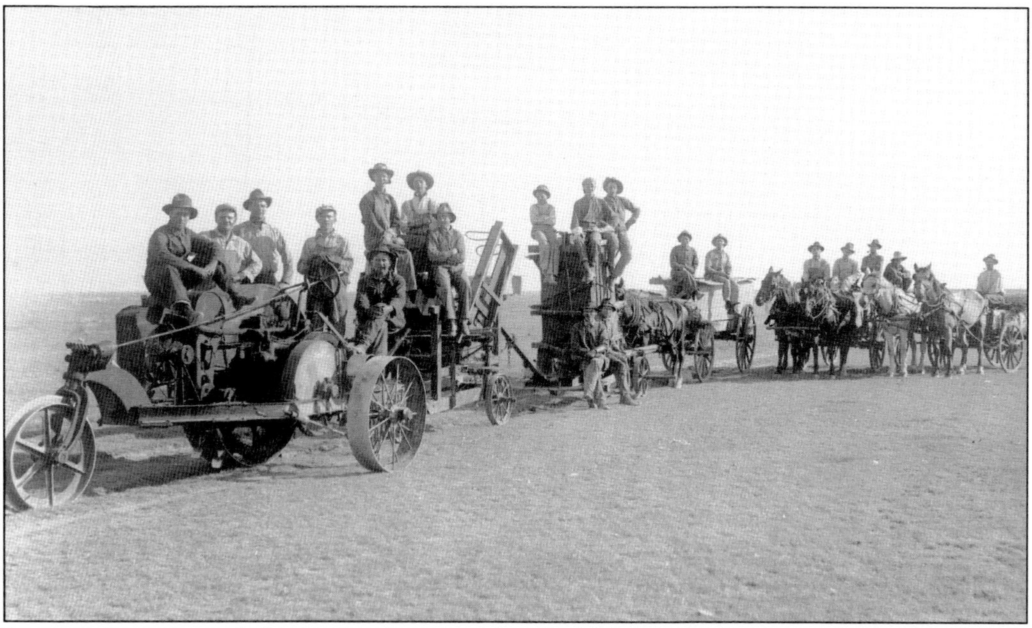

Raising wheat was work, but nothing compared to the labor involved in broomcorn harvest. Men would walk between two rows and break or "pull" the top of the broomcorn brush off the stalk. The brush was then placed in every five rows to dry. The men would go back to the field, cut the brush off the stalk, and haul the brush to a machine that would grind the seed from the brush. The brush was then shocked and compressed into bales weighing 350 to 400 pounds. The broomcorn was then taken to town, purchased by a broomcorn buyer, and shipped by rail to factories. The tractor pictured is a 1912 Samson model. (Courtesy of Seward County Historical Society.)

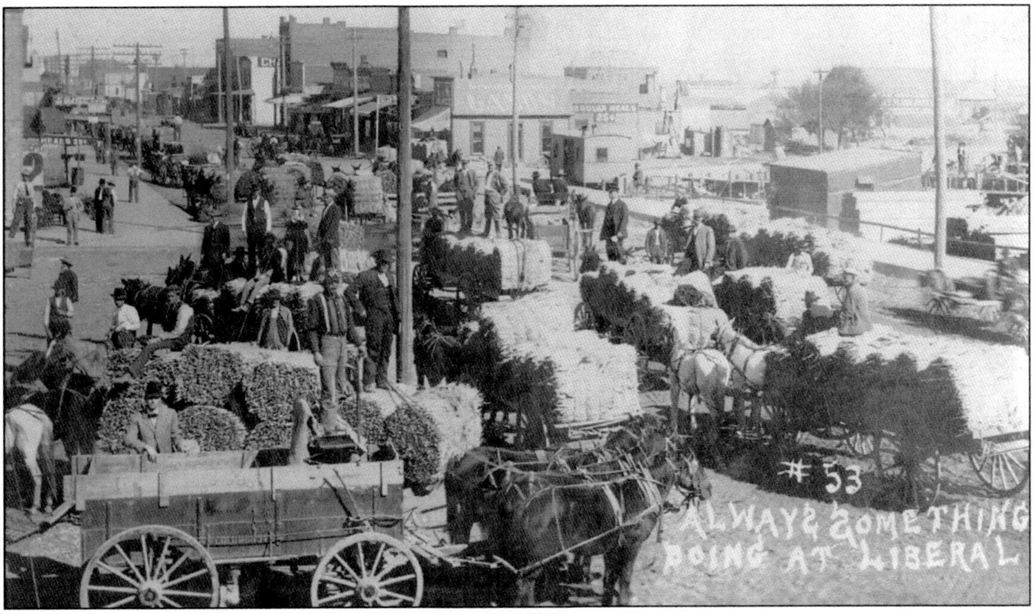

Liberal was touted as the broomcorn capital of the world in 1918. Over one million tons of broomcorn was harvested in Seward County. This photograph shows an abundant harvest loaded on wagons lined up at the Rock Island depot. The men in suits are broomcorn buyers who purchased the crops directly from the farmer.

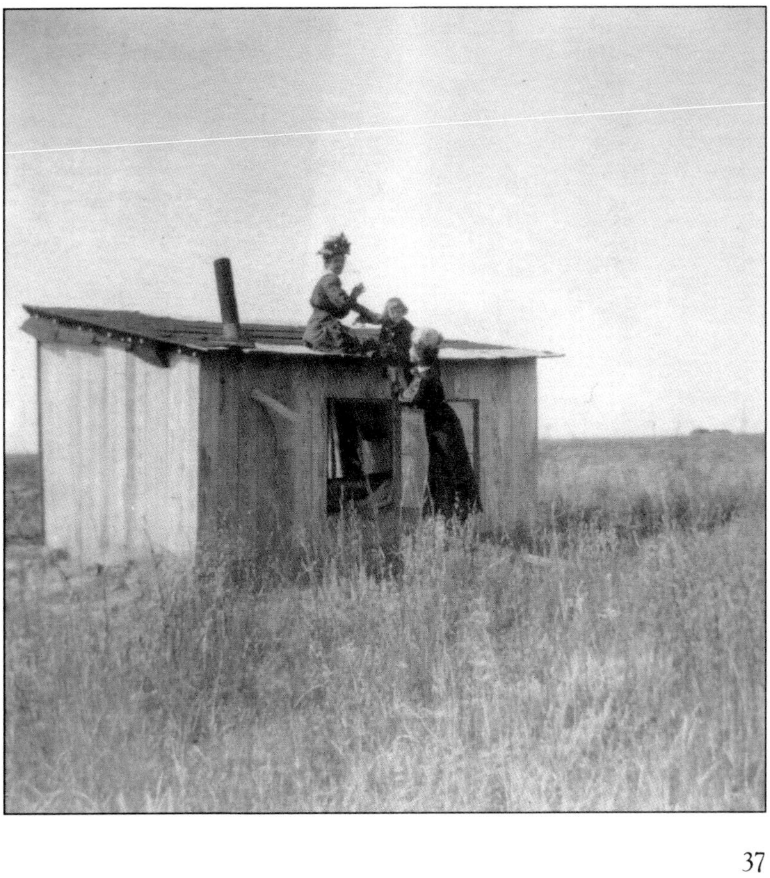

Visiting the claim shack of Jack Vickers is his mother, Belle Vickers (on the roof), cousin Clair Williams (toddler), and sister Irene Vickers. Jack left Liberal to pursue a career in grain commodities, but after oil was discovered in Butler County, Kansas, he changed his interest to oil production. Vickers Oil became a large presence in the Midwest. The company was known for its low gasoline prices and its spokesperson, Lonesome George Gobel. (Courtesy of Seward County Historical Society.)

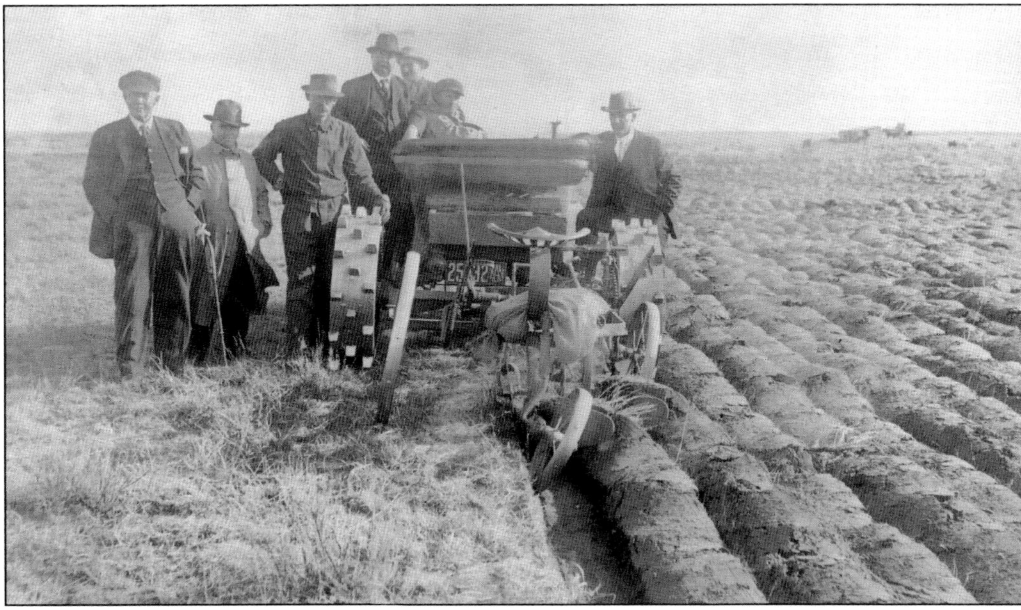

Massive changes to agriculture came after 1910 when large, open-geared tractors came into use. However, the family Model T Ford was also put to use by hitching up plows and planters. With the back end jacked up, the Model T's rear wheels became a belt pulley and could power a small thresher or a corn sheller. Joe Trindle is holding a rifle, John E. George is fourth from the left, and Ed Wood is on the far right. (Courtesy of Seward County Historical Society.)

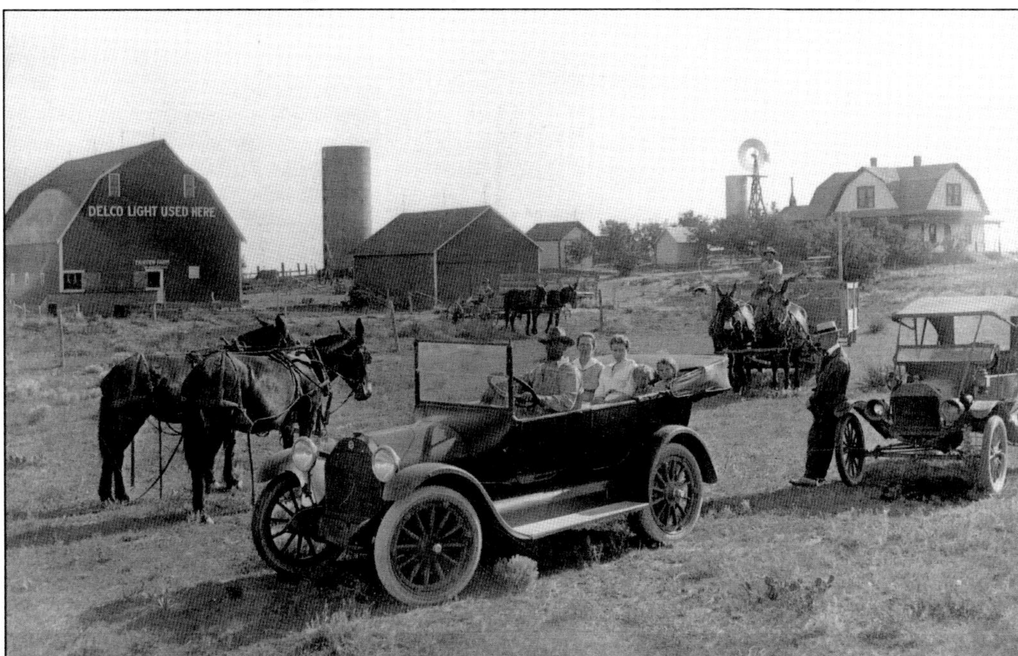

The Fairview Farm, located four miles northeast of Liberal, was obviously a successful one. The barn and home still survive northeast of Liberal. This F.M. Steele photograph shows a gambrel-roofed barn, also echoed in the roofline of the two-story home. (Courtesy of Seward County Historical Society.)

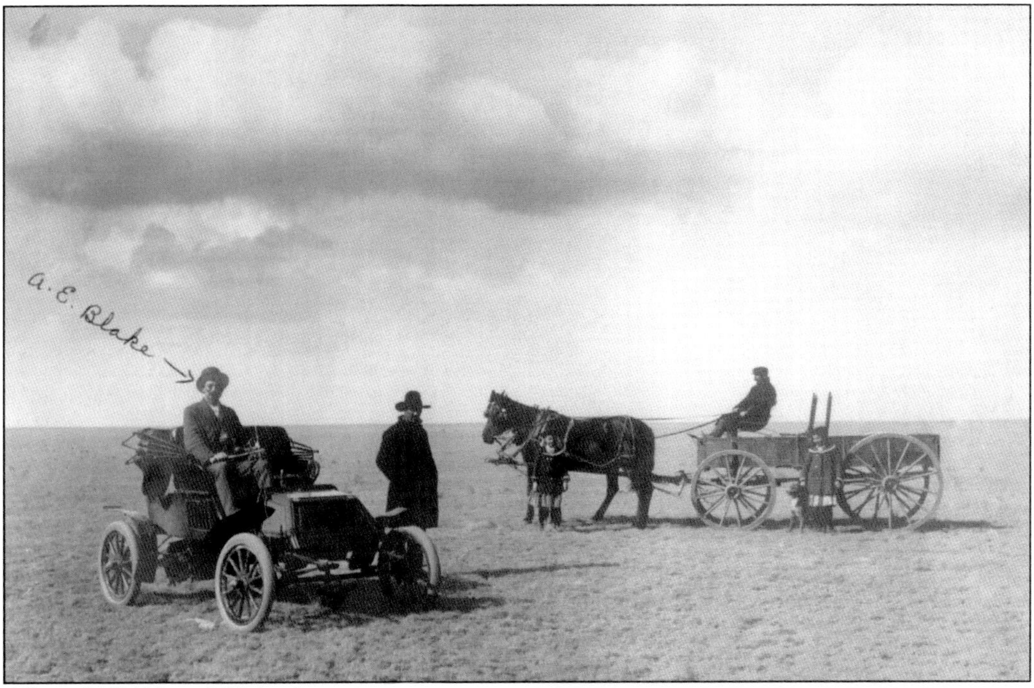

Albert "Al" Edward Blake, born in Canada, moved as a young man to a claim south of Old Tyrone. In 1897, Blake married Alice Steen, and the couple moved to Liberal where they opened a hardware store. Blake constructed a building for the post office at 24 West Second Street. After several years, the post office moved, and Blake decided the building would make a perfect structure for a bank. Through his efforts, the Peoples Bank began business June 14, 1914. Blake is shown in his 1903 Rambler, the first automobile in Liberal. (Courtesy of Seward County Historical Society.)

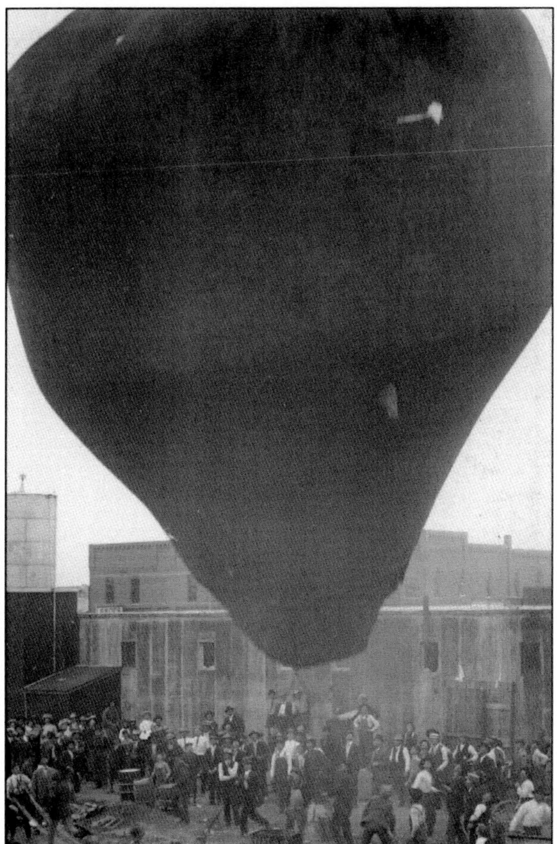

May 10, 1910, was sales day in Liberal. To make it more festive and—of course—to draw a crowd, a balloon and pilot were hired by the Liberal Service Club. The balloon was enormous. It was made of 2,000 yards of dark silk, and the liftoff created such havoc that the event was described as frightful.

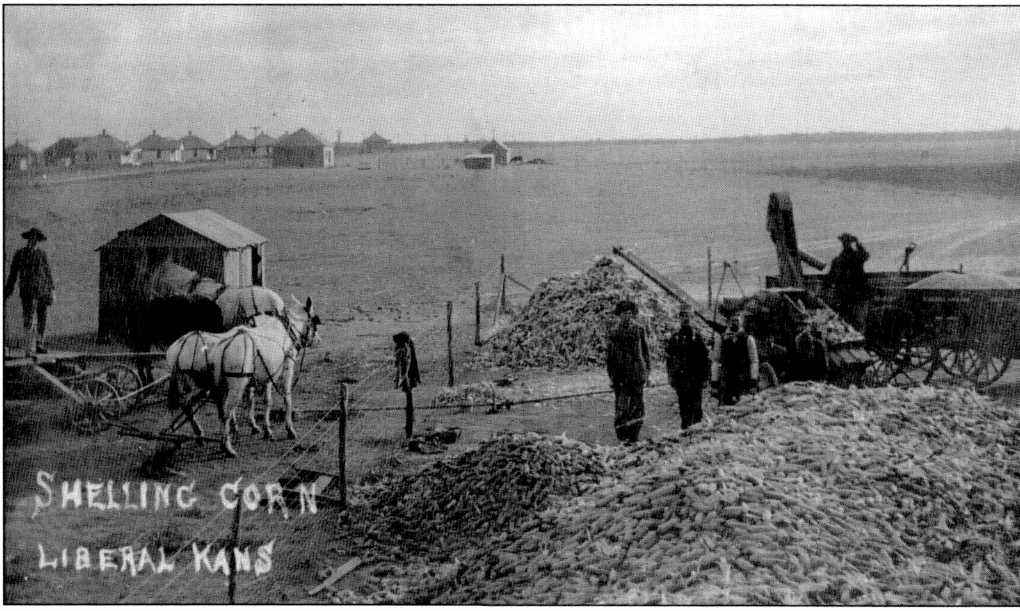

By 1918, Seward County farmers had planted 6,900 acres to corn. Southwest Kansas typically was too hot and dry for corn, but 1915 and 1918 were wet enough to tempt farmers into planting the profitable crop. These men were utilizing a horse-powered, disk-type corn sheller to finish their harvest.

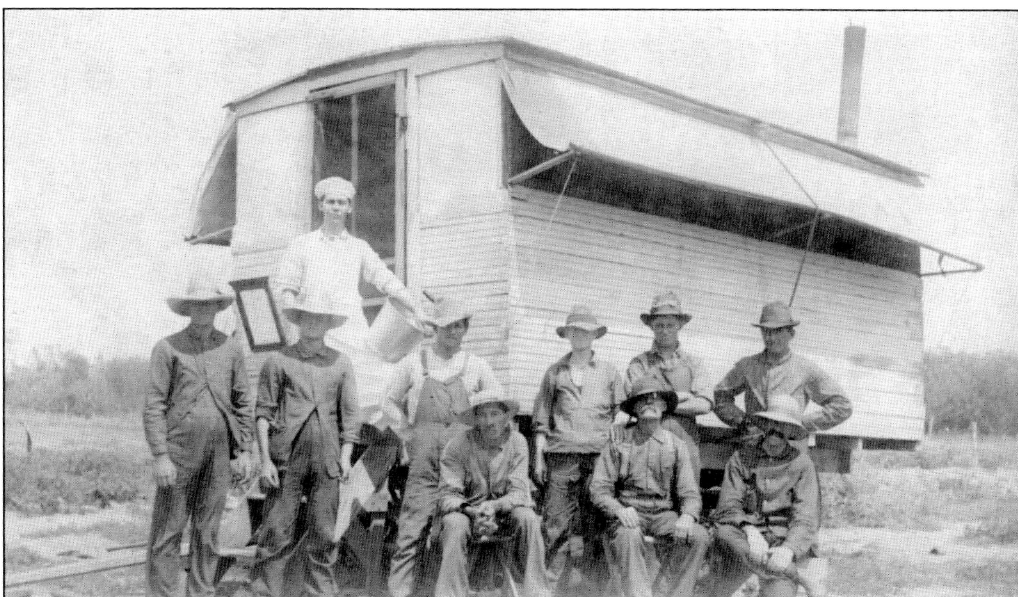

When a crop was ready for harvest, there was no room for delays. With long hours and nonstop labor, meals were often served in the field from the cook shack. Small, portable buildings with flip-up windows were fitted onto a wagon chassis; outfitted with a work counter, stove, pots, and pans; and hauled out to the harvest. Wives, daughters, and hired girls were typically who produced three hearty meals a day for the harvesting crews. This image, however, taken in northern Seward County, shows a male cook with some of his diners. (Courtesy of Seward County Historical Society.)

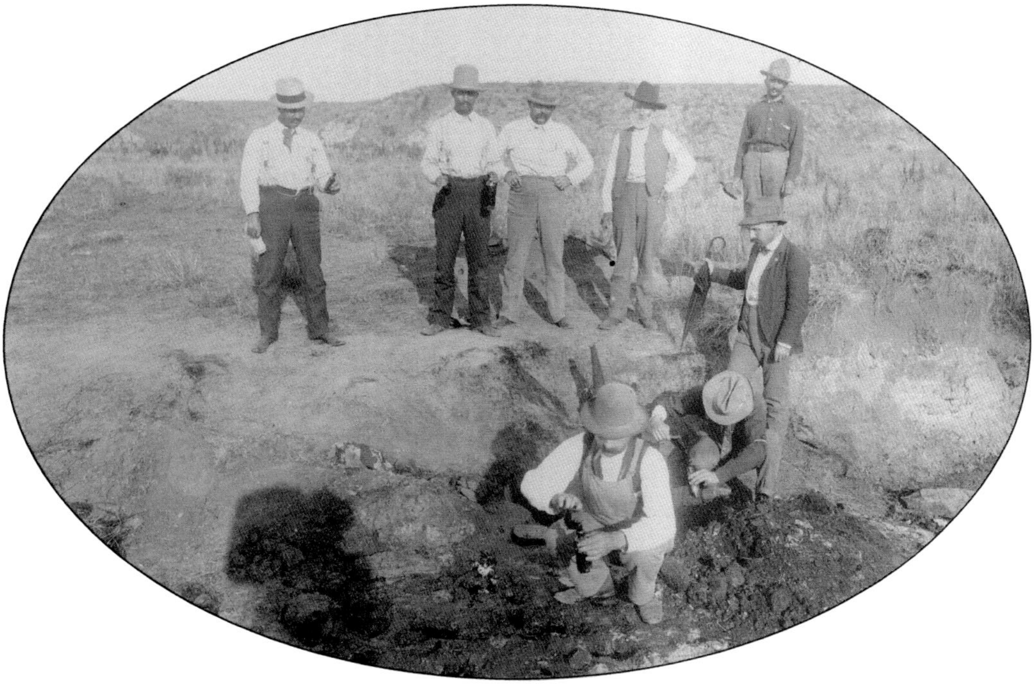

This F.M. Steele photograph captures unidentified men collecting oil in bottles from a shallow well in Seward County. The location, participants, and occasion are unfortunately unknown. (Courtesy of Seward County Historical Society.)

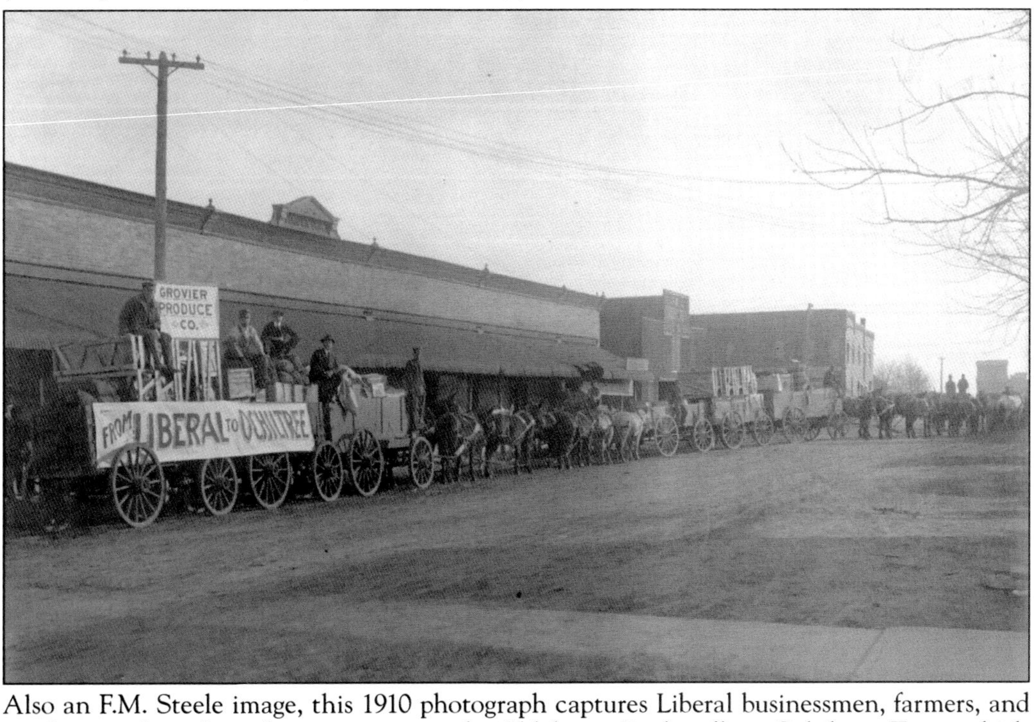

Also an F.M. Steele image, this 1910 photograph captures Liberal businessmen, farmers, and ranchers ready to drive their teams across the Oklahoma Panhandle to Ochiltree, Texas, which took three days travel time from Liberal. (Courtesy of Seward County Historical Society.)

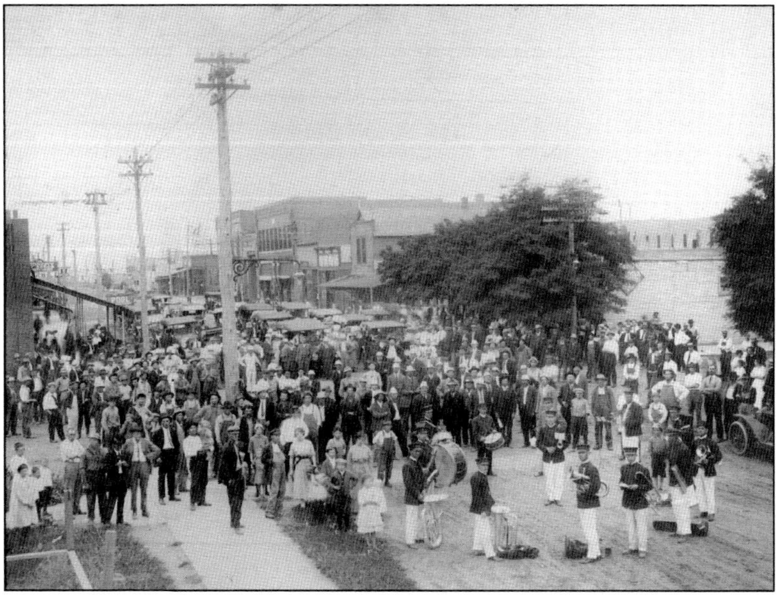

The Liberal Boosters were the early-day chamber of commerce that often traveled to neighboring towns to boost the advantages of trading in Liberal. This F.M. Steele photograph shows a large gathering at Third Street and Kansas Avenue, complete with the Liberal Booster Band, in 1914. (Courtesy of Seward County Historical Society.)

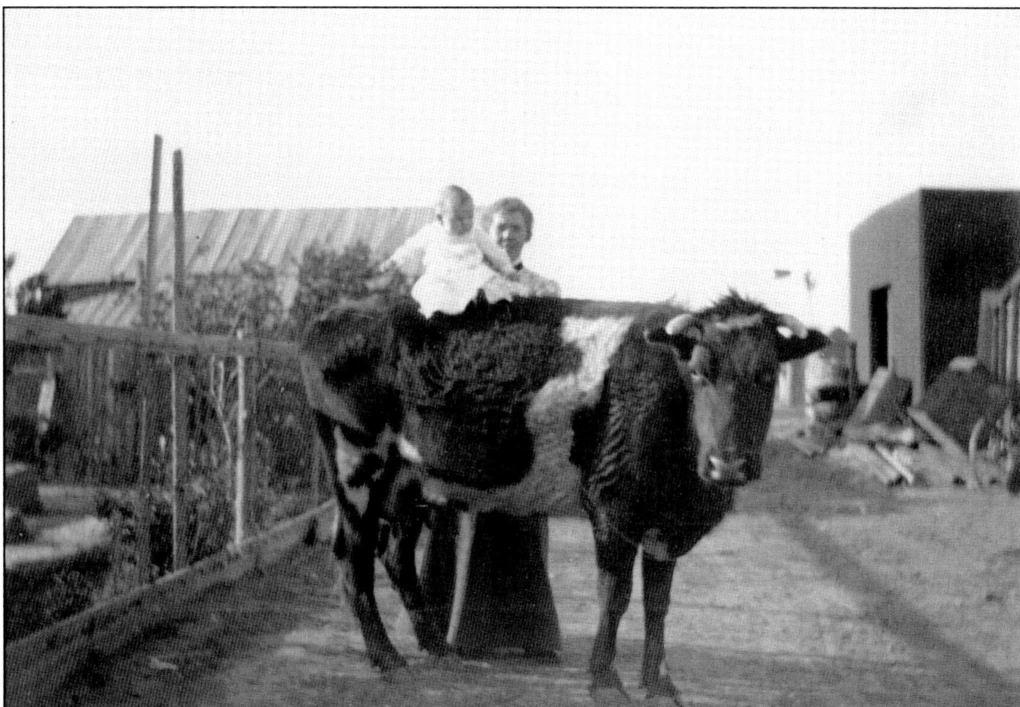

It was common for Liberal town residents to have their own windmill, outhouse, and milk cow. Pictured in their alley is Agnes Rea (the baby), Helen Rea, and Bertha the cow. Bertha had a reputation for standing in the middle of the railroad tracks and daring the trains that were leaving the Liberal depot. Bertha always stood her ground until personally shooed off the tracks by the engineers. (Courtesy of Mary Brewington.)

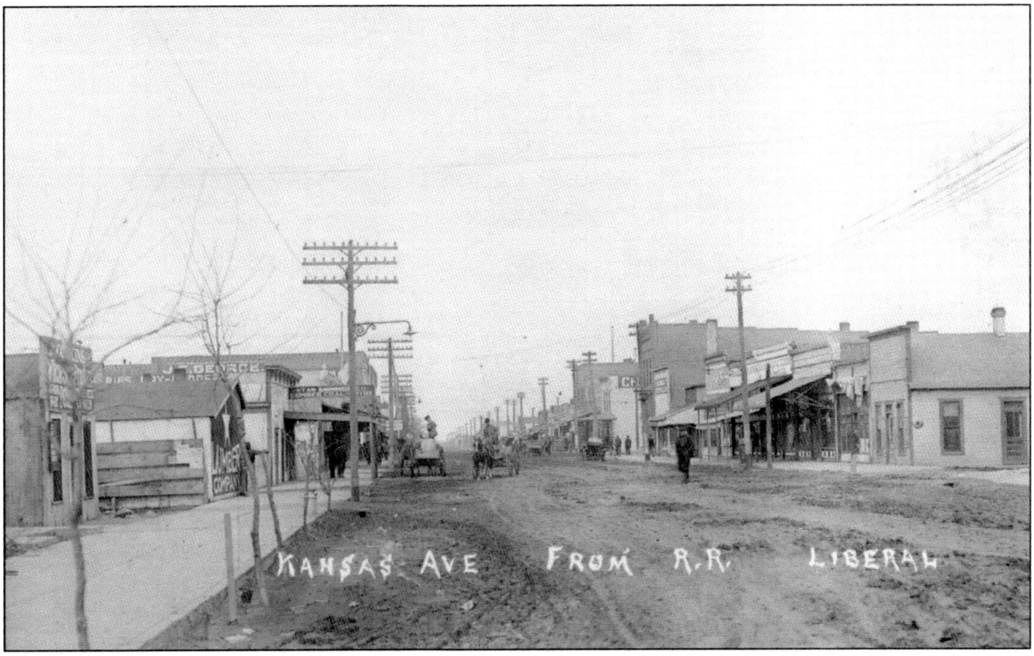

When this 1912 photograph was taken, Liberal had grown into a lively trading center. Looking north from the railroad tracks, Kansas Avenue businesses had electrical and telephone lines, street lamps, and boardwalks.

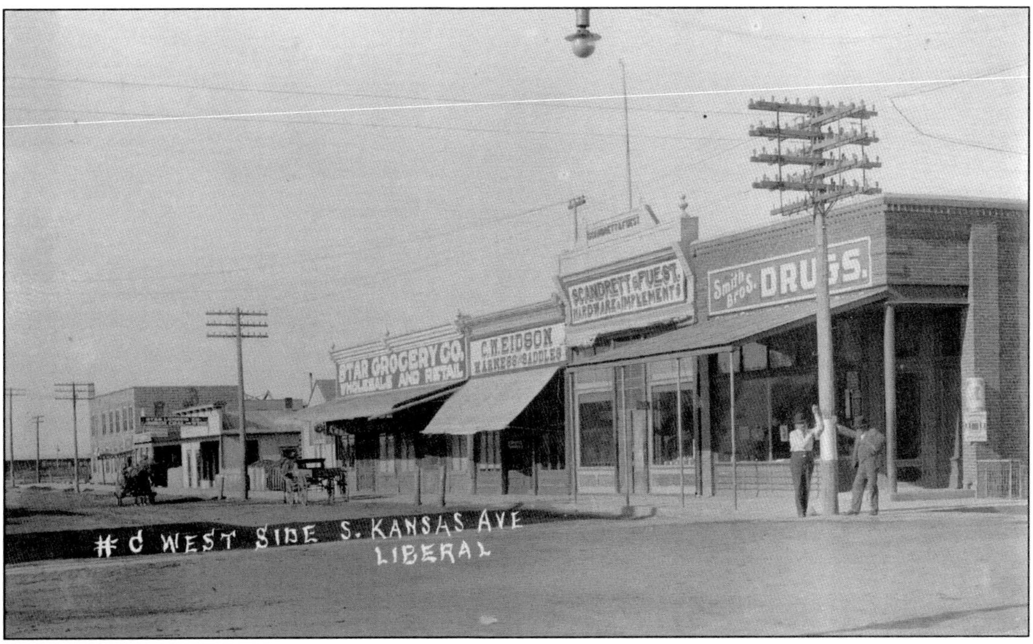

The telephone arrived in Liberal in 1897 with a single line and five telephones. The telephones were at the Rock Island depot, Cort Brown's home, the Smith Brothers Drug Store, the O.K. Ranch, and the Smith brothers' ranch on Sharps Creek in the Oklahoma Panhandle. The rural line was partially laid on top of convenient fence posts. In 1906, Dr. George Smith and his pharmacist brother Tom applied for the telephone franchise. The drugstore's phone number was 1.

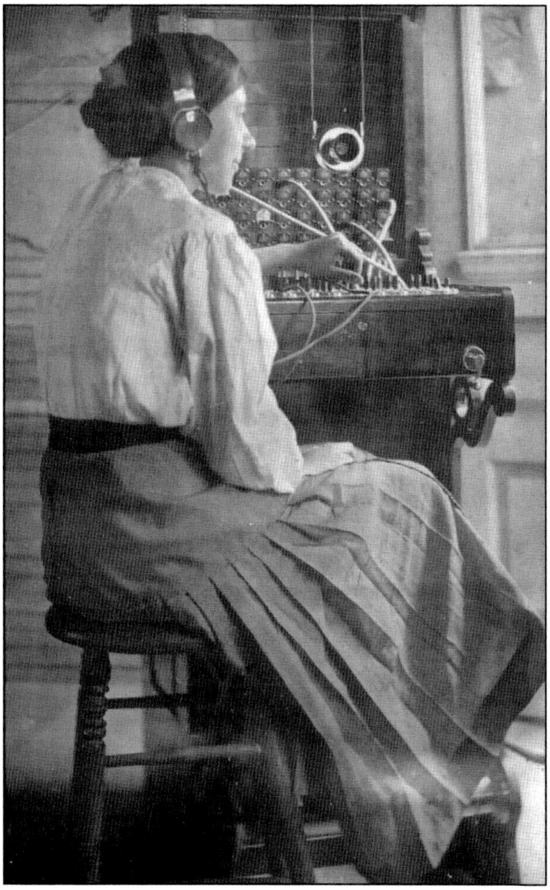

Sarah West sits at her switchboard in the upstairs telephone office at 10 West Second Street. The telephone company was purchased from the Smith brothers in 1909 by L.W. Stevensson. By this time, the company had lines to Beaver, Hooker, and Meade. Later, Stevensson constructed his own building one block north on Third Street.

Liberal Light, Ice & Power was established in January 1908 with H.W. Magruder as manager, Henry Walker as secretary, and E.E. Cook as electrician. Power was furnished by a steam engine and two boilers, which produced 200 kilowatts. The ice plant produced 20 tons of ice daily, most of which was used by produce trains. Ice was also delivered throughout Liberal to home iceboxes. In 1921, Felix Cadou became manager. Cadou reputedly came from a French and English royal family.

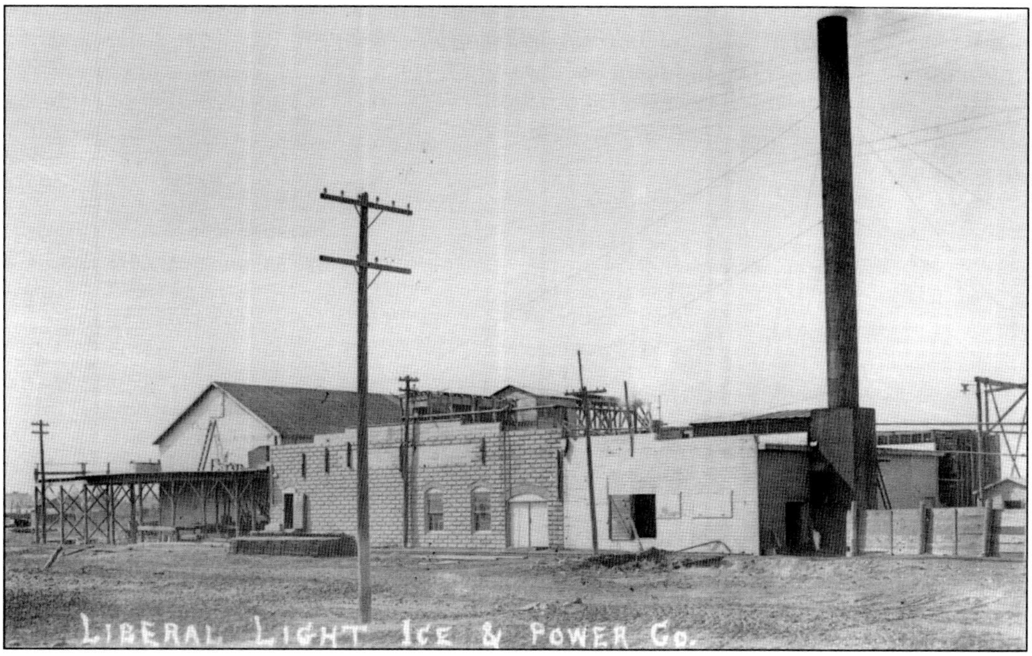

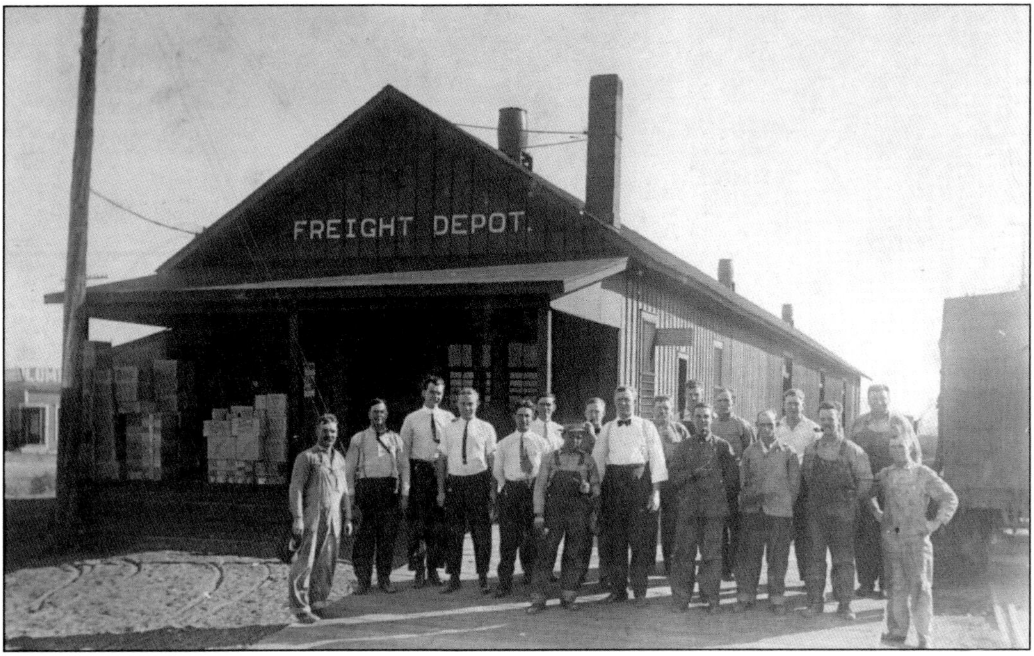

The freight depot was the important place in Liberal. Practically everything was shipped to Liberal over the rails, including cars, groceries, books, and building supplies. This simple building was located to the east of the depot. The photograph was taken in September 1914.

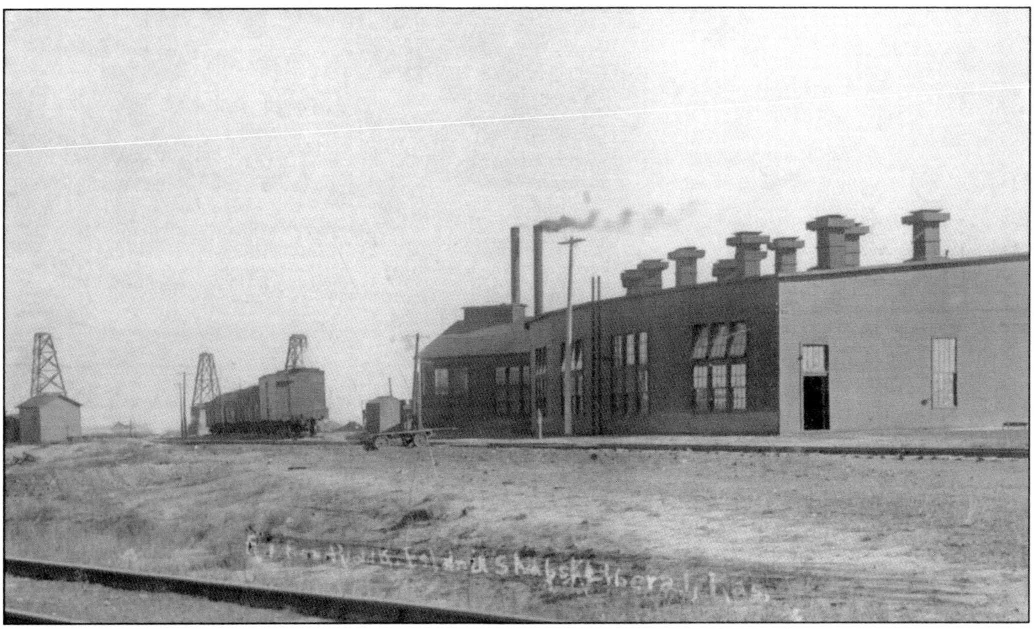
The brick Rock Island roundhouse was built in 1889 and originally had one employee. Steam locomotives were so massive that the turntable was essential for maneuvering the engines so they could be repaired and returned to service. After diesels became common, railroads had little need for roundhouses and the building was torn down. The turntable from the Liberal roundhouse, however, is still employed (even though upside down) as the Massoni Bridge, which spans the railroad cut between Liberal and Kismet. (Courtesy of Seward County Historical Society.)

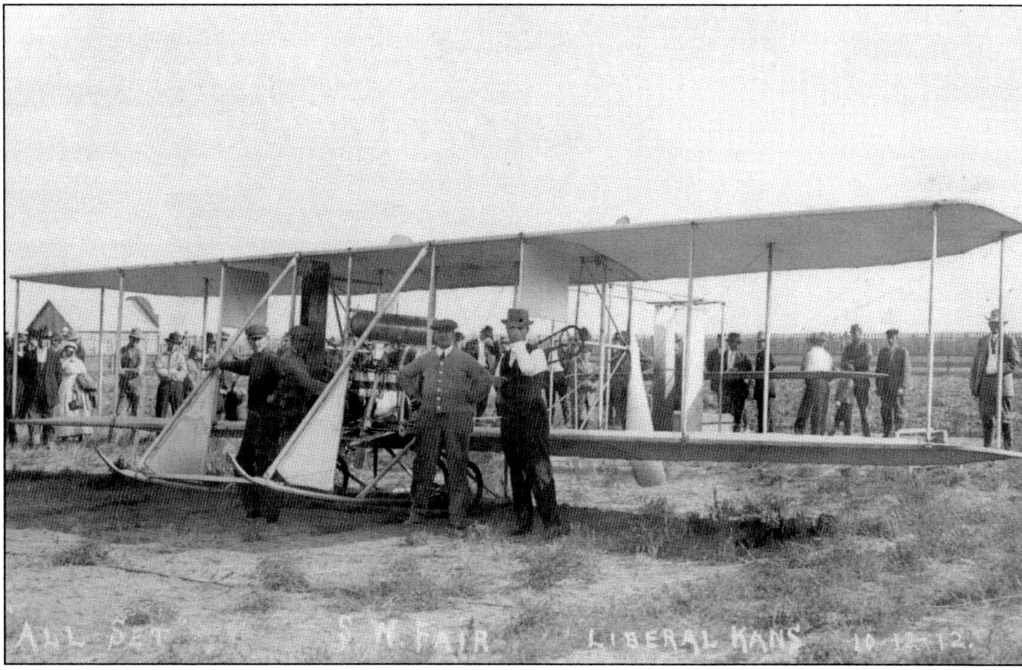

The Southwest Fair Association was organized March 5, 1913, but earlier in mid-October 1912, a fair was held. People came mainly to see the "new-fangled airships." The grandstand is filled to capacity with spectators waiting to see the Wright Flyer in action.

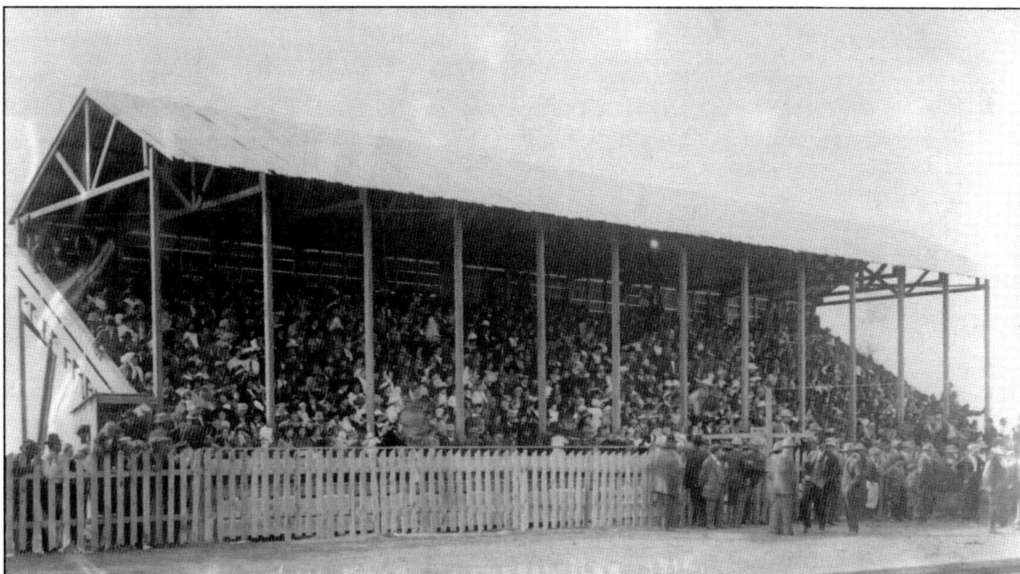

Cars were uncommon in Liberal, and an airplane was something of an once-in-a-lifetime sight. Consequently, the fairgrounds grandstand was filled to capacity. The Southwest Fair Association was the idea of Warren Farmer, J.F. Funk, Lee Larrabee, and C.D. Gasaway for farmers and producers to show off their crops and to entertain those who attended. The fair was discontinued in 1918 at the beginning of World War I. In 1919, all buildings were sold, except for the grandstand. Seward County purchased the grandstand and land for $2,000.

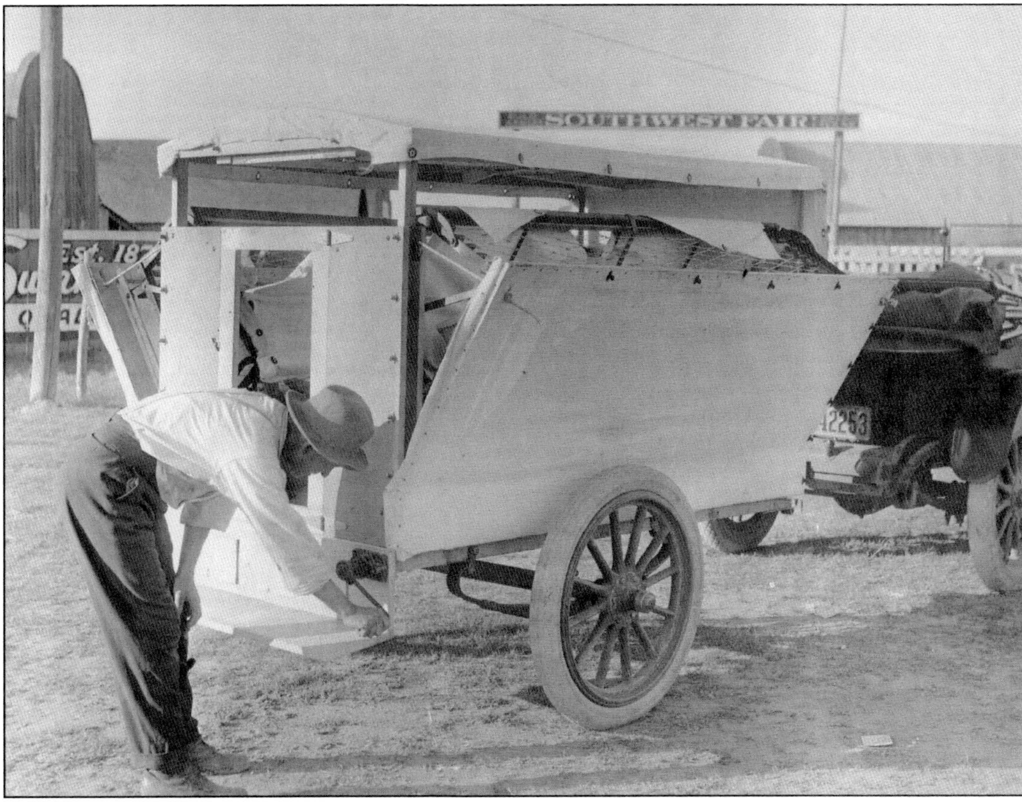

Charles E. Hancock arrived in southwest Kansas in 1886 and was one of few who saw the last wild herd of bison in No Man's Land. Hancock, who became a builder, constructed 114 homes between 1914 and 1920, mainly in the Sunnyside Addition in Liberal. He was also an inventor. In preparation for a trip to Missouri, Hancock placed a platform over a small two-wheel trailer, constructed sidewalls and ends out of canvas, attached everything together and devised a crank that would raise and lower all the comforts of home. This F.M. Steele photograph shows Hancock demonstrating his early camper at the Southwest Fair. (Courtesy of Seward County Historical Society.)

Baseball has always been an enjoyable pastime for Seward County folks. One of Liberal's teams was the Yellow Jackets. Lee Larrabee (in the striped shirt and stockings) is being roughed up by an unidentified player. Lee's official position—other than being the team's jester—is not known. (Courtesy of Seward County Historical Society.)

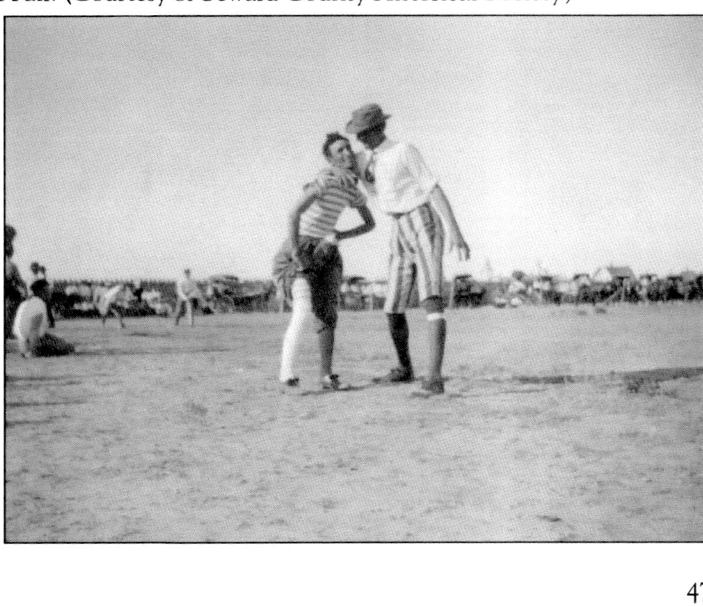

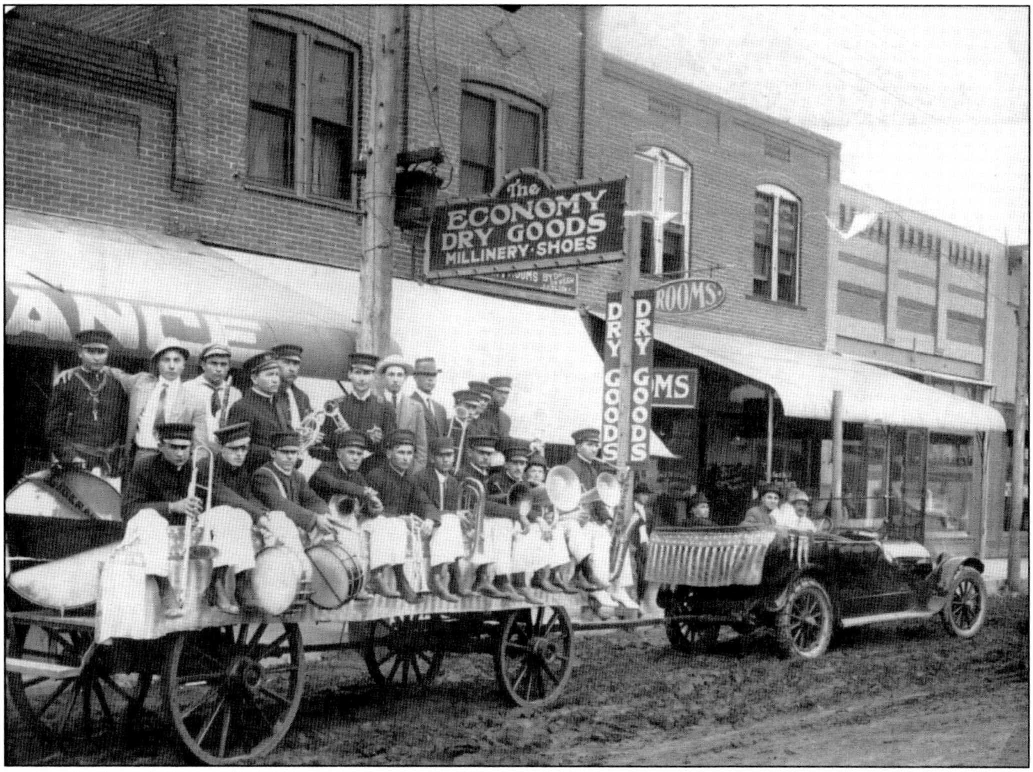

Liberal's band formed in 1912 and was considered a good source of entertainment. The band played for meetings and the Liberal Boosters and was towed about town by John Baughman's Apperson 8. Baughman is in the driver's seat.

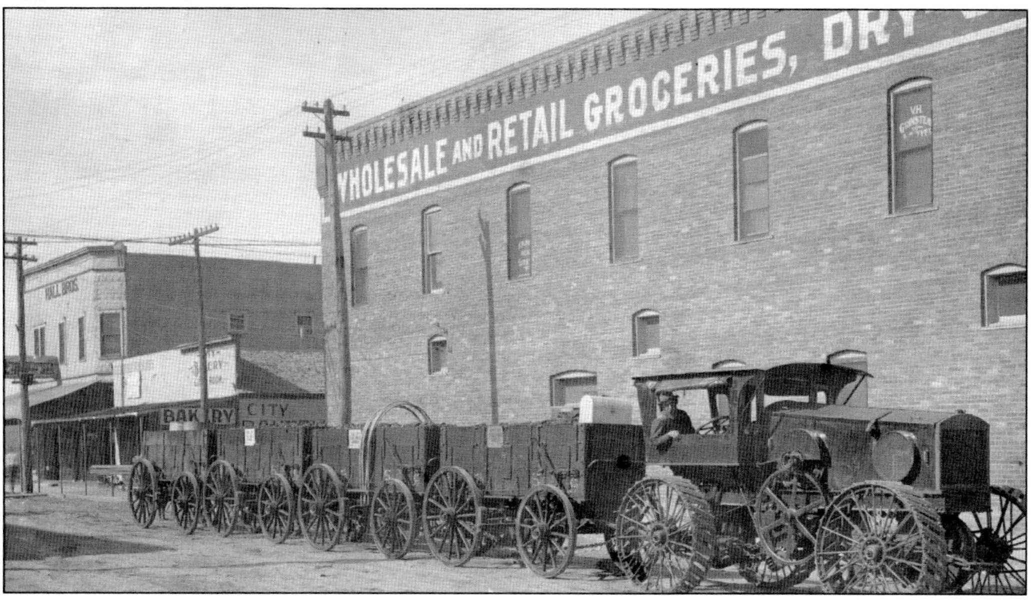

This gentleman is headed out onto Liberal city streets to deliver coal. The wagons are hitched to an unusual Heer tractor. The image was taken on West Second Street adjacent to the J.E. George building.

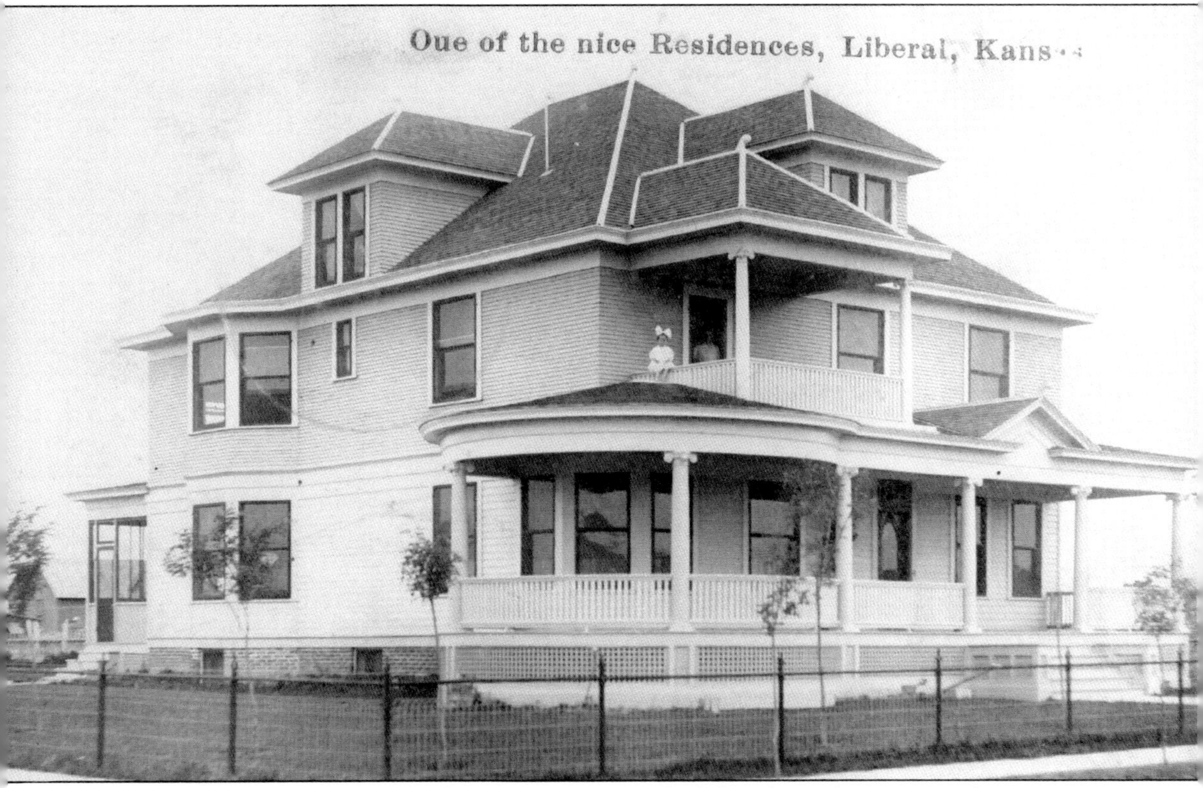

This grand residence at 506 North Sherman Avenue was built by Abe and Hattie Stoufer in 1906. Abe was the editor of the *Liberal News* and served as postmaster. The home features considerable rooms, a double staircase, and a third-story ballroom. It has been said that when the Stoufers entertained in the summer, all windows and doors were thrown open, and people danced and laughed the night away. Margaret Stoufer is on the balcony.

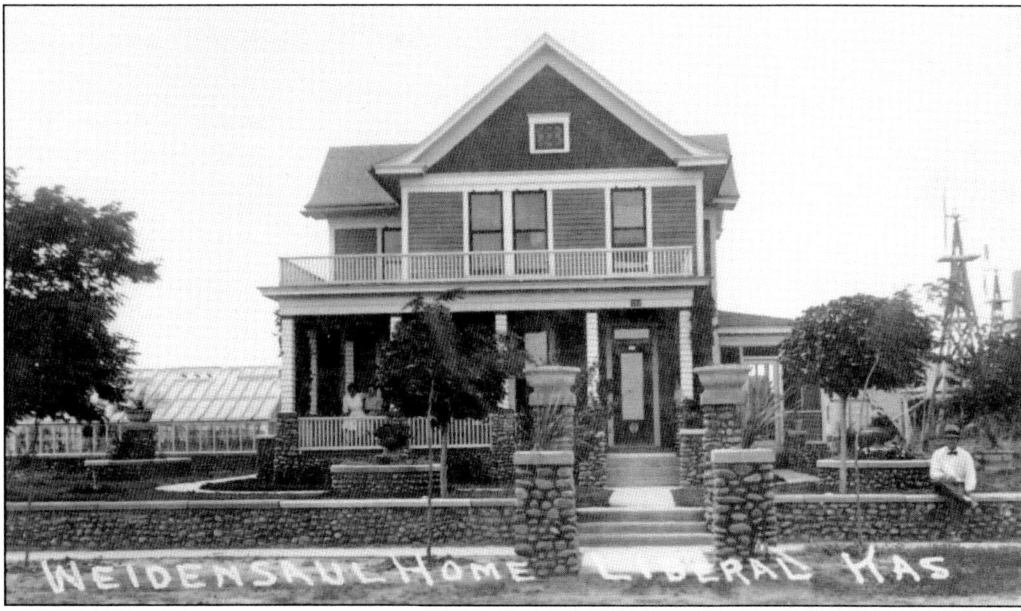

The Weidensaul home was built by L.D. "Wiggly" Weidensaul at the cost of $30,000. Wiggly came to Liberal in 1904, followed by his two sisters Blanche and Zula, who were milliners and florists. Wiggly was a cartographer, specializing in local maps and plats. He also invested in real estate and loved to garden. Notice the greenhouse and the extensive use of river rock.

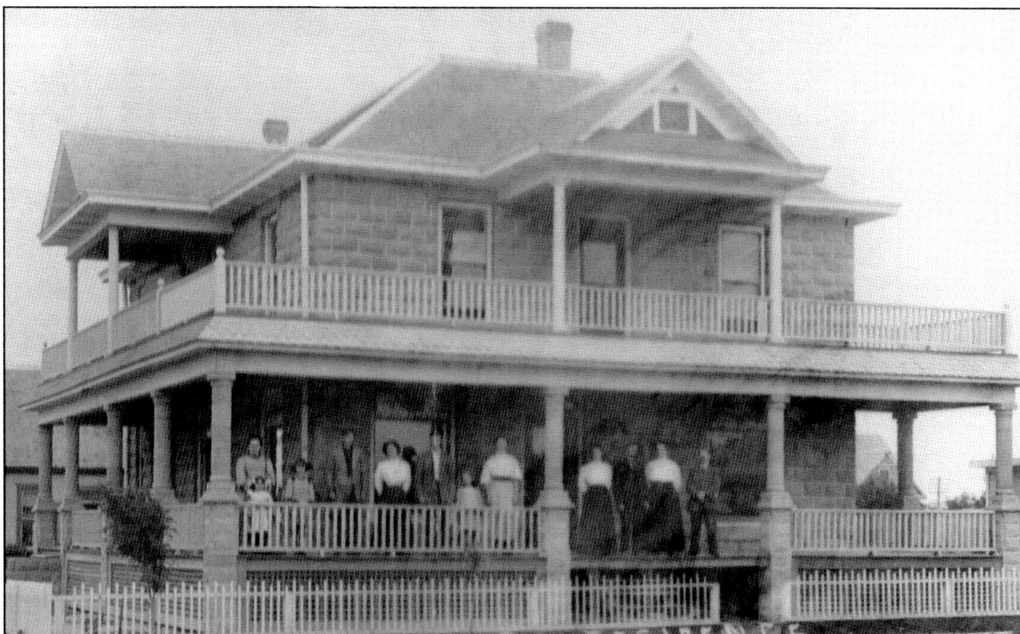

John and Agnes Printz built this home, located at 323 North Sherman Avenue, but never lived in it. John was a well-known contractor, constructing many residences and buildings in the Liberal area. Handmade cement stone was used for this dwelling. John's penchant for dentil molding is evident in many of his homes. The Liberal Gas Company building, at 18 West Third Street, was his last project. (Courtesy of Dessie Jenkins.)

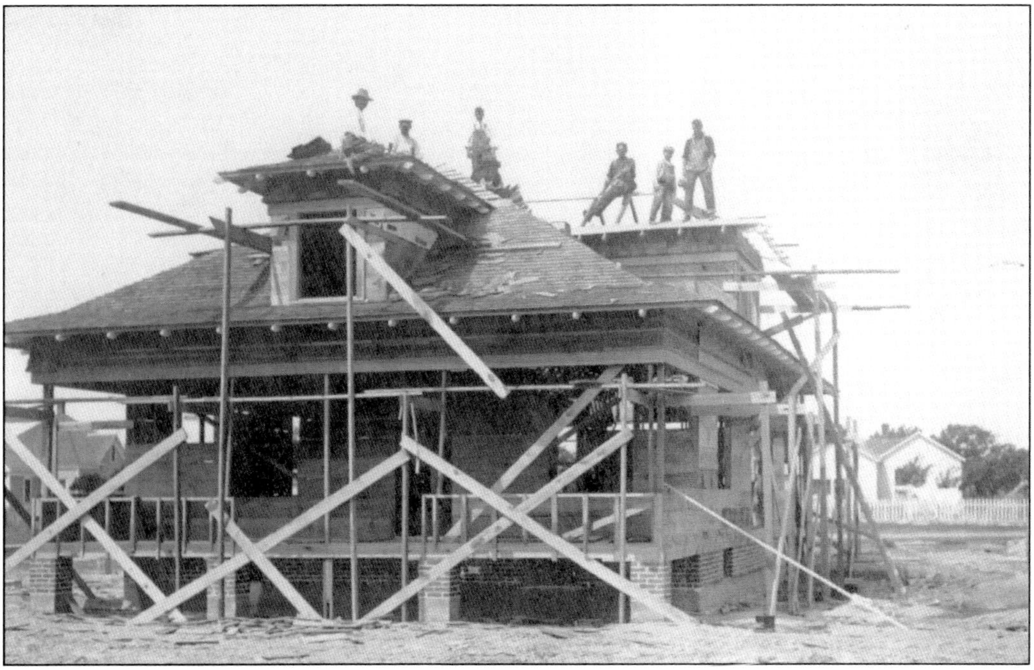

Another John Printz project was this home located on North Grant Avenue. The entire Printz family pitched in to help John with construction. On the roof are, from left to right, John Printz, Mr. Cude, Milous Printz, unidentified, Lloyd Printz, and Earl Printz. (Courtesy of Dessie Jenkins.)

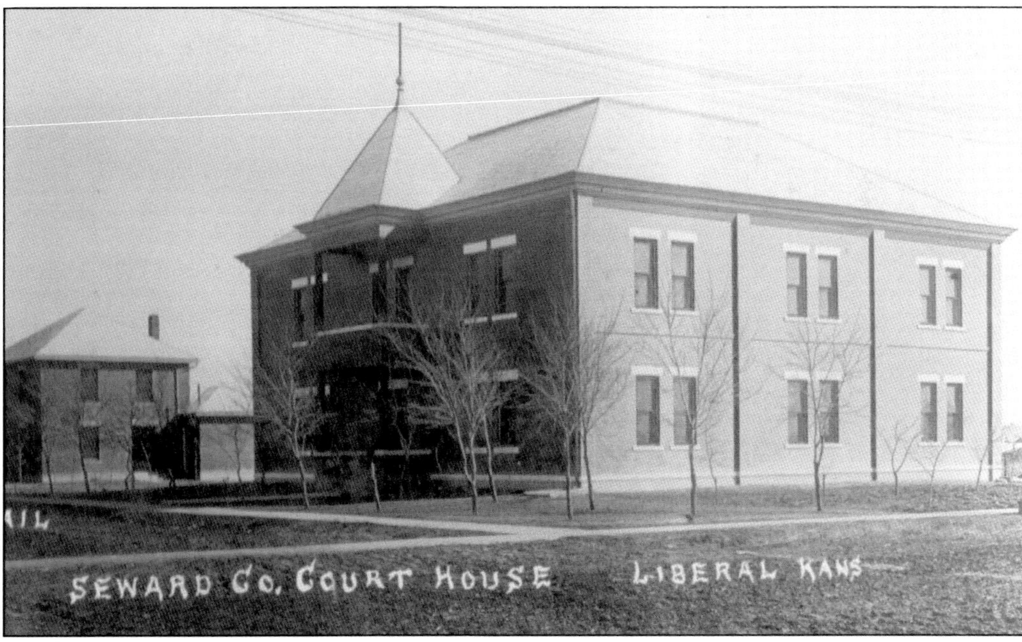

This two-story brick building in the 400 block of North Washington Avenue was completed in 1908. The courthouse cost the taxpayers $12,000. The building had fireproof vaults and was heated by a basement boiler. The building also had an unusual floor plan. The bathrooms were located upstairs, so when someone was in need of the restroom, they had to traipse through the courtroom, halting many a solemn trial. A brick jailhouse was located adjacent to the north.

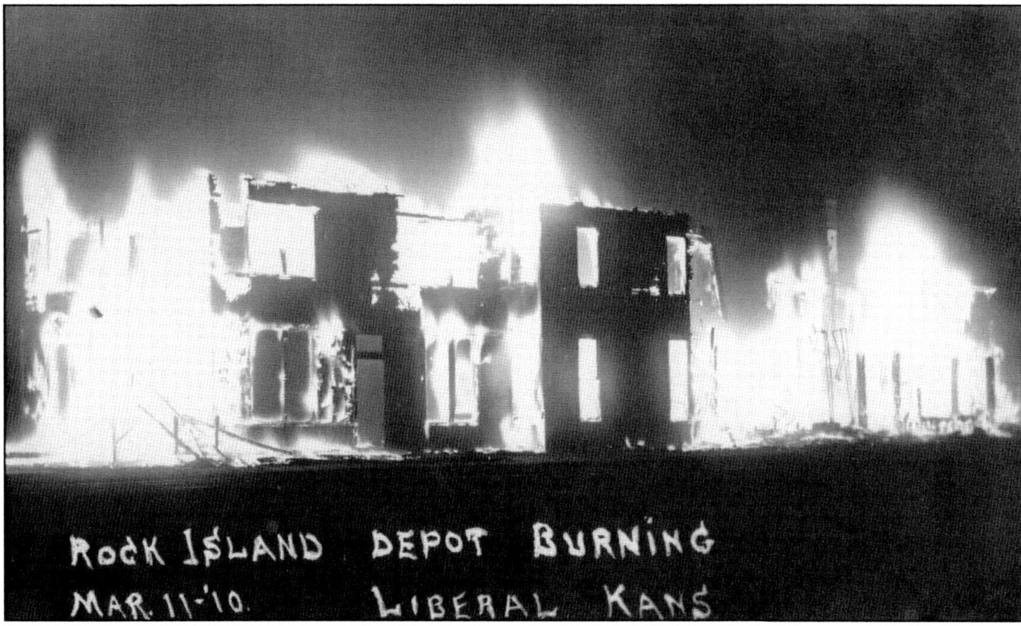

A long blast from a resting Rock Island locomotive signaled something was wrong at the depot. On March 11, 1910, a fire destroyed the wooden depot. The limited resources of the fire department and a hastily formed bucket brigade were not enough to save the building. The next morning, townspeople saw nothing more than a blackened mass of timbers and twisted brass bedsteads.

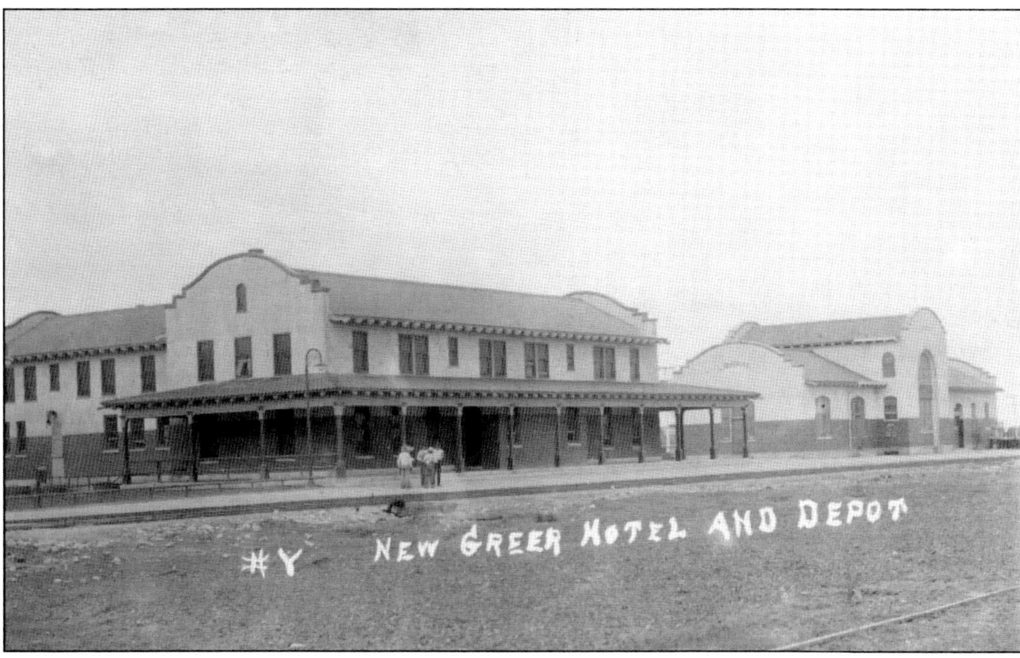

The new Grier House and Rock Island depot opened for business in 1911. The stucco and tile building to the east housed the ticket office, waiting room, railway express, and railroad offices. The west building held a formal restaurant, lunch counter, kitchen, laundry facilities, and a hotel.

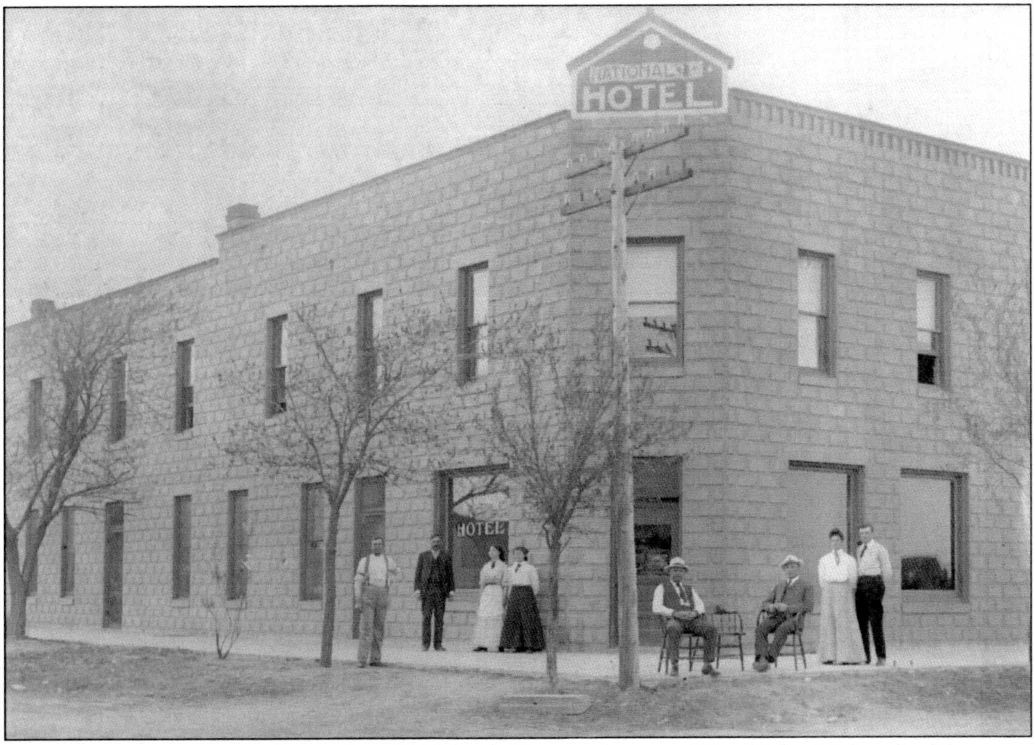

The National Hotel was located at 300 North Kansas Avenue. The 50-by-80-foot building was constructed of cement blocks made locally by A.A. Lien and E.E. Byland. The general contractor was L.H. Sutton, who also built the Seward County Courthouse and the Smith Brothers Drug Store. Cash Waters, the owner, is second from the left. The National later became the Sanford Hotel and last served as the Morrow Hospital. (Courtesy of Seward County Historical Society.)

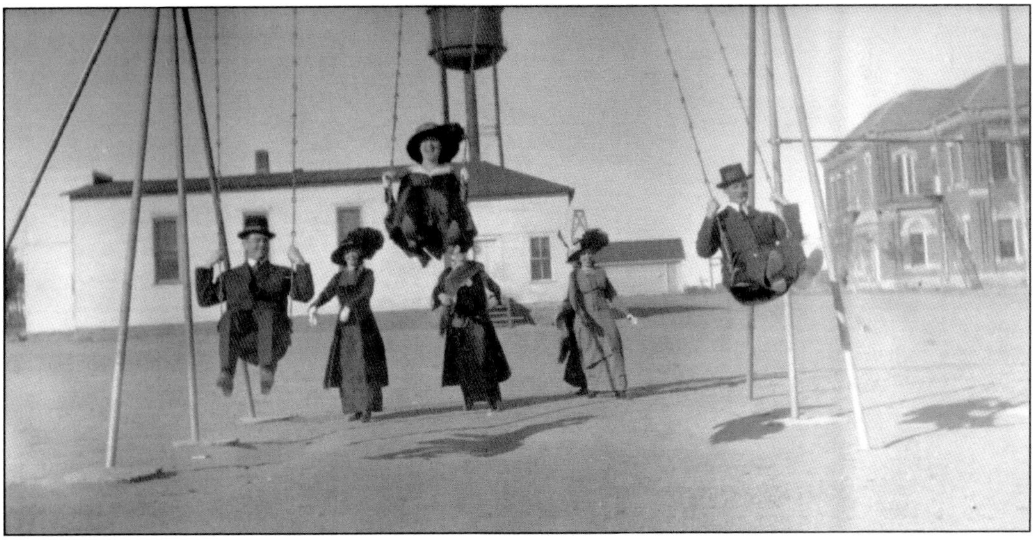

Vegetation may be scarce, but smiles are not as a couple of guys take their turns in the swings at the school playground on North Lincoln Street. The first metal water tower in the city is in the background. It was located on the northeast corner of Seventh and Lincoln Streets. (Courtesy Seward County Historical Society.)

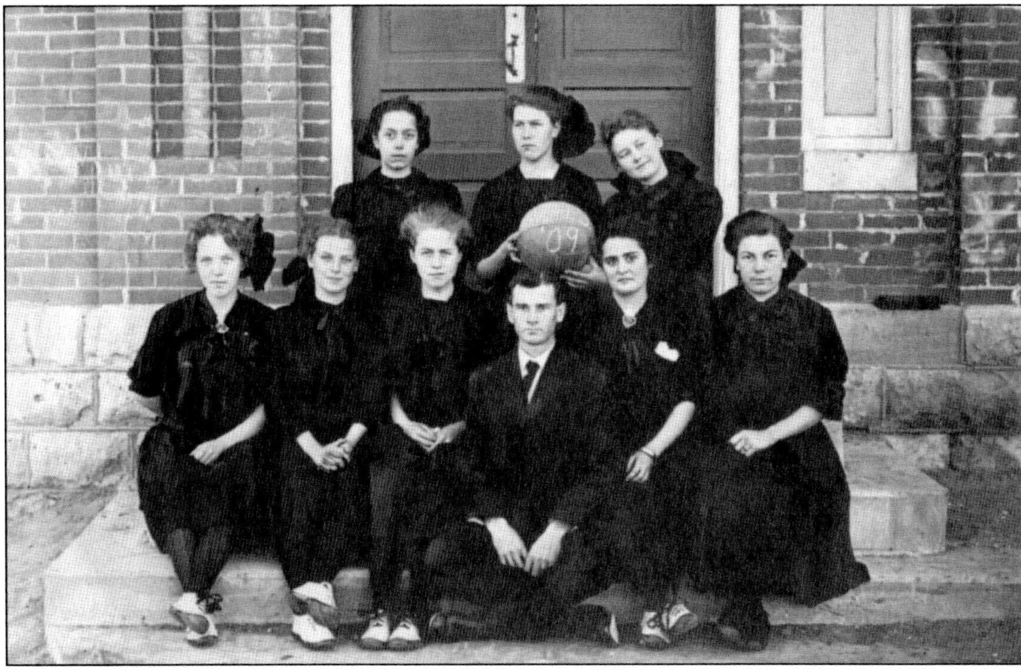

The 1909 girls basketball team poses for a photograph on the front steps of the Liberal School. From left to right are (first row) Lafaun Wilkins, Hazel Scandrett, Mae Stevensson, Professor Rindom, Laura Wood, and Edna Fuest; (second row) Maurine Long, Edna Stevensson, and Mildred Hood.

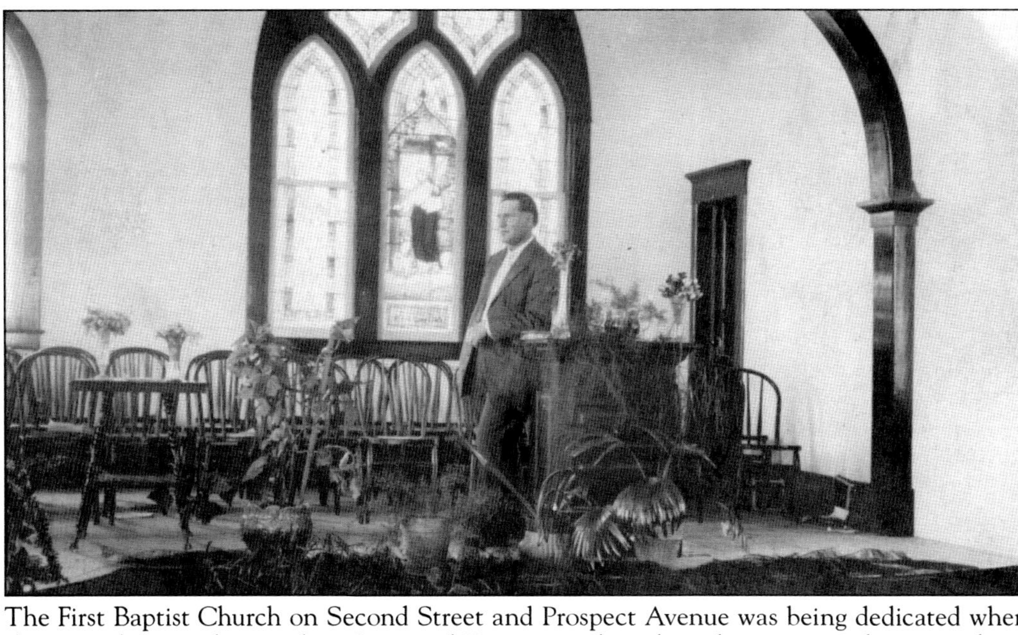

The First Baptist Church on Second Street and Prospect Avenue was being dedicated when this 1910 photograph was taken. Reverend Harper stands at the pulpit amongst the many plants well-wishers had sent. The structure cost $5,500 and was thought to be the nicest church building in western Kansas.

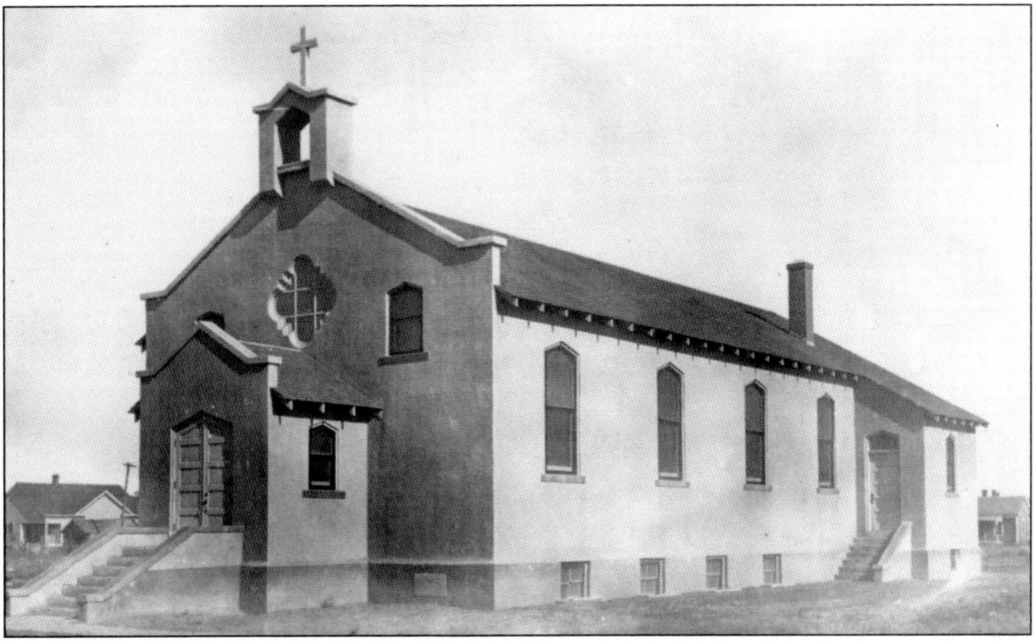

The first St. Anthony's Catholic church was built and dedicated at First Street and Prospect Avenue in June 1916. Before construction began, Had Lane held services in his home for the 48 parishioners. Fr. Anthony Herrman served as first pastor, followed by Fr. Emil Meyers. The church was destroyed by fire in 1949. (Courtesy of Seward County Historical Society.)

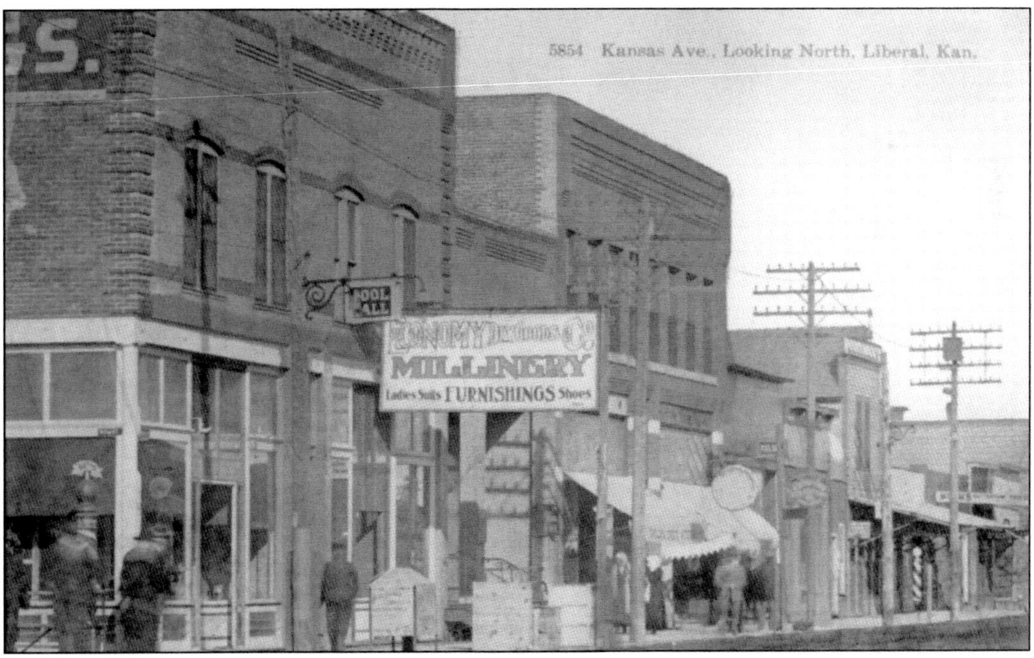

The 200 block of Kansas Avenue had an impressive array of businesses. This view shows the west side of the street. From left to right are the J. E. George Furnishings Store, the Woolley Pool Hall, Economy Dry Goods, First National Bank, and Taylor Drugs. Many more offices and services occupied the upper and basement levels of these buildings.

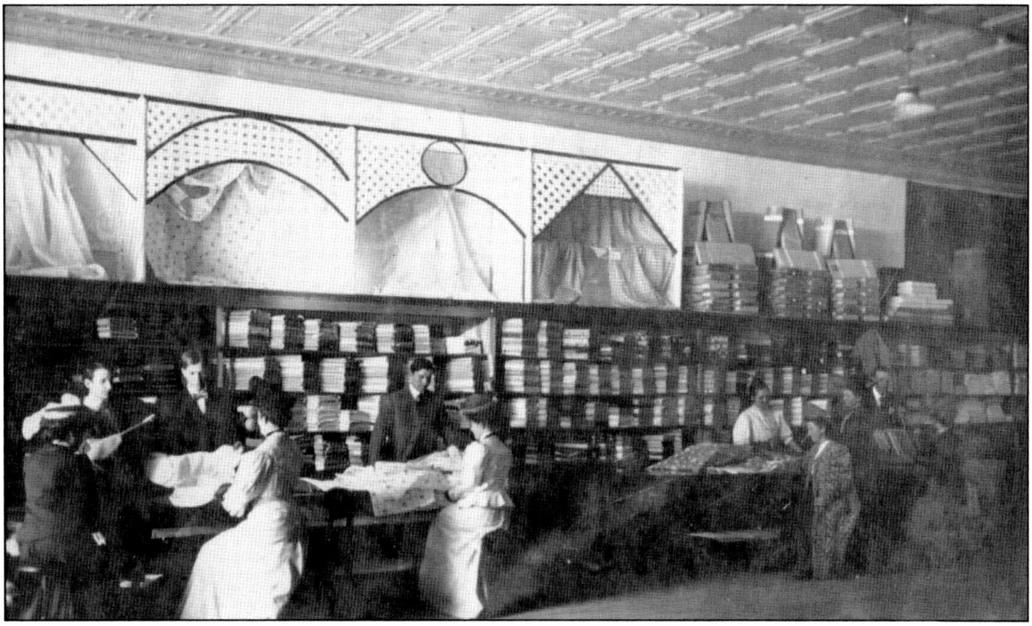

The interior of the Charles Summers Store at 202 North Kansas Avenue was spacious enough to handle hundreds of bolts of fabric for the discerning lady shopper. Judging by the number of clerks and their attentive posture, customer service was an important feature at the Summers Store.

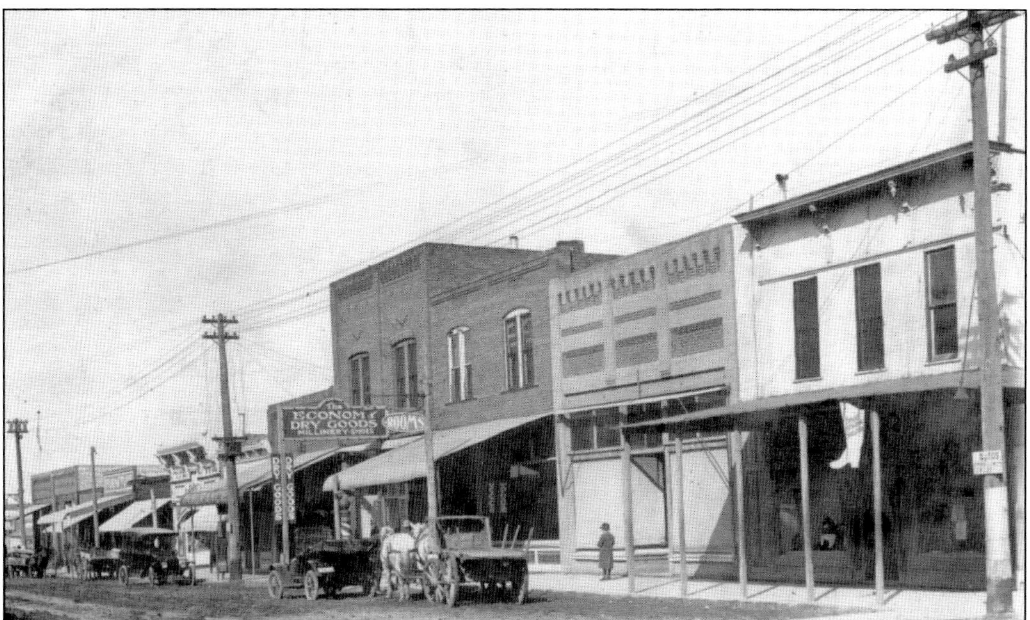

Cars were becoming as common as the horse and wagon in this early-1918 photograph. The view of the 200 block of Kansas Avenue shows both modes of transportation. A sign on the telephone pole warns automobile motorists not to exceed 10 miles per hour.

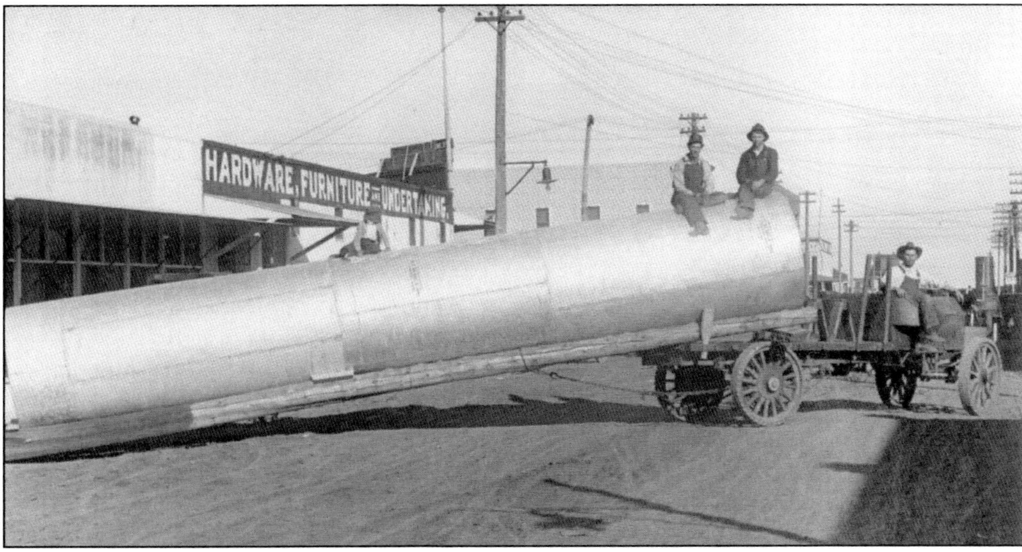

On the corner of West Second and Lincoln Streets, farm implements could be purchased from the Blake and Sons Store owned by B.E. and A.A. Blake. The building measured 140 feet by 165 feet and carried wagons, furniture, tools, seeds, and pumps and offered undertaking services. The business also distributed lubricating and illuminating oil.

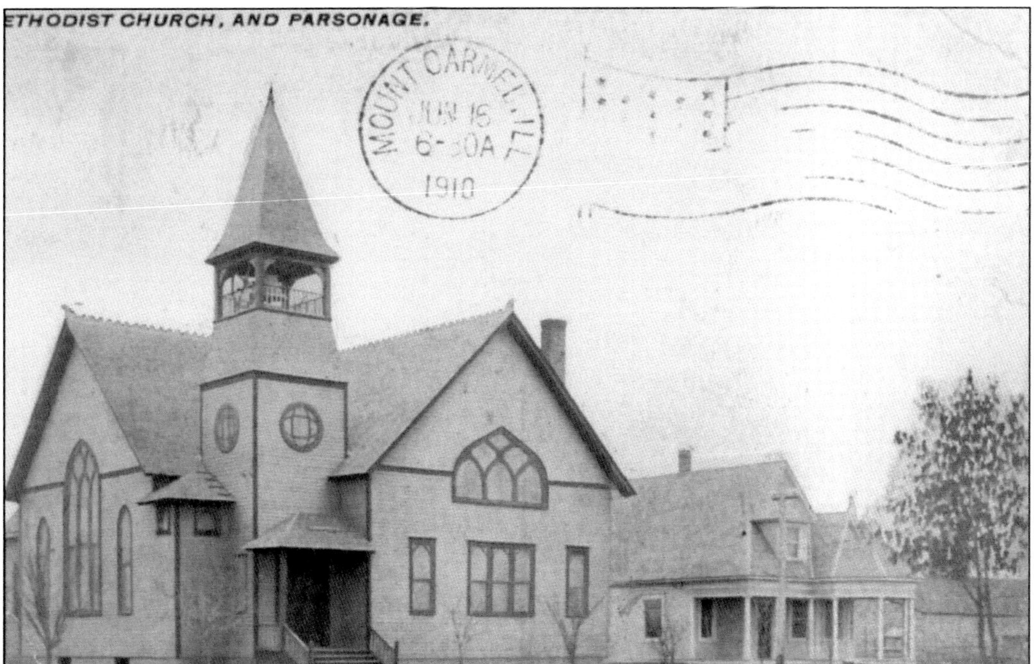

In 1885, the First United Methodist Church began in the sod home of Mr. and Mrs. G.W. Light. The church later moved into a sod schoolhouse in southeast Liberal. A tabernacle was constructed in 1888, but in the early 1890s, many people left the area, forcing the church to sell the building. The Presbyterians extended an invitation to the congregation to worship with them, a plan that worked well for years. In 1907, the Methodist church was built and dedicated at Second Street and Sherman Avenue.

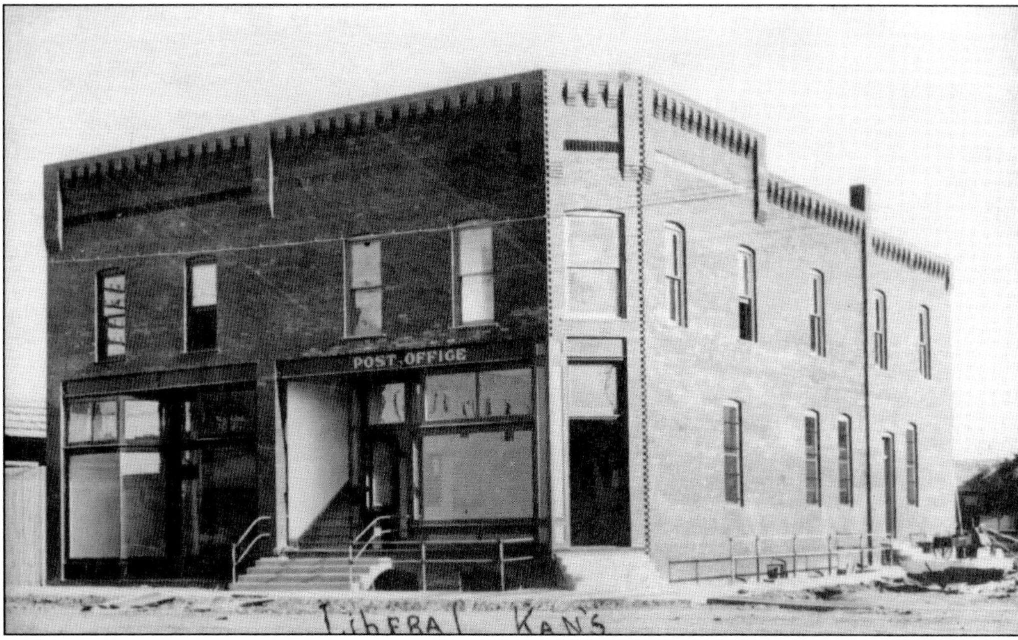

Al Blake constructed this brick building at Second Street and Lincoln Street in 1908 to house the post office, charging nothing for the first year's rent. In 1914, the postal service moved their office to Third Street and Kansas Avenue. The building then became the first home of Peoples State Bank until 1951.

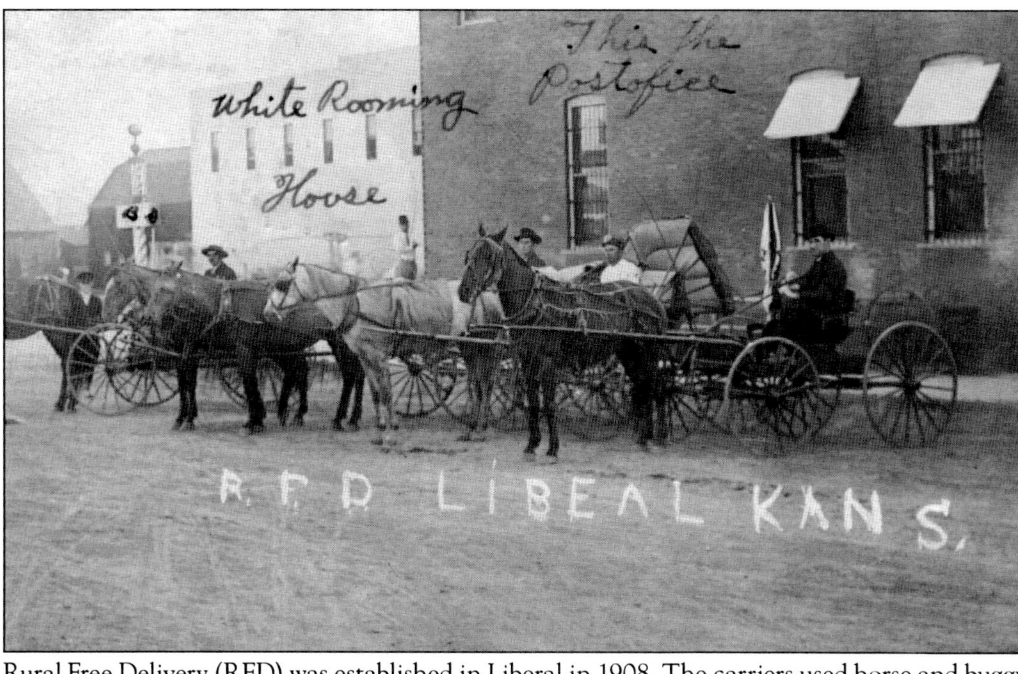

Rural Free Delivery (RFD) was established in Liberal in 1908. The carriers used horse and buggy to deliver to four Star Routes that covered hundreds of miles. The routes were Shade's Well in Oklahoma; Hugoton, Kansas; Beaver, Oklahoma; and Ochiltree, Texas.

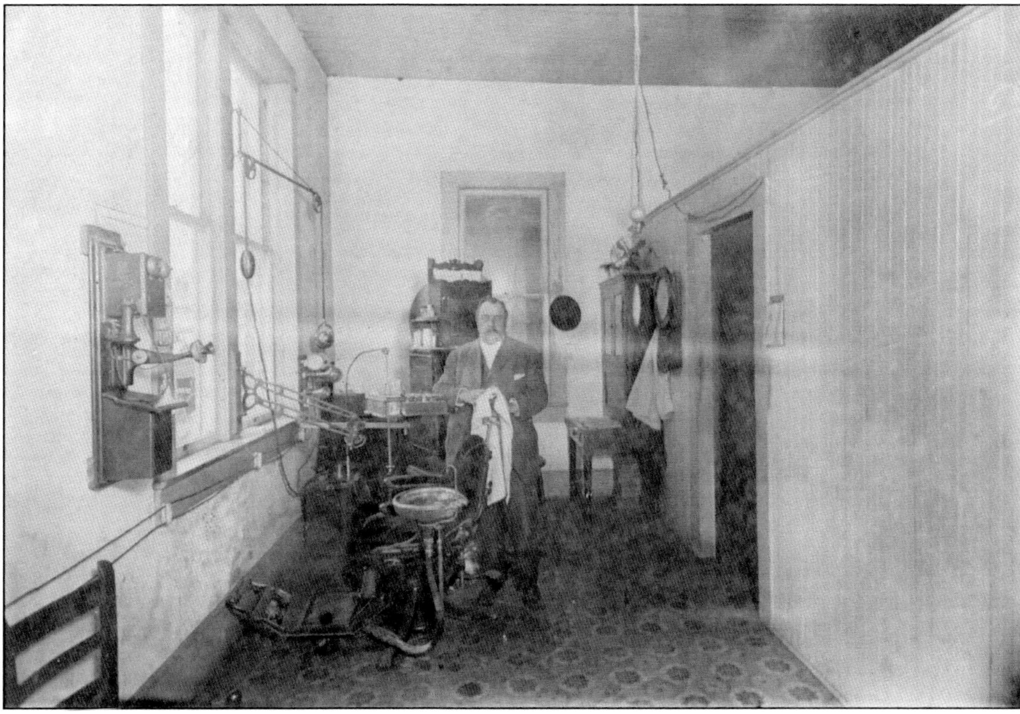

Traveling "painless" dentists would come through Liberal every three months and usually had a crowd waiting for them. This unidentified dentist, shown here as he sets up for the next patient, was well equipped. The photograph was taken in the Miller building in the 200 block of North Kansas Avenue.

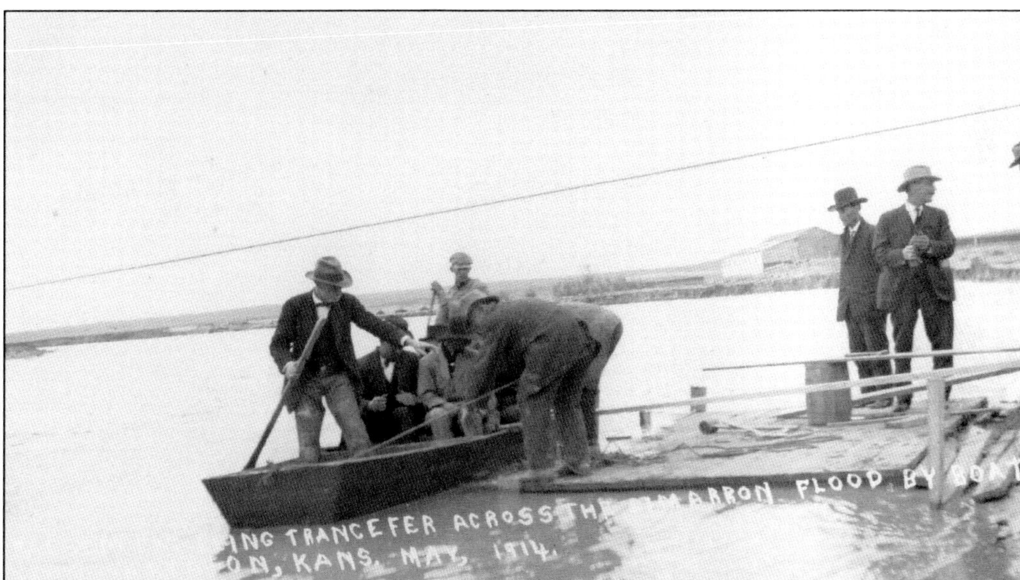

This image, taken near Arkalon in May 1914, shows train passengers being transferred by boat across the flooded Cimarron River. This method was used until the floodwaters receded and the railroad could repair their bridges. This flood also wiped out the telegraph line, causing a major pause in communications.

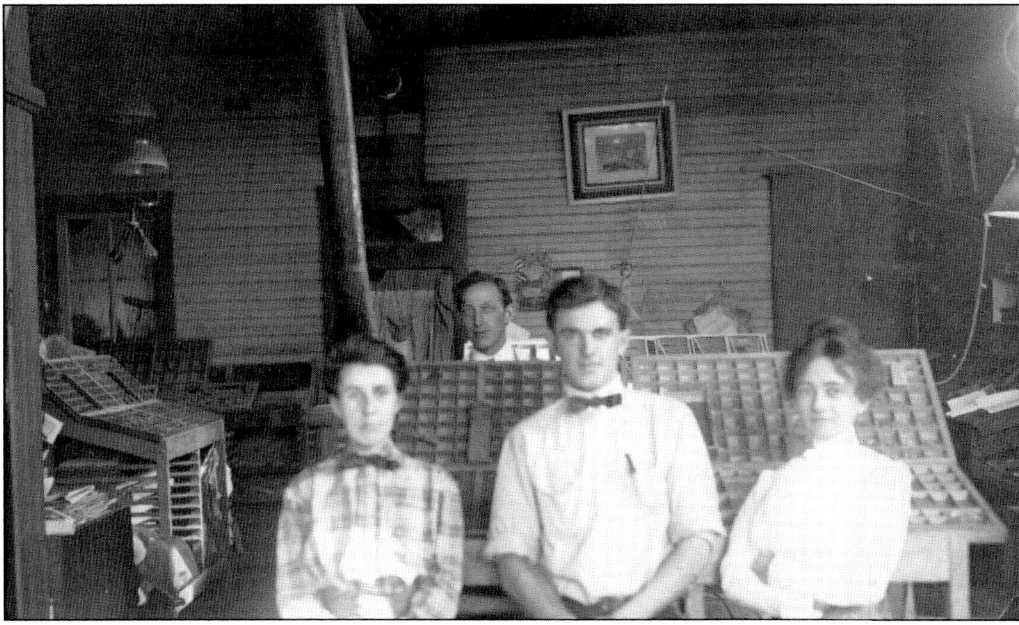

The *Liberal News* office was located at 209 North Kansas Avenue. The *Liberal News* was established by Abe Stoufer, who moved the newspaper from Fargo Springs to Arkalon and finally to Liberal in 1892. The crew in this 1912 photograph includes, from left to right, Emma Jacquins, Henry Fleck, Earl Fuller, and Miss Sinclair. Jacquins worked as a typesetter. Not pictured is Ray Millman, the editor.

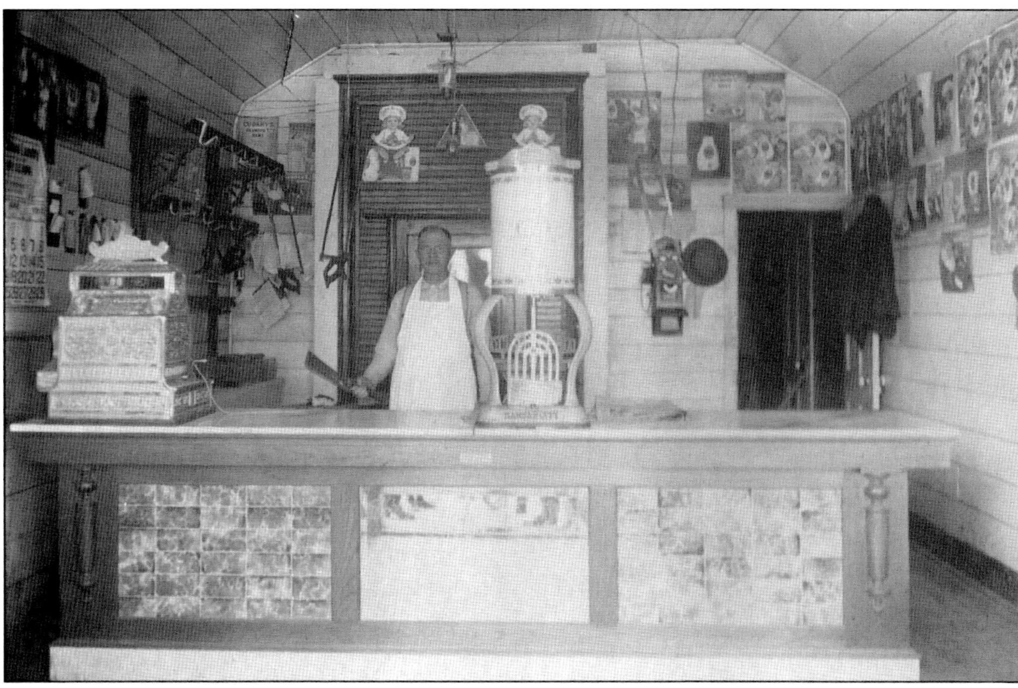

The butcher stands ready to prepare a choice cut at the South Side Grocery, located at 313 South Kansas Avenue. On the wall are pictures of sample cuts, various saws, and a calendar from Eureka Steam Laundry. The ornate item in the middle of the counter is the butcher's scale.

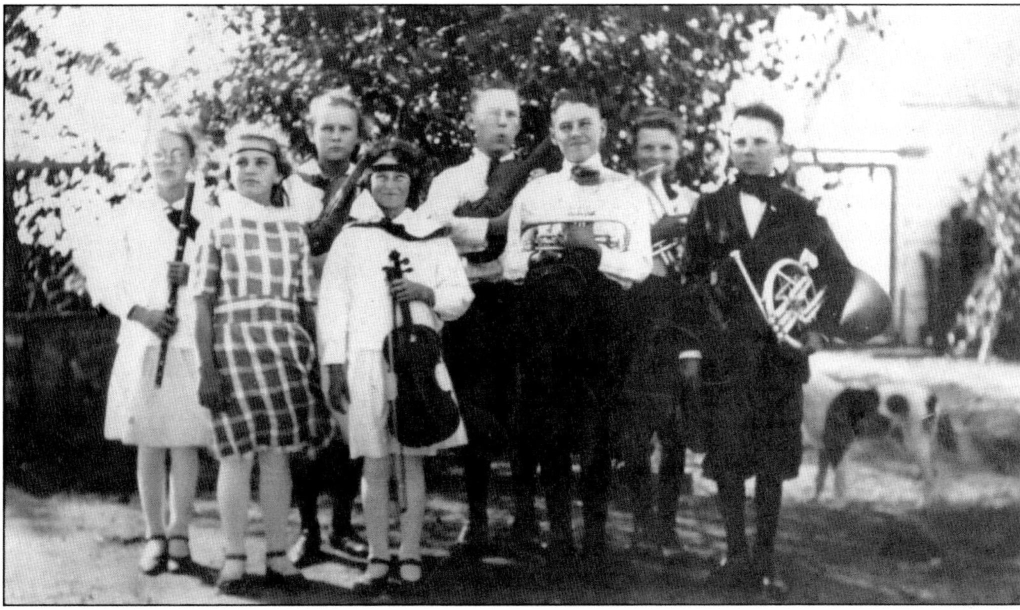

These 11-year-old musicians gave concerts in Kismet and Seward County. From left to right are Ruth Hess, Margaret Nelson, Lucille Mooney, Lula Hess, Nora Moody, Denzil Hobbs, Ralph Hess, and Oliver Brown. Price of admission to their concerts was 35¢. (Courtesy of Seward County Historical Society.)

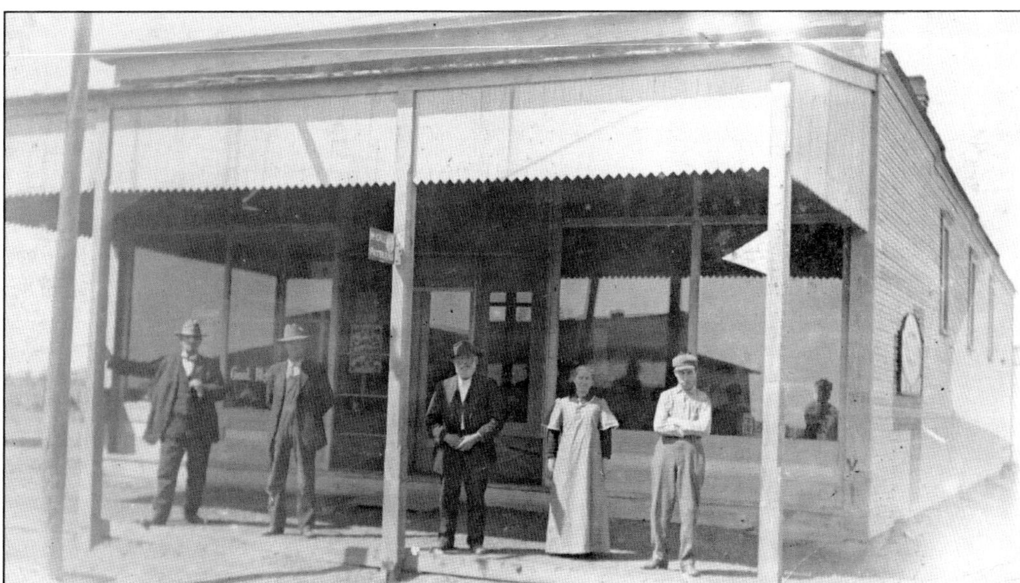

Kismet was originally a siding and boxcar depot for the Rock Island Railroad in 1886. A.C. and Emeline Olin founded the town of Kismet in 1907 when the couple purchased 40 acres from John Baughman. The Olins opened this store on the west side of Main Street with Emeline Olin as manager. The store had a stock of dry goods, a women's ready-to-wear selection, and McCall's patterns for those making their own garments.

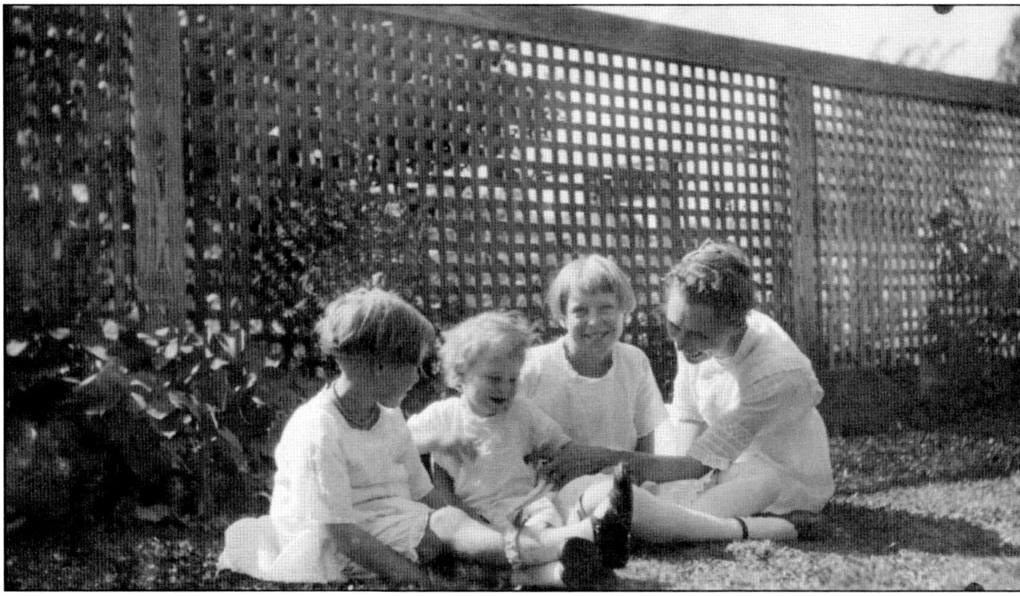

"In every land, in every clime, it C.D. Gasaway, all the time!" Charles D. Gasaway arrived in Liberal by train in 1907. Gasaway was a successful broomcorn buyer and broker. Charles and Myrtle built a home at 532 North Sherman Avenue where they raised their three children. Charles served as mayor and helped Liberal purchase its first gasoline fire truck. Pictured are, from left to right, Martha, Howard, Charlotte, and Myrtle Gasaway. (Courtesy of Seward County Historical Society.)

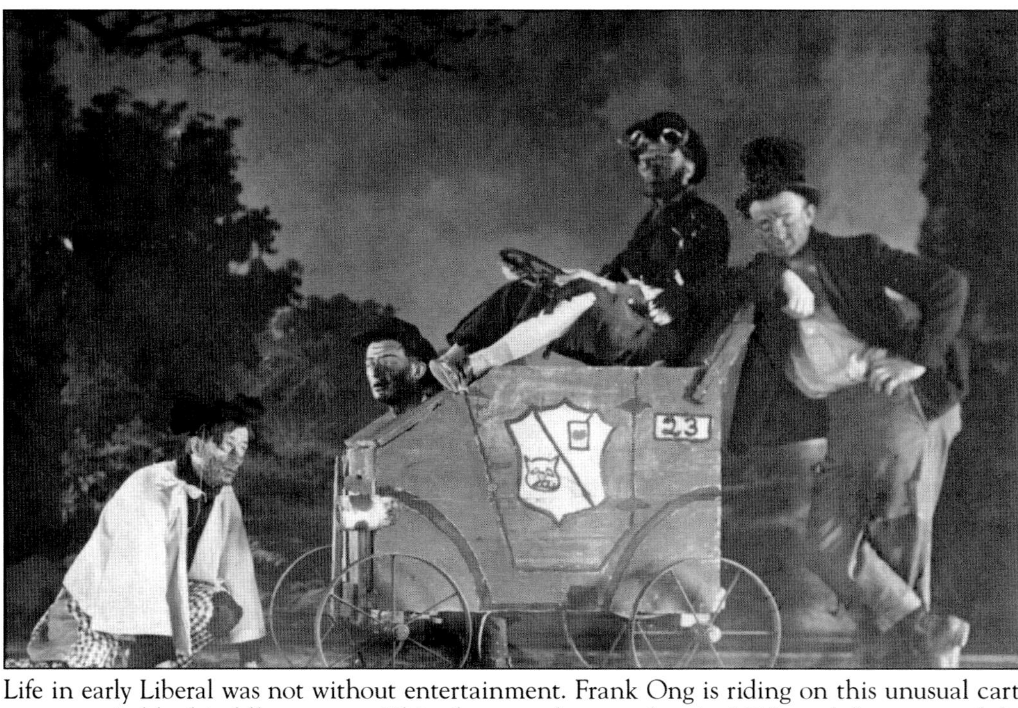

Life in early Liberal was not without entertainment. Frank Ong is riding on this unusual cart, accompanied by his fellow actors. This photograph was taken in 1913, and the name of the production shall remain unknown.

Three

The Good Years 1920–1930

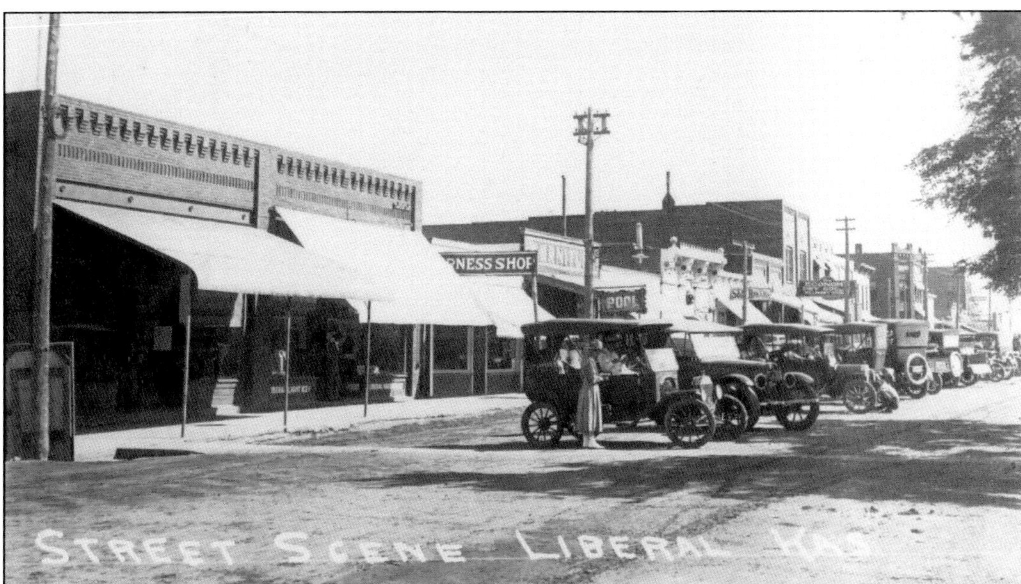

During the 1920s, Liberal and Seward County had the beginnings of a stable economy. Mechanized farming, communications, and better transportation made life a bit easier. This view is the east side of Third Street and Kansas Avenue, looking south.

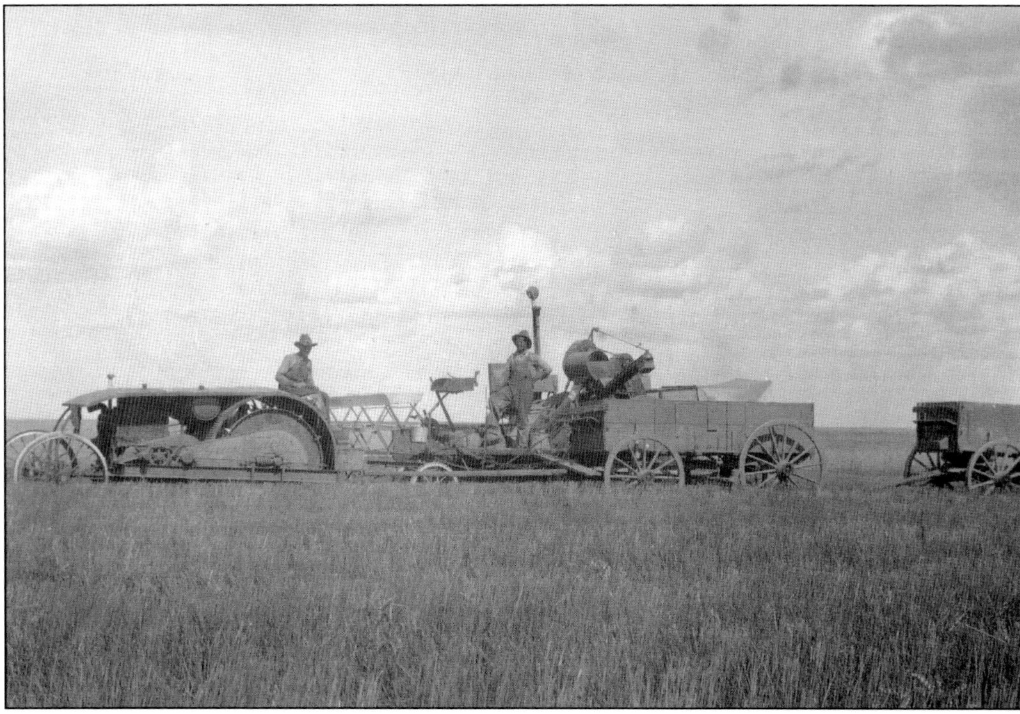

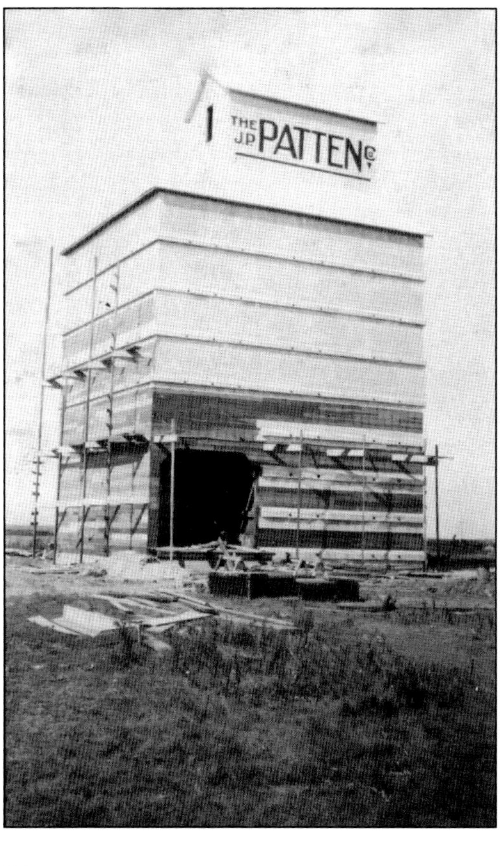

The old and the modern are shown in this image, taken in 1920 in western Seward County. These farmers are pulling their combine with a 36-horsepower Gray tractor manufactured in Minneapolis. The tractors, when new, had a price tag of $2,250. Wagons were still being used for hauling the harvested wheat.

This tin-clad wooden elevator had a capacity of 25,000 bushels equipped with a 10-horsepower motor, a five-ton wagon scale, and an elevating capacity of 1,800 bushels per hour. The elevator was located on the south side of the Rock Island tracks, a half block from Kansas Avenue.

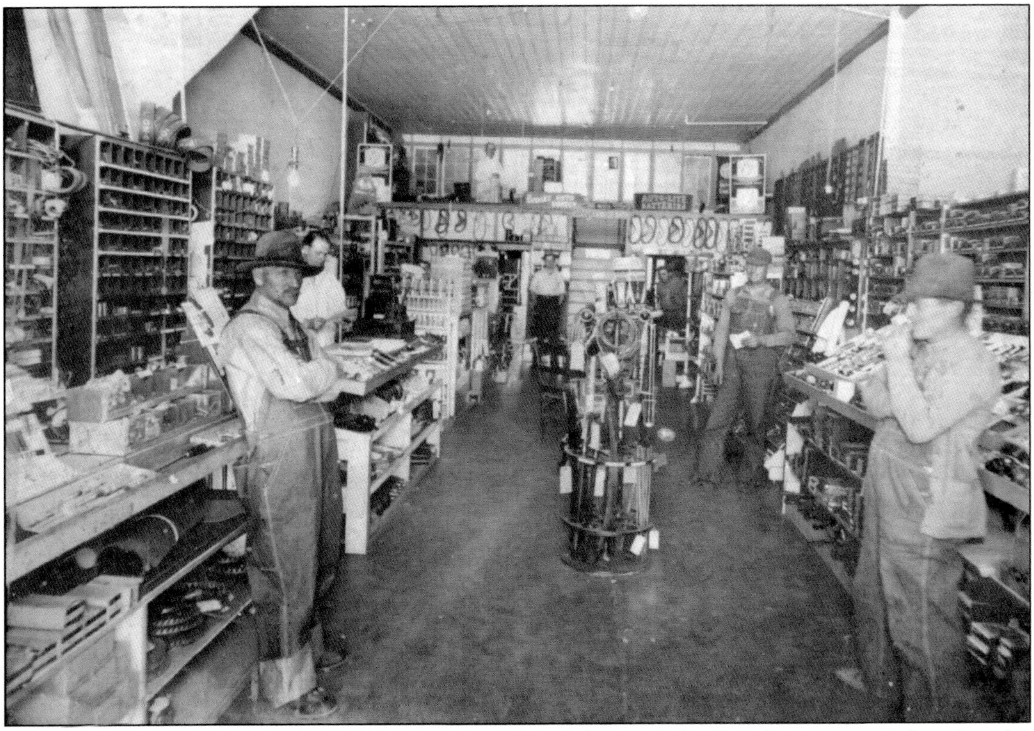

Cars were becoming commonplace and so were breakdowns. John Brooks came to Liberal in the early 1920s and opened his well-equipped automobile supply store first at Third Street and Kansas Avenue; he later moved the business to 319 North Kansas Avenue. Brooks also sold real estate and insurance. From left to right are an unidentified man, Jess White at the cash register, John Brooks upstairs in the loft, Leslie Littlefield in the left door, Cy Littlefield in the right door, and two unidentified men. (Courtesy of Seward County Historical Society.)

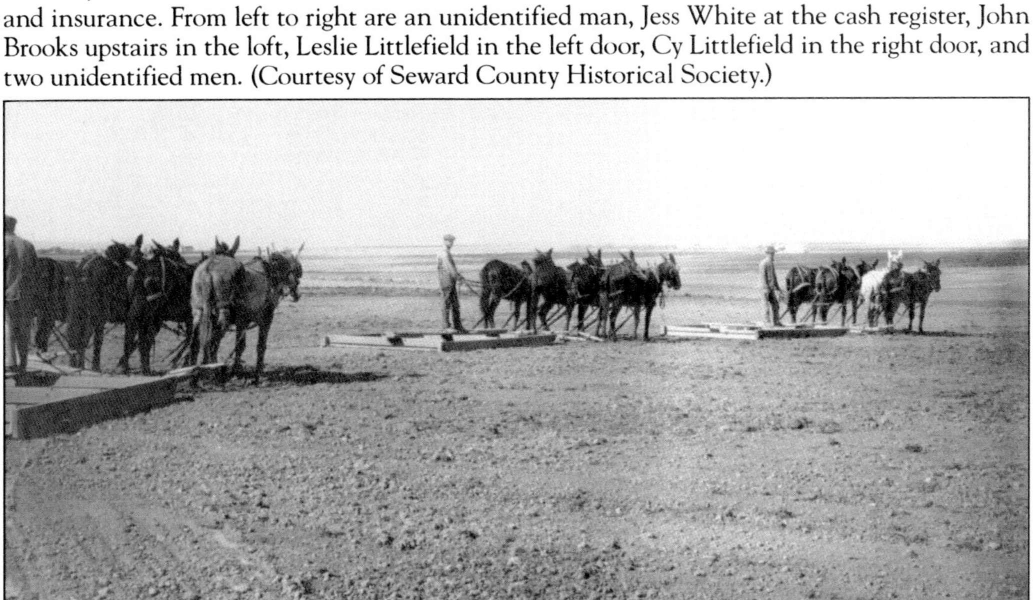

With more cars using Seward County and Liberal's streets and roadways, men, fresnos, and mules were ready to do the maintenance. Liberal's Kansas Avenue, Lincoln Street, and other main ways were beginning to be bricked in 1919. However, most of the remaining streets were dirt. (Courtesy of Seward County Historical Society.)

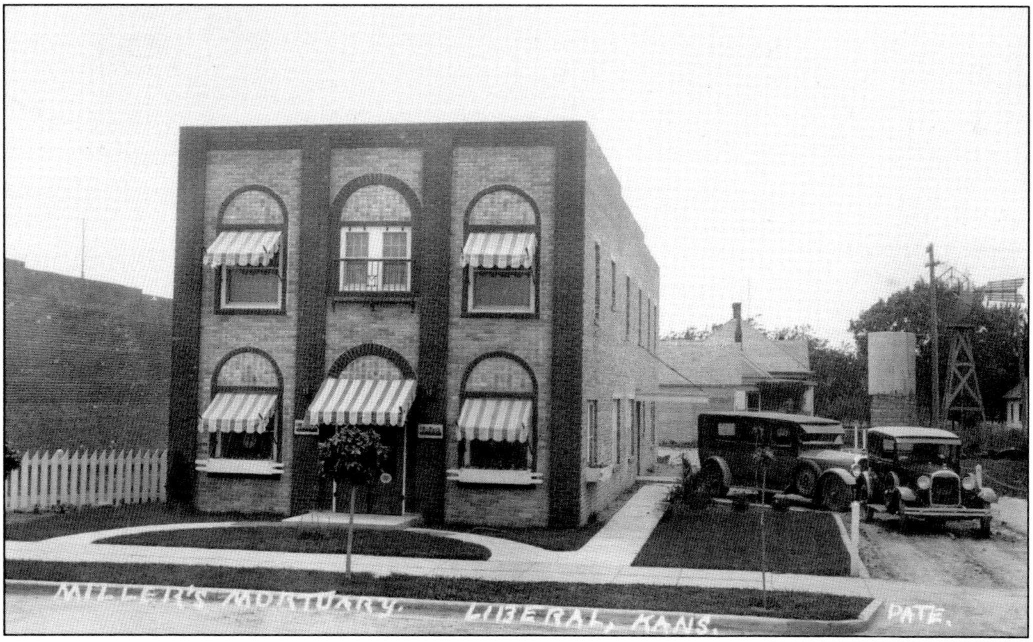

Miller Mortuary was established in 1913 by S.A. Miller. Tom Tegarden convinced him to come to Liberal. The funeral home was advertised as "modern with a reception room, restroom, and the largest stock of funeral goods west of Hutchinson." The building was located at 514 North Kansas Avenue until 1933 when it relocated to 908 North Lincoln. (Courtesy of Mary Brewington.)

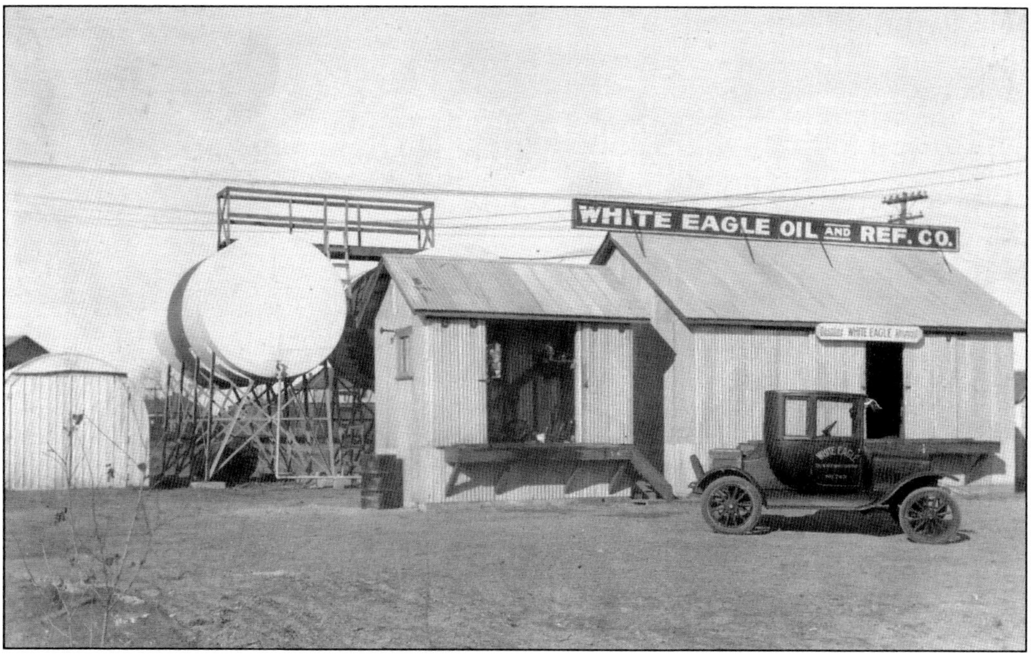

R.C. Foutz managed the Ford Agency in Turpin, Oklahoma, before becoming the area representative of the White Eagle Oil and Refining Company. Located in the 200 block of South Kansas Avenue, the White Eagle also had branches on West Second Street and North Kansas Avenue. The company car was a Ford Model T coupe. (Courtesy of Seward County Historical Society.)

What boy did not want to broadcast the latest news over his own radio? *Boy's Magazine* in the early 1920s encouraged young men to make their own crystal radios. Necessary supplies included a lead galena crystal and a cat whisker to find the signal. This L-shaped tower was built in February 1922 to broadcast the news from Clifford Sawyer and his brother. Their home was located at 402 North Prospect Avenue. (Courtesy of Seward County Historical Society.)

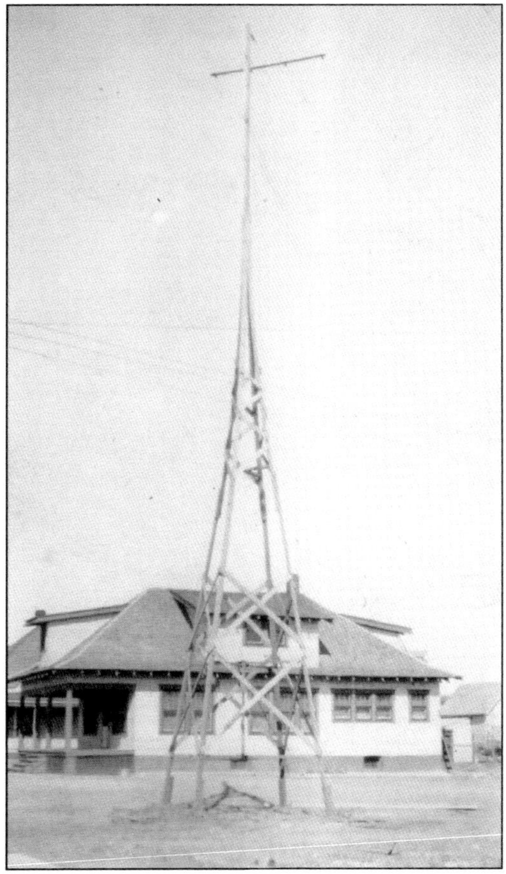

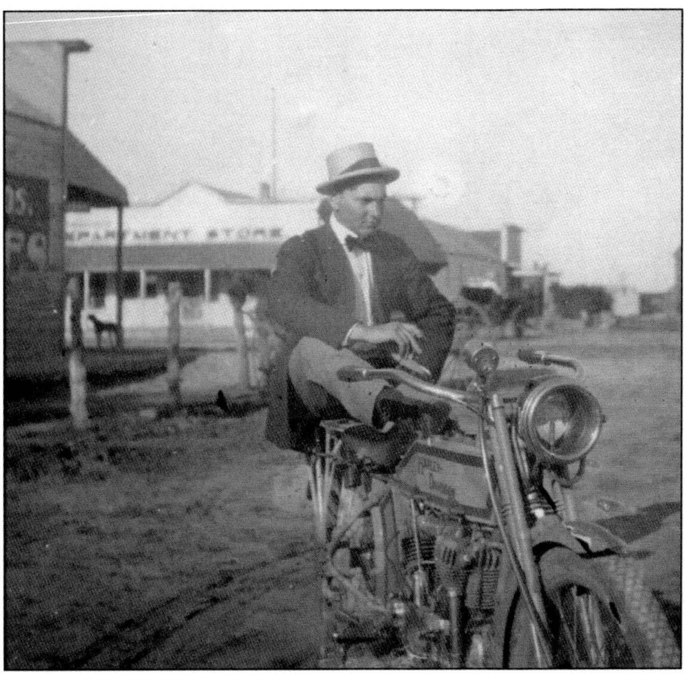

Toby Tobias arrived in Liberal in 1919 to join J.A. Brooks in an insurance and real estate business. In 1924, he established the Hudson-Essex and Terraplane dealership. Tobias met his wife, Flossie, in 1922 when he brought an ill friend to the hospital where she was a nurse. In 1936, Tobias became postmaster. He is pictured with his favorite Harley-Davidson. (Courtesy of Seward County Historical Society.)

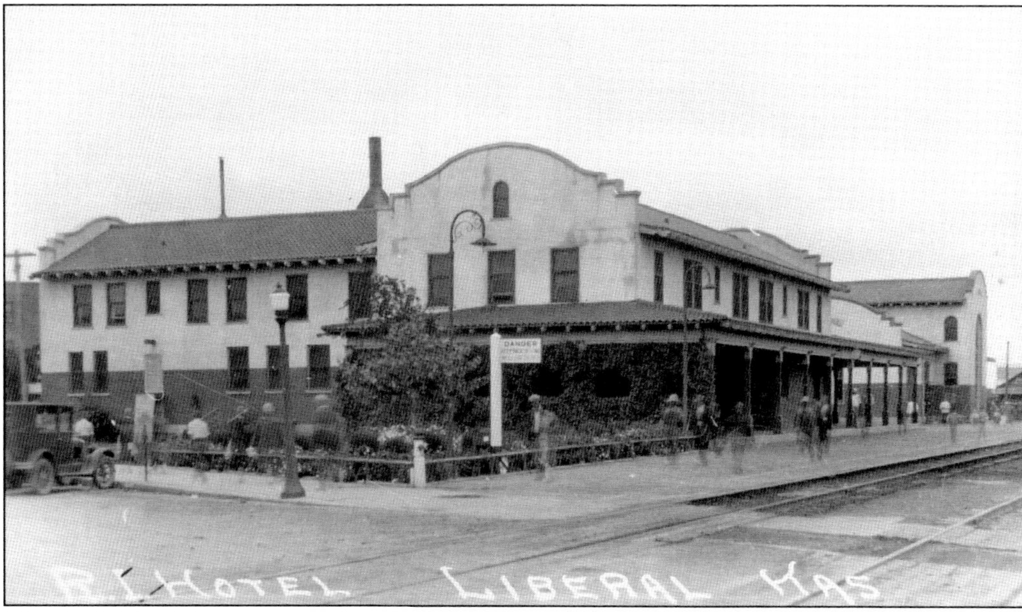

The Rock Island depot remained the center of activity for the area. This 1926 photograph shows plenty of townsfolk shopping and waiting to see who is getting on and off the train.

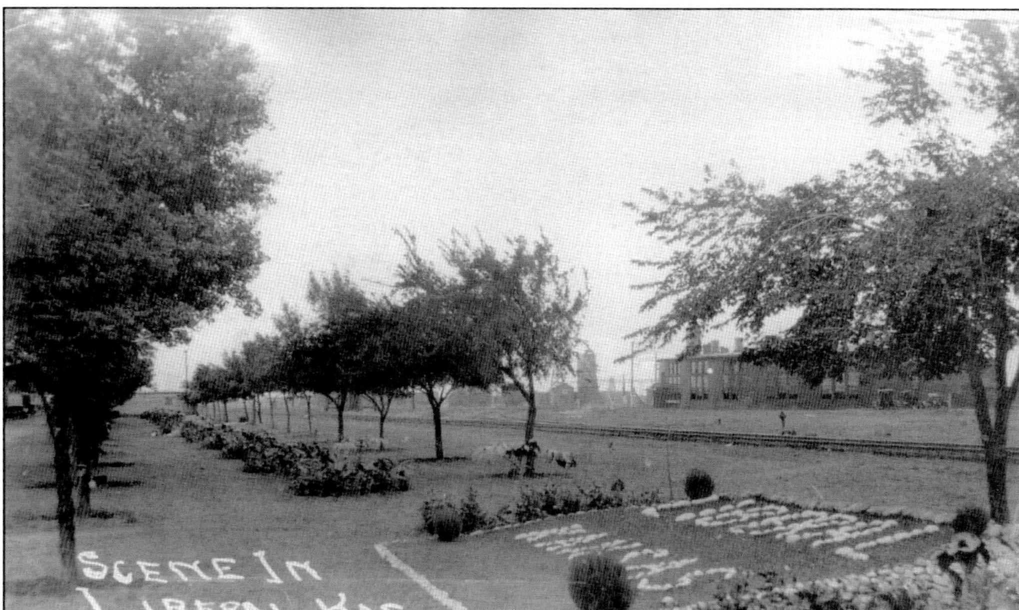

Across from the depot and between the two main railroad tracks, train passengers were greeted by a beautiful park with mature trees and planned flower beds. The gardener even took the time to identify the stop on the Rock Island line.

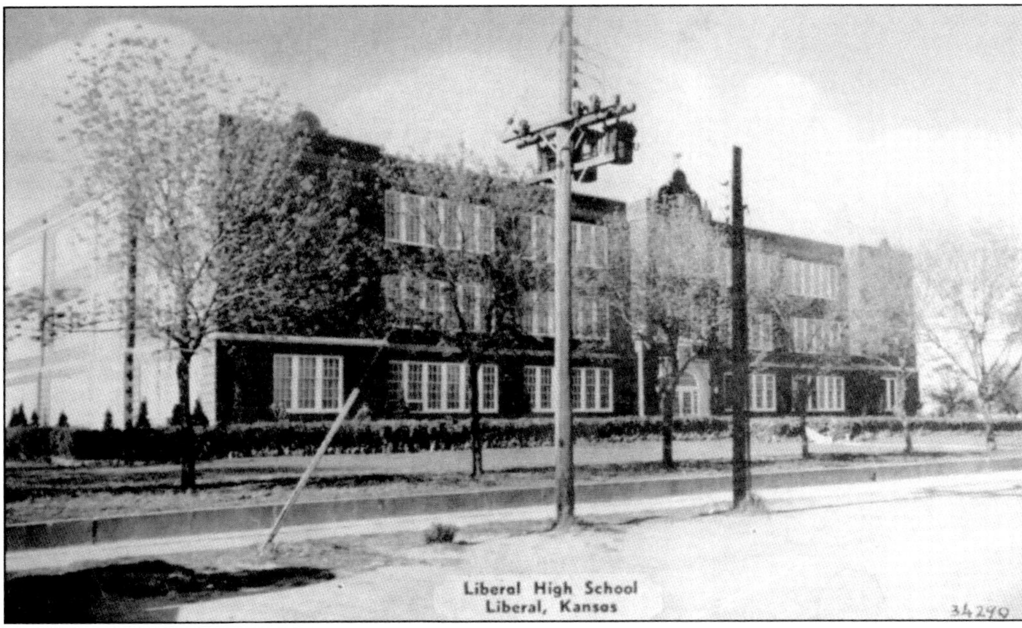

Population growth was reflected in the student enrollment at Liberal High School. In 1920, the original school was torn down to make way for the new three-story brick building at Sixth and Lincoln Streets. Construction was completed the summer of 1922. N.B. Mahuron was superintendent, and Oscar Brownlee was principal. In 1925, coach E.E. Shupe led the football team to an undefeated season with no ties and only five points scored against the team.

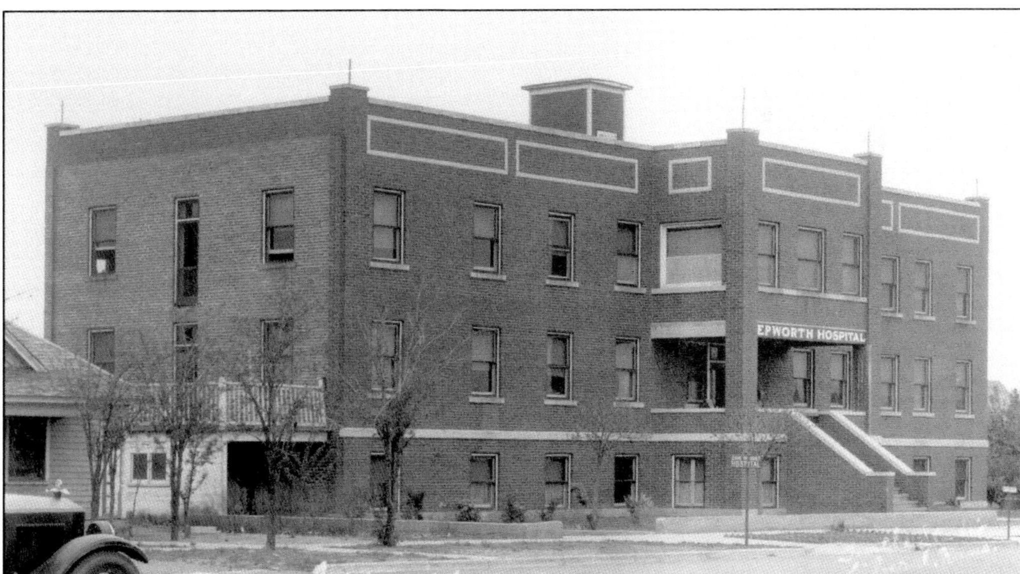

In 1924, the Liberal Hospital became Epworth Hospital. Drs. Day, Jones, Morrow, and Huddleston joined the staff and practiced at the hospital until retirement. In 1925, two sun porches located on the south side of the building were converted into wards. In 1949, the wards were demolished and a new wing was erected. The Epworth Hospital was the area's primary health care center until the Southwest Medical Center was built in 1964.

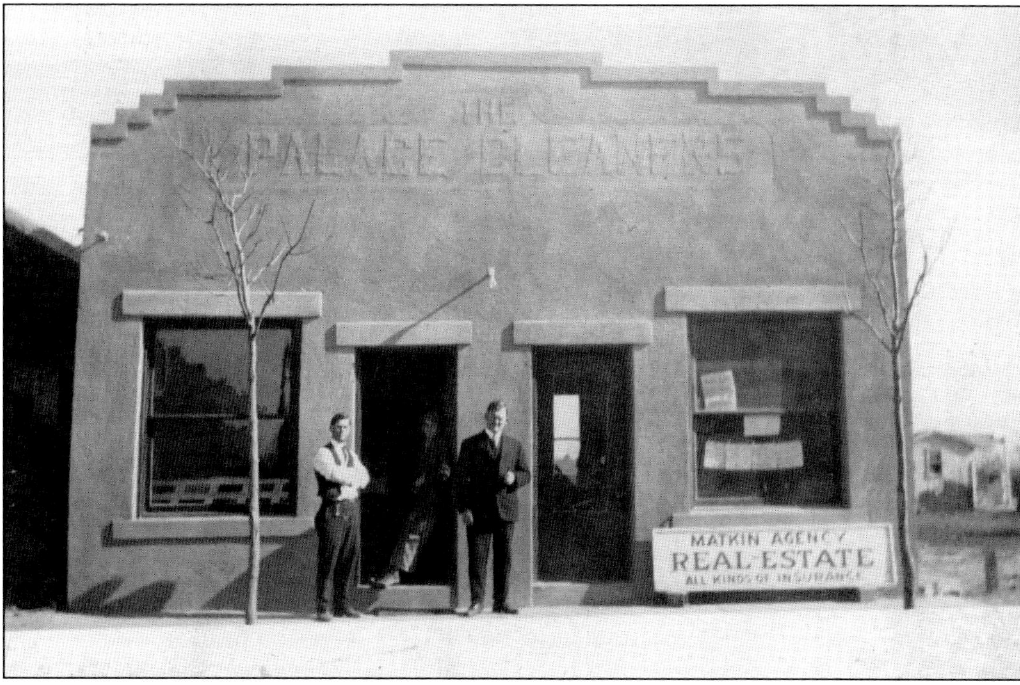

The Palace Cleaners building was located at 301 North Kansas Avenue, also housing the Matkin Real Estate office. From left to right are A.B. Mitchell, Leonard Kent, and John Ralston. This building was removed when the Warren Hotel started construction. (Courtesy of Seward County Historical Society.)

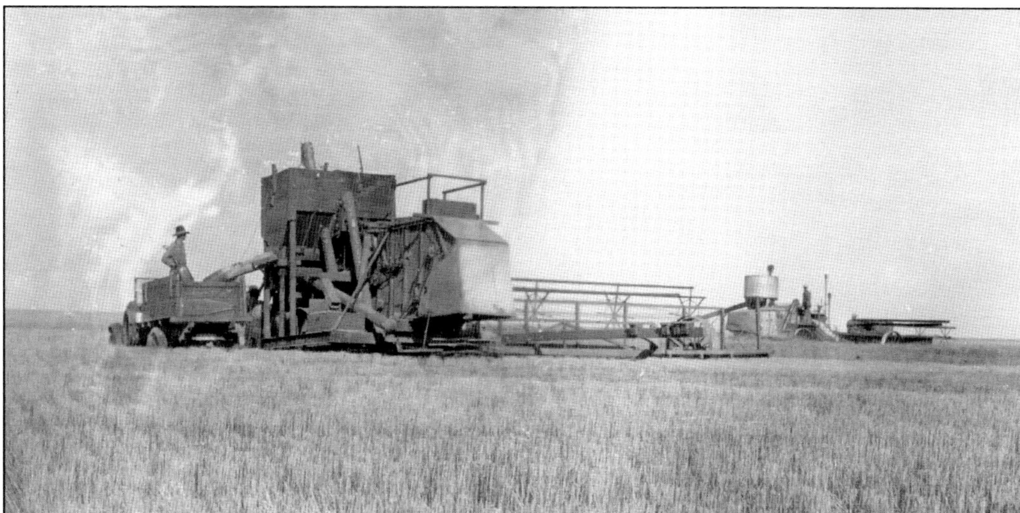

Thomas and Emma Hopkins moved from Bisbee, Arizona, to homestead in Seward County. Emma's sisters came along to join in land ownership. Homesteaders had to prove owner occupancy of their 160 acres of land, so the Hopkins' solution was to build one house at the junction of all four land quarters. Thomas was able to sleep on his quarter, Emma on hers, sister Anna on hers, and sister Nannie on hers. Thomas farmed all four quarters for the family without a shred of experience. He gradually acquired additional land and became known as the Wheat King. This image shows the Hopkins' 24-foot, self-propelled combine. (Courtesy of Seward County Historical Society.)

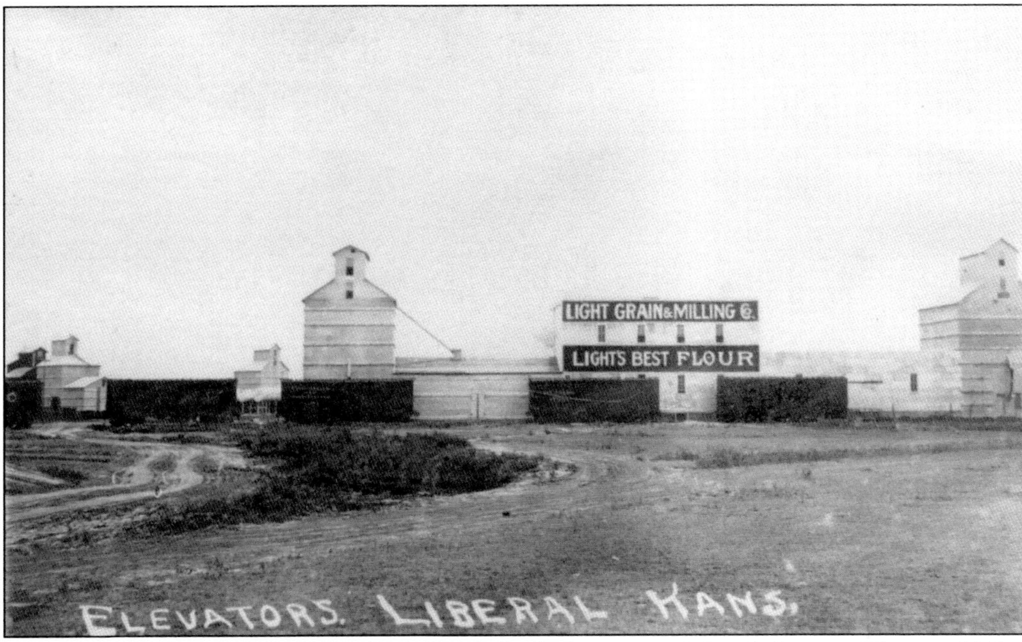

Charles M. Light Grain Company had already built elevators in Liberal, Satanta, Pleasant Valley, and Beaver, Oklahoma, and had acquired existing facilities at Turpin, Guymon, Hooker, and Tyrone. In 1918, Light Grain & Milling Company built the flour mill that furnished Light's Best Flour to bakers for years. This 1928 photograph shows boxcars waiting in front of the elevators and warehouse. The company employed 55 people.

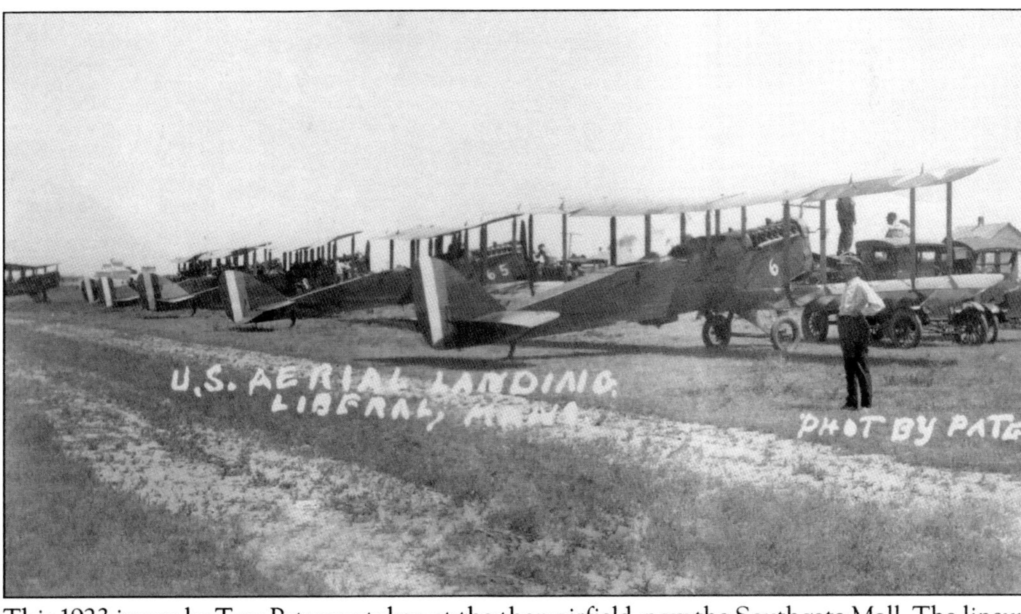

This 1923 image by Tom Pate was taken at the then airfield, now the Southgate Mall. The lineup consists of Curtiss Jennies and Laird Swallows. The planes were in Liberal for the Flying Frolic.

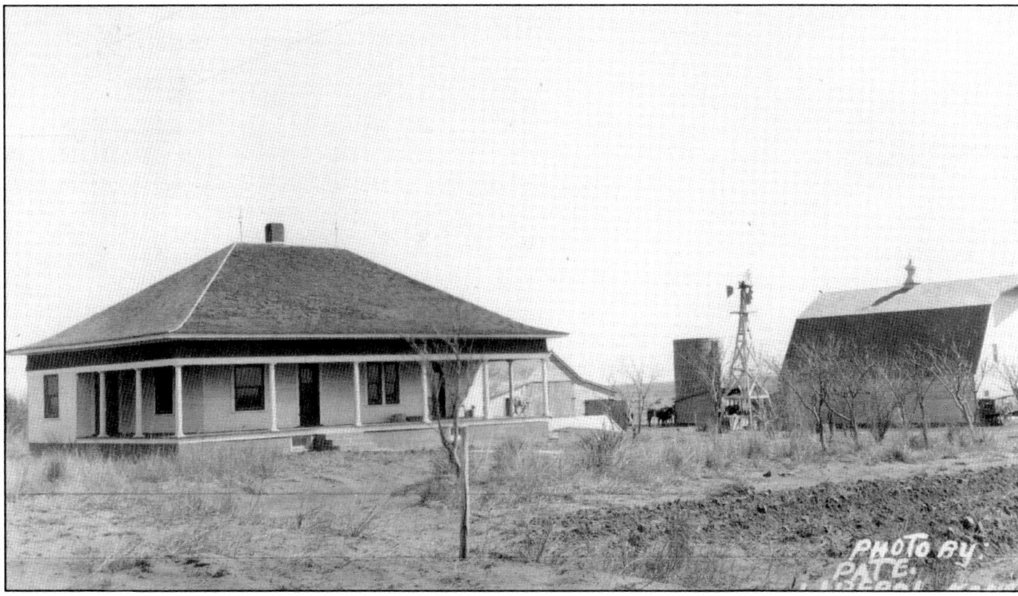

John and Della Priefert came to Seward County in 1907, living first in a two-room shack. During the winters, the family would move into their one-room cellar. As their fortunes improved, the Prieferts built this home three miles north of Liberal in 1920. Mr. Moser was the contractor. Frank Higgins built the barn at the same time the house was being constructed. When this barn caught fire and burned, Higgins returned and an exact replica of the first barn was built, which still stands today. (Courtesy of Seward County Historical Society.)

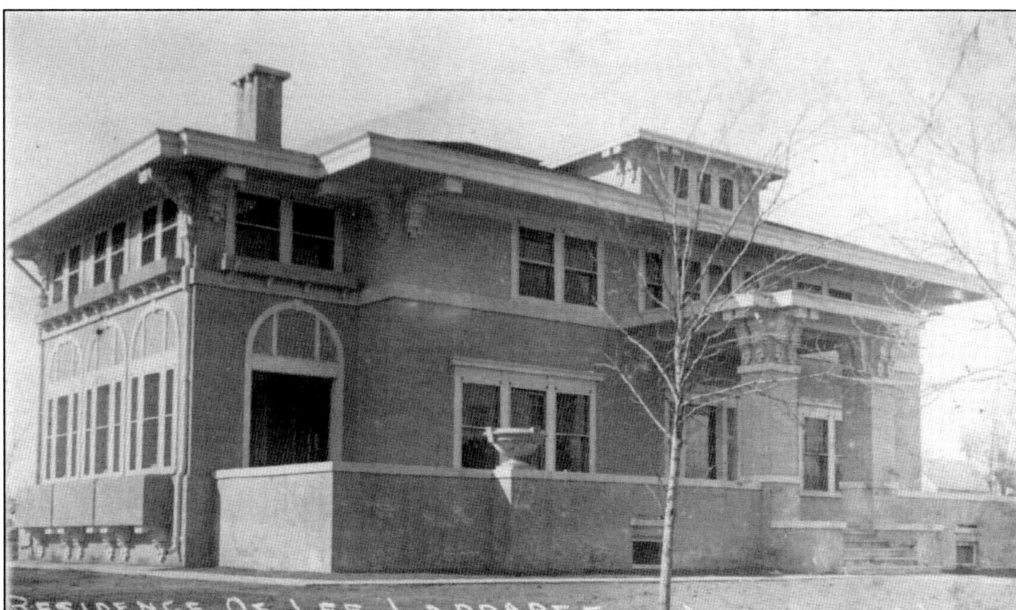

The Lee and Nettie Larrabee home was located at 510 North Lincoln. Of Prairie-style design, the home's interior featured light oak woodwork, hardwood floors, two staircases, and a maid's quarters. The Larrabee home was relocated to 567 East Cedar Street when it was donated to the Seward County Historical Society. The move was the largest of its kind when the intact house inched its way down Kansas Avenue in 1961.

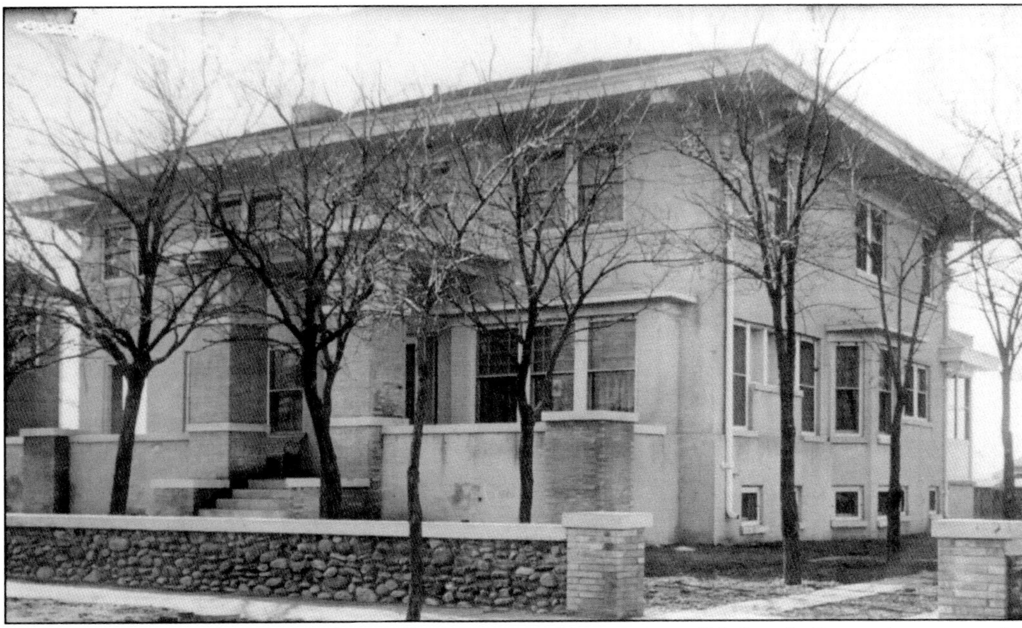

Similar to the Larrabee home, but still in its original location at 120 South Grant Avenue, is the John E. and Bella George residence. John and Bella came to Liberal in 1899 from Beaver County, Oklahoma. They purchased the Odell and Company Grocery Store, changing the name to the J.E. George Grocery Company. George also was president of the Liberal State Bank, which later became the First National Bank. Local legend has it that the Larrabees and the Georges had a friendly competition on who had the fancier house. The Georges lived in the home until a tornado heavily damaged it in 1933.

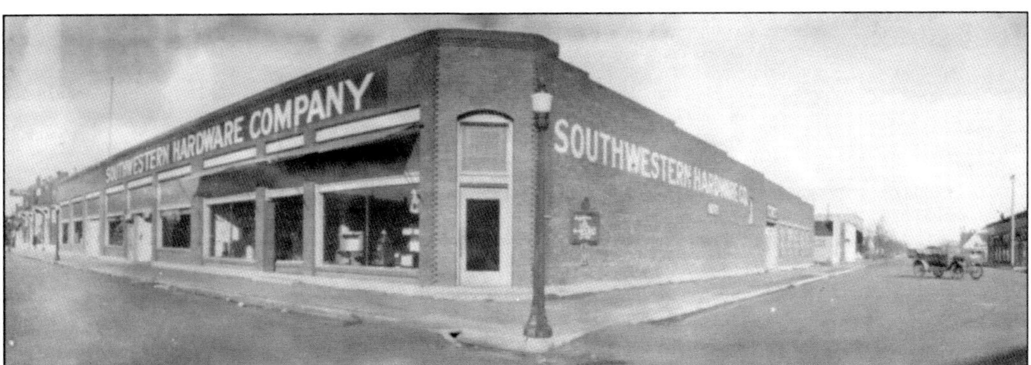

This store was described as the busiest concern in Liberal, especially during harvest. Robert Evans graduated from Liberal High School in 1907, attended Kansas Agricultural College, and came back to Liberal to clerk at Southwest Hardware for $15 per week. He became manager and owner five years later. The store offered McCormick-Deering and International Harvesters along with all types of motorized and horse-driven farm machinery. (It was not until 1955 that tractors outnumbered draft animals in Kansas.) The hardware company was located at 103 West Second Street.

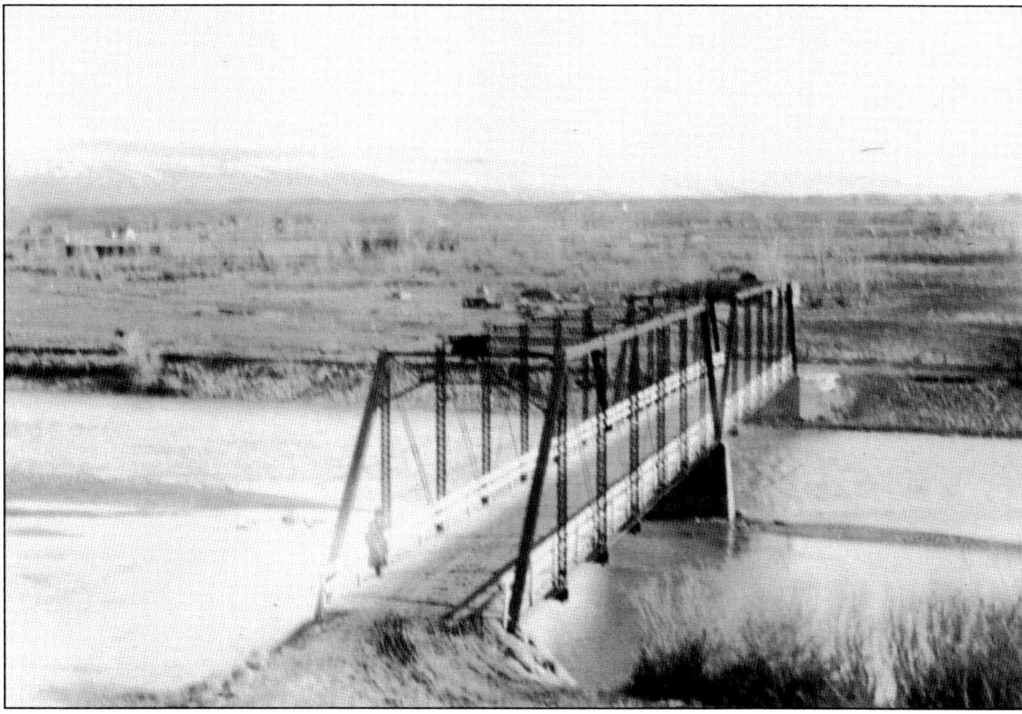

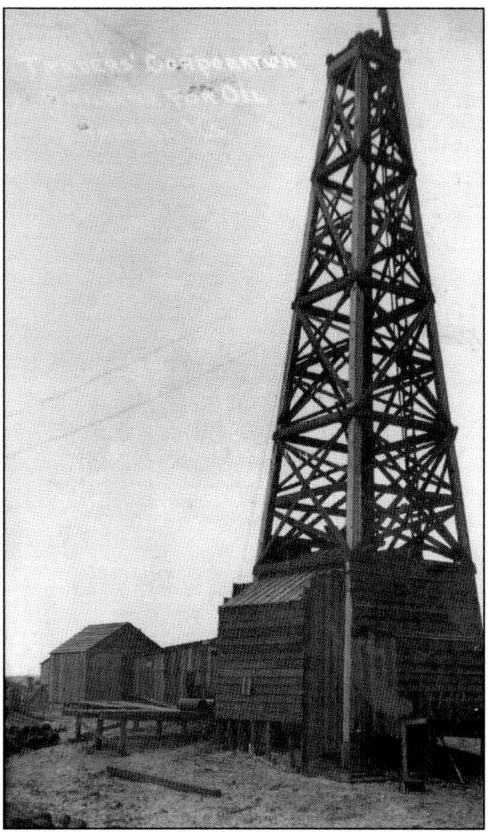

This bridge across the Cimarron River made getting from east to west much easier for travelers. The bridge was located upstream from the present Sampson Bridge. It was subject to the Cimarron River's flooding and, consequently, often was closed.

On the John Bole's farm, four and a half miles west of Liberal, a couple of wildcatters drilled a well using a small cable tool rig. The men drilled into the Permian Period dolomite but did not hit the oil they were hoping for. Instead, the wildcatters had tapped into the Hugoton dry gas field, which eventually became one of the largest gas fields in the country. A second well was drilled on the Boles lease, and in 1927, a gas distribution system was installed, heating homes and businesses in Liberal.

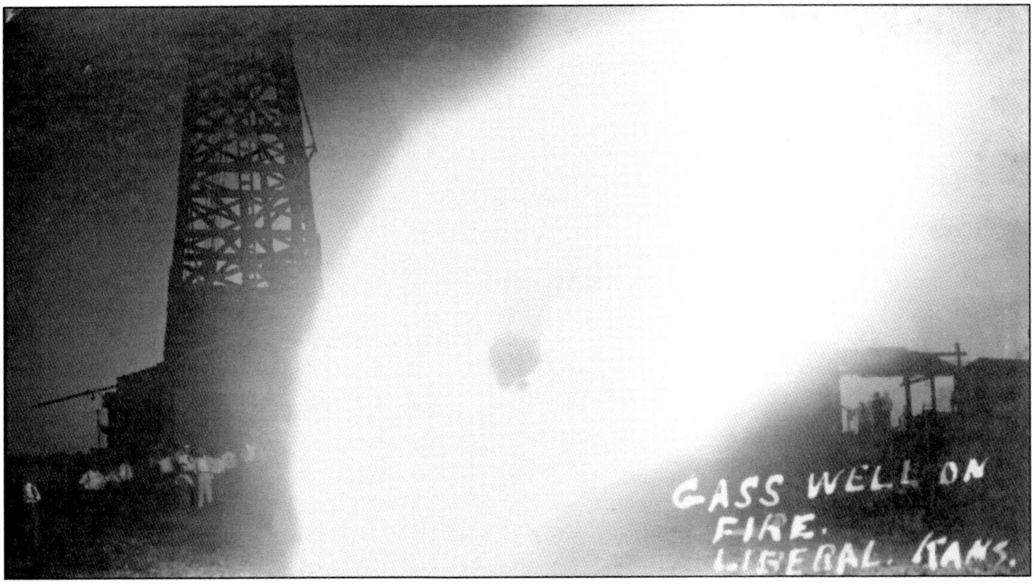

In the summer of 1920, Frank Boles and Ray Millman decided to show the people of Liberal that natural gas would burn. The two men laid a length of pipe from the Boles No. 1 to a riser. Unknown to Boles and Millman, the pipe had a leak, which let natural gas gather in a shallow spot along the line. When the fellows put a match to the riser, the leaking gas ignited, sending a huge flame into the crowd of over 500 that had gathered. No one was injured, but for the next several years, the burning well became a novelty, attracting thousands of curiosity seekers.

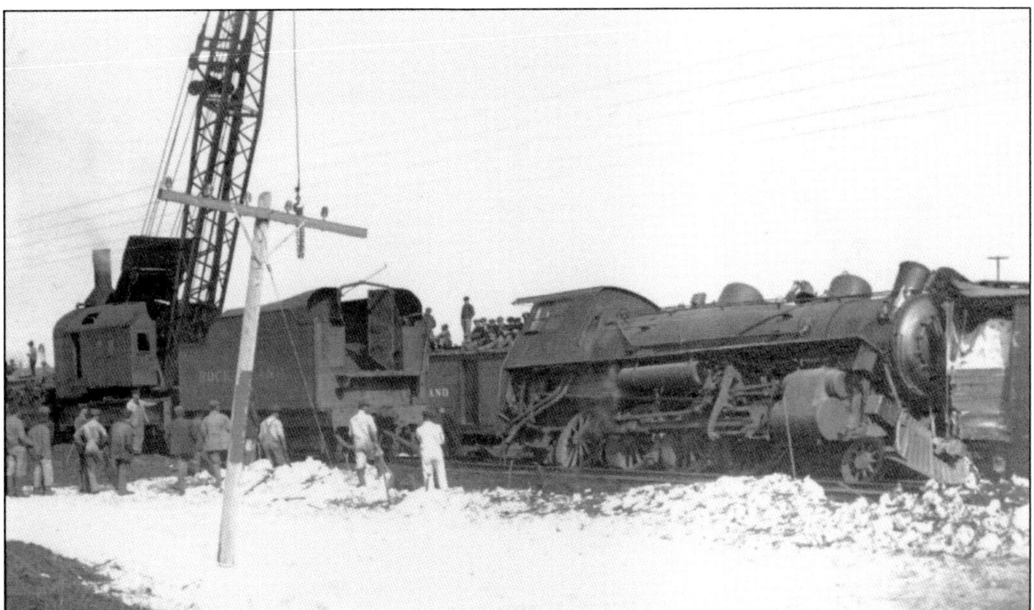

Train accidents were a rare occurrence, but this Rock Island engine No. 951 has derailed and separated from its tender after ramming another train. The accident happened in the Liberal rail yard in the mid-1920s.

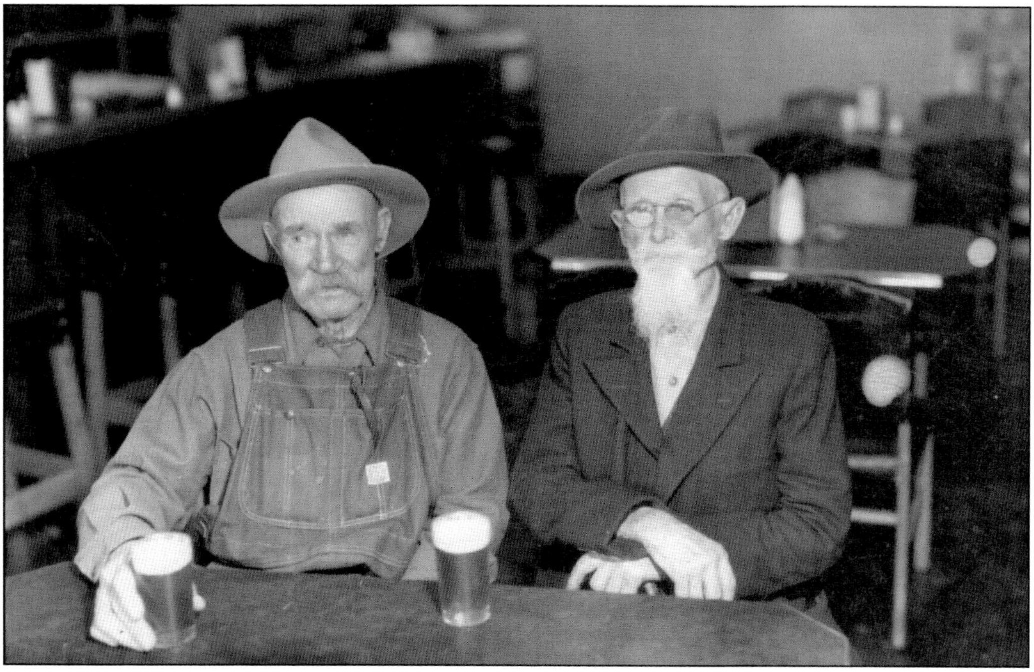

Lee Rhiness (left) and Alex McCoid were both early pioneers of Seward County. McCoid came to Springfield to file a preemption claim. With his last $14, he bought lumber to roof his sod house and left to retrieve his family. In March 1886, McCoid returned with his family only to find the roof had been stolen. McCoid also filed for a tree claim, giving him an additional 160 acres. The McCoids eventually sold their claims and moved to Liberal. Lee Rhiness was an old-time cowboy and an excellent baseball catcher. (Courtesy of Seward County Historical Society.)

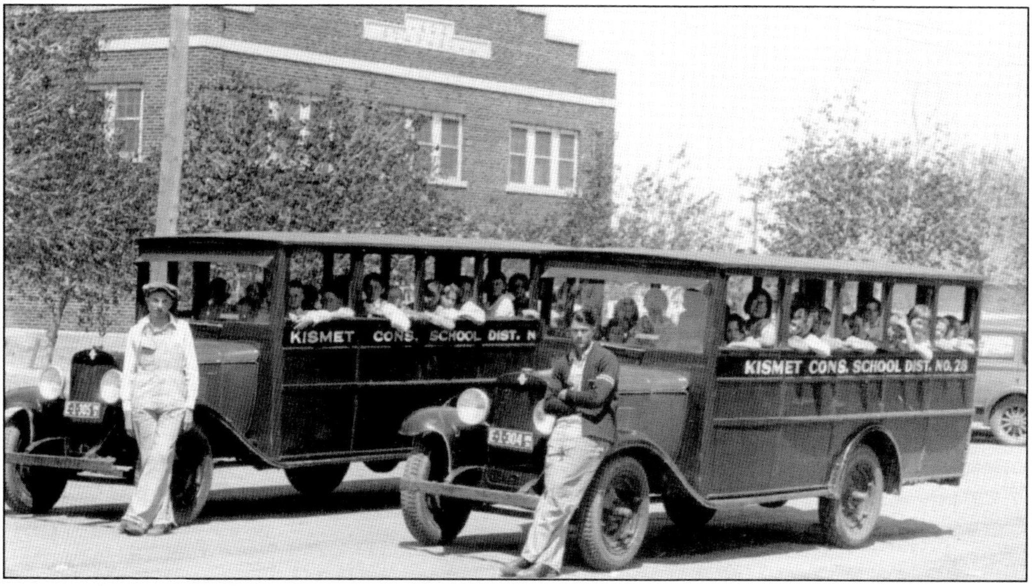

In 1918, the Kismet School Board worried about getting students to and from school, as smaller rural schools were consolidating with Kismet. Several years later, the problem was solved when these two modern school buses were purchased by School District 28. Students, drivers, and buses are parked in front of the Kismet Rural High School. (Courtesy of Seward County Historical Society.)

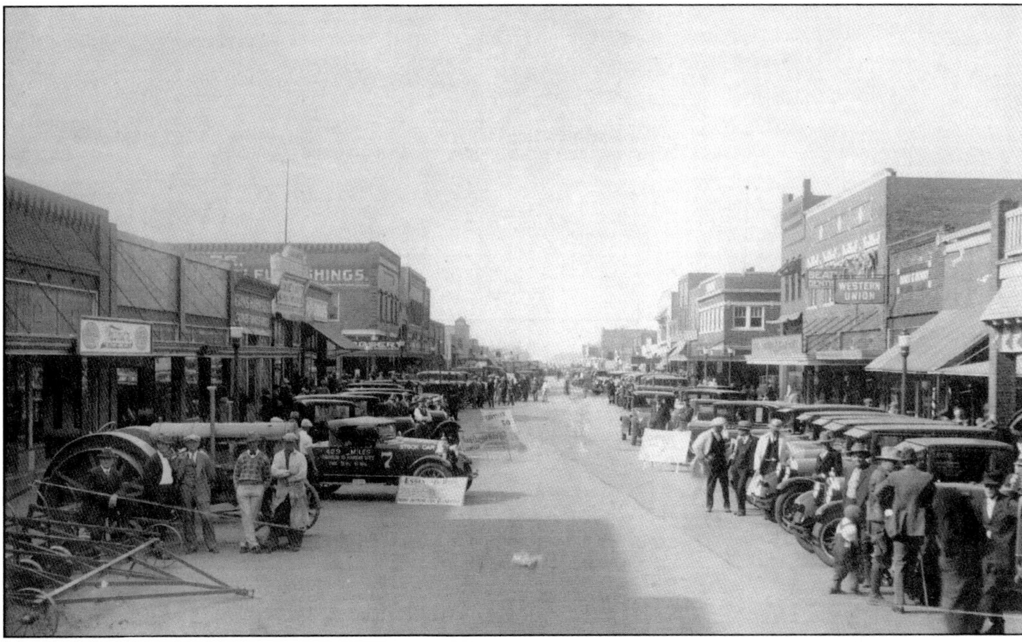

The mid-1920s were a promising turning point for area farmers and businesses. Farm machinery and automobiles were selling, and this automobile and tractor show on Kansas Avenue attracted a crowd. The Essex Bobtail Speedabout Roadster was featured by the A.B. Hunt Motor Company, while the Hood-Clagget Company brought out their Chryslers. (Courtesy of Seward County Historical Society.)

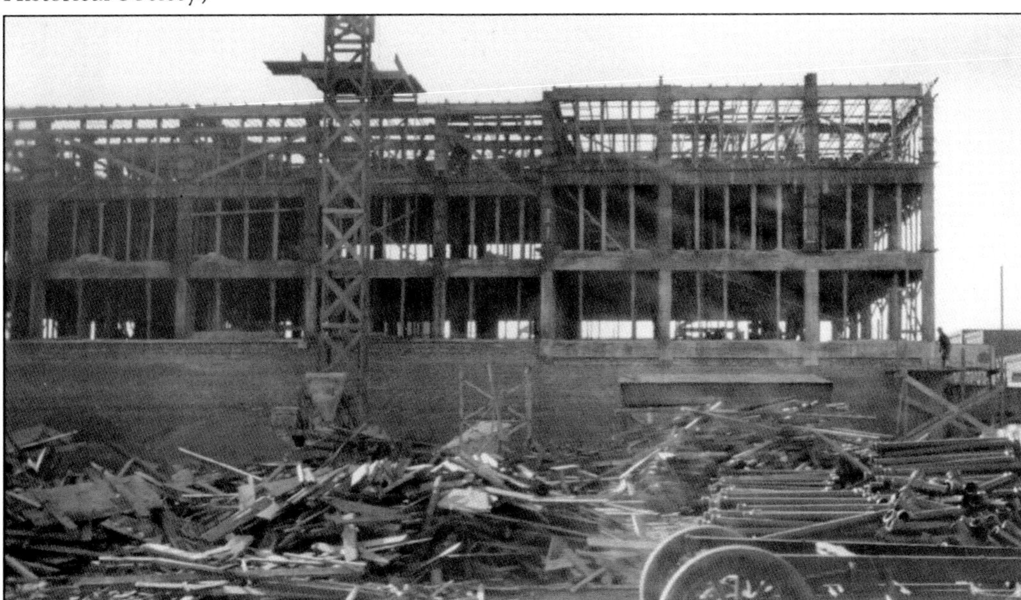

Liberal had become a busy regional trading center by the late 1920s. Improved farming practices, successful crops, and a promising oil and gas business meant Liberal was busy day and night. The Liberal Hotel Company, formed in 1929, recognized the shortage of hotel rooms and set about building an 80-room, four-story hotel complete with main-level commercial space, a coffee shop, a formal restaurant, and an elevator. (Courtesy of Seward County Historical Society.)

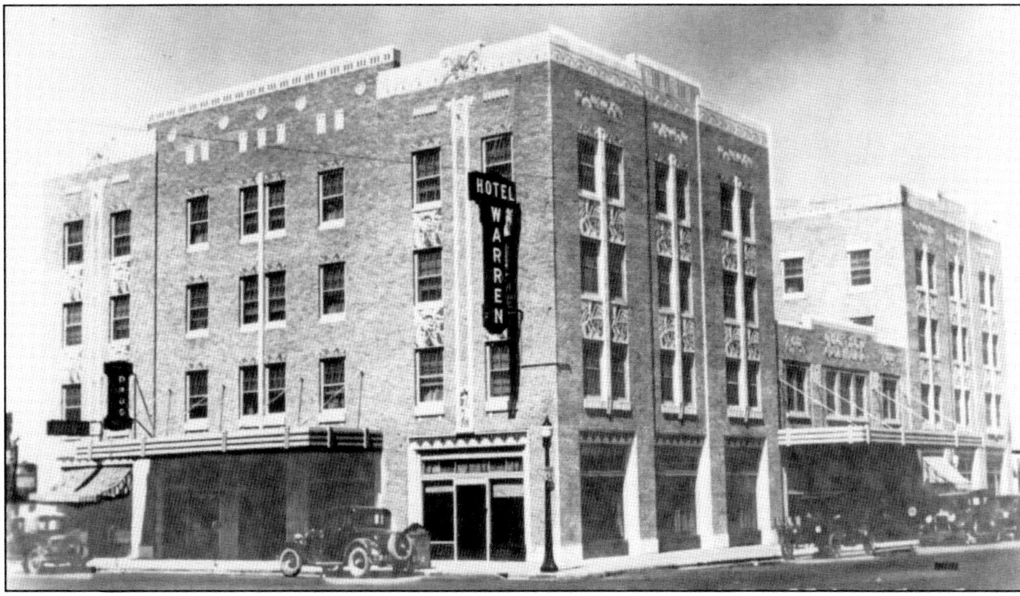

Hotel Warren was completed in April 1930. Architect Ellis Charles designed this high-style Art Deco building. The Liberal Hotel Company consisted of John Baughman, Frank Boles, Bert Dubois, C.M. Light, Paul Light, Thomas Smith, and Thomas Hopkins, along with other Liberal stockholders. When the hotel was near completion, the directors held a contest to name the structure. Charles Tucker and Peirce Munsy won with their suggestion, the Wheatland. However, when Guy Helvering and Warren Smithers, of Salina, leased the new hotel, they changed the name to Hotel Warren to conform to other hotels the men operated.

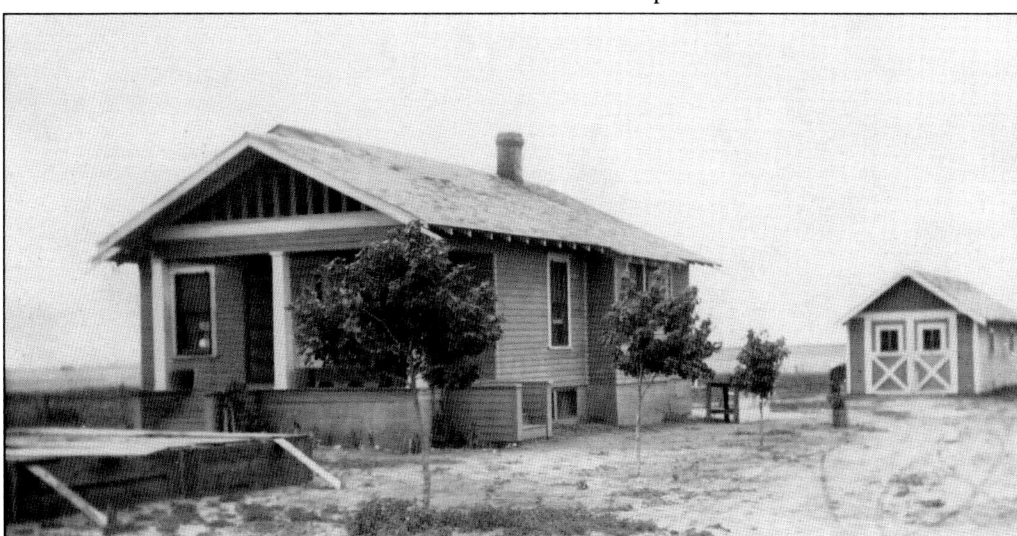

On land Ralph and Cora Heath purchased in 1907, this bungalow became the first home in the new town of Archer. Archer was formed when the K&O Railroad came from Liberal, headed northwest to Milner, angled over to Archer, and ended in Woods in Stevens County. The short line railroad had a crew of three who would offer rides on their grain runs to and from Liberal and would pull out the occasional stuck automobile with their locomotive. (Courtesy of Seward County Historical Society.)

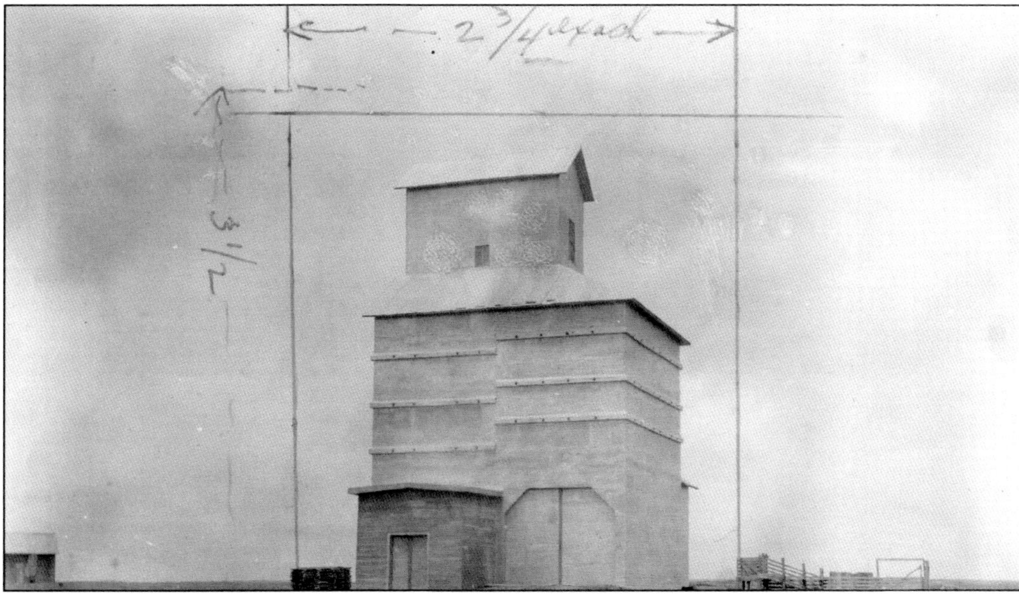

Awaiting the arrival of the K&O Railroad, this tin clad wooden elevator was built in the early 1920s by Howard Wheaton, of Hugoton, Kansas. After the K&O was abandoned, the elevator was moved upright by Lloyd Chance to the Shuck farm where it resides today. (Courtesy of Seward County Historical Society.)

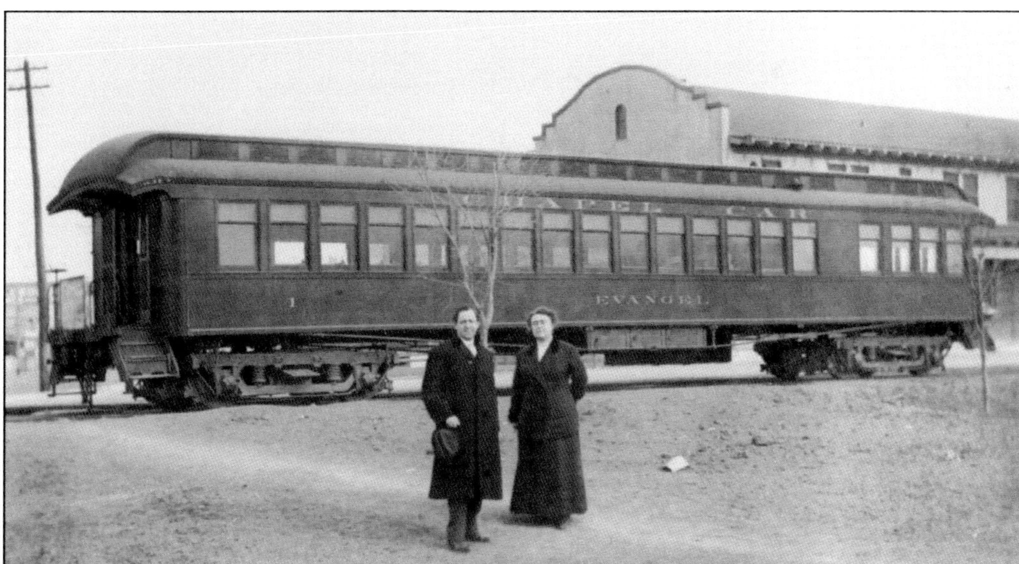

Mr. and Mrs. Kullian stand in front of their chapel car near the Rock Island depot. The white curtained area in the back of the railcar was their living quarters, while the front portion served as the chapel. The mission of the chapel car was to minister to people who lived close to the railroad tracks and railroad crews who could not attend church on a regular basis.

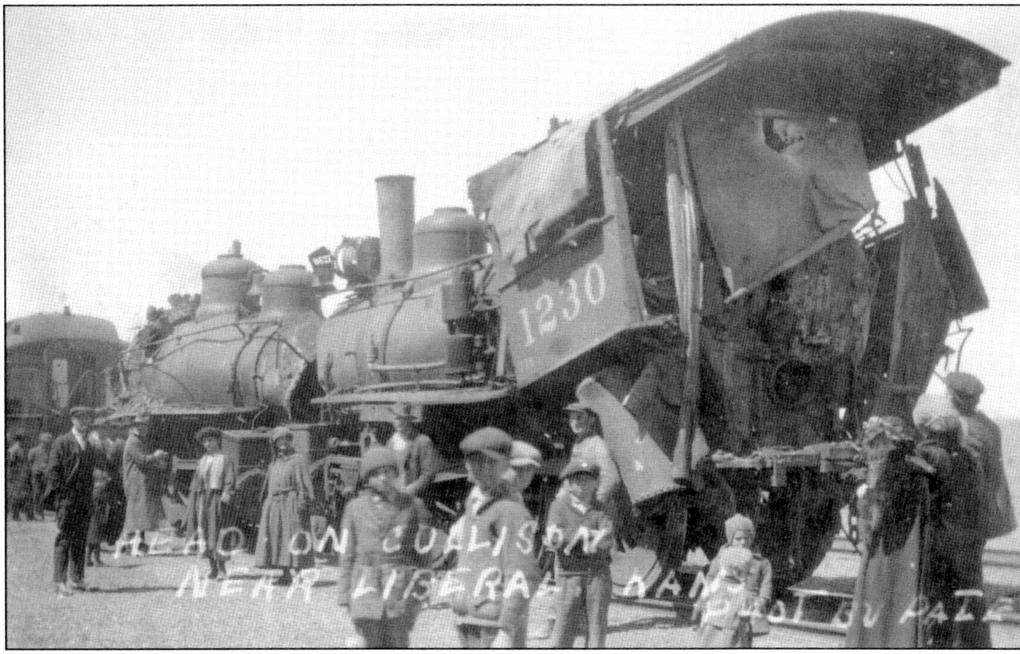

Tom Pate took this photograph of a head-on collision between Rock Island train Nos. 311 and 312 on April 19, 1922. The accident happened three miles east of Kismet. Both engineers, Frick and Weidman, were killed. Confused train orders were the cause of the tragic accident.

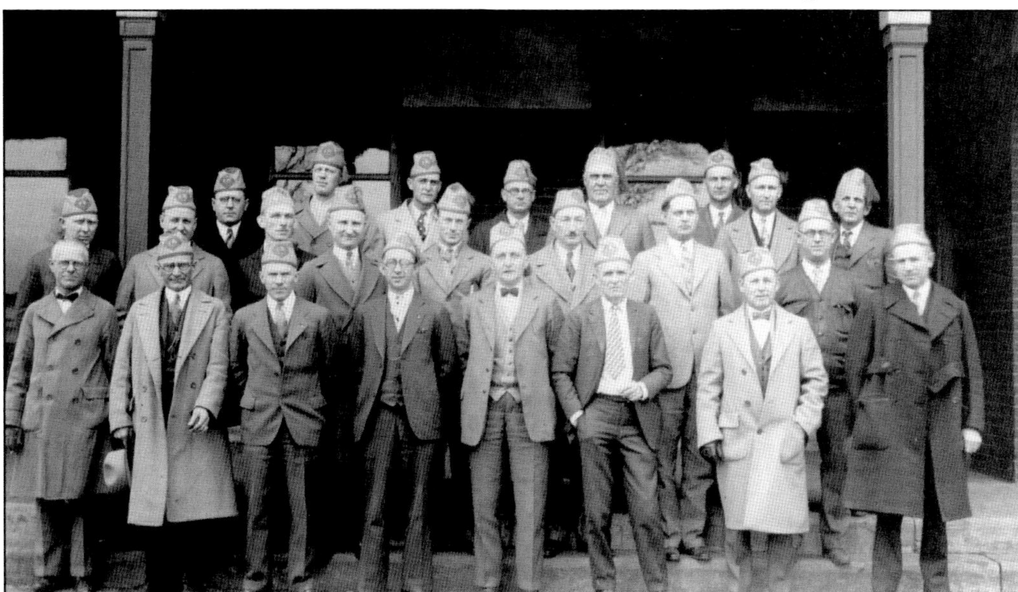

In 1925, the local Lions Club donned their fezzes and posed for a photograph in front of the Rock Island depot. From left to right are (first row) Dr. Phillip, Henry Goss, Napoleon Bonaparte Mahuron, Dr. H. Penny, Harry Pruitt, Oscar Grossman, Ray Kennedy, and L.L. Holland; (second row) E.P. Rustman, Charlie Taylor, Dr. Eugene Pellette, C.W. Law, Herman Salley, Dr. F.M. Beatty, Vern Griffith, and Perry Buckley; (third row) Warren Zimmerman, Eldon Shupe, Cliff Leete, Judy ?, F.O. Rindom, Sam Dodd, Rev. J.N. Gibble, and W.D. King.

Four
THE DEPRESSION
1930–1940

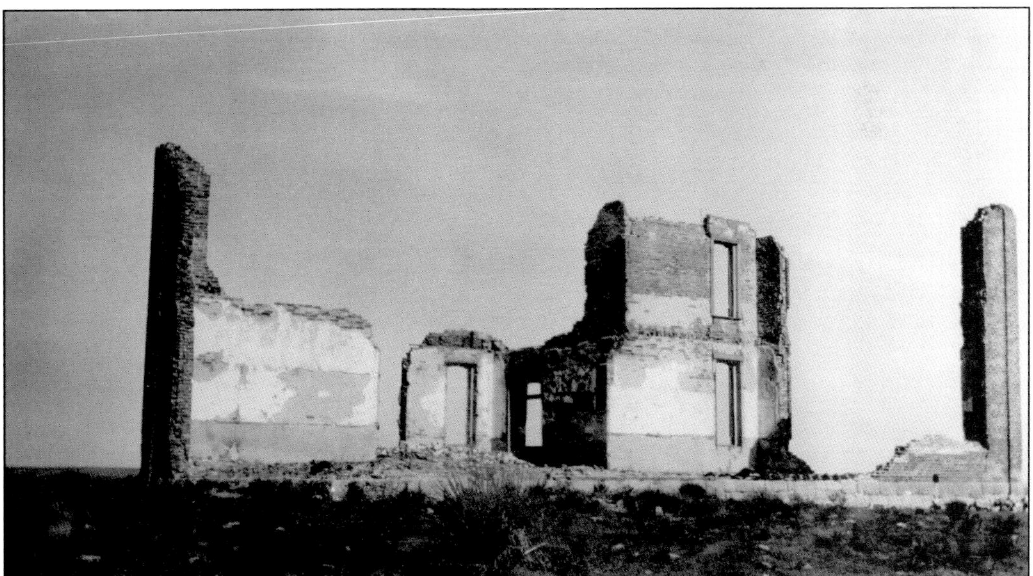

Seward County's former county seat was almost gone by 1930. Maurine Long Tate took this photograph of the remains of the old Fargo Springs schoolhouse on Decoration Day 1930. (Courtesy of Seward County Historical Society.)

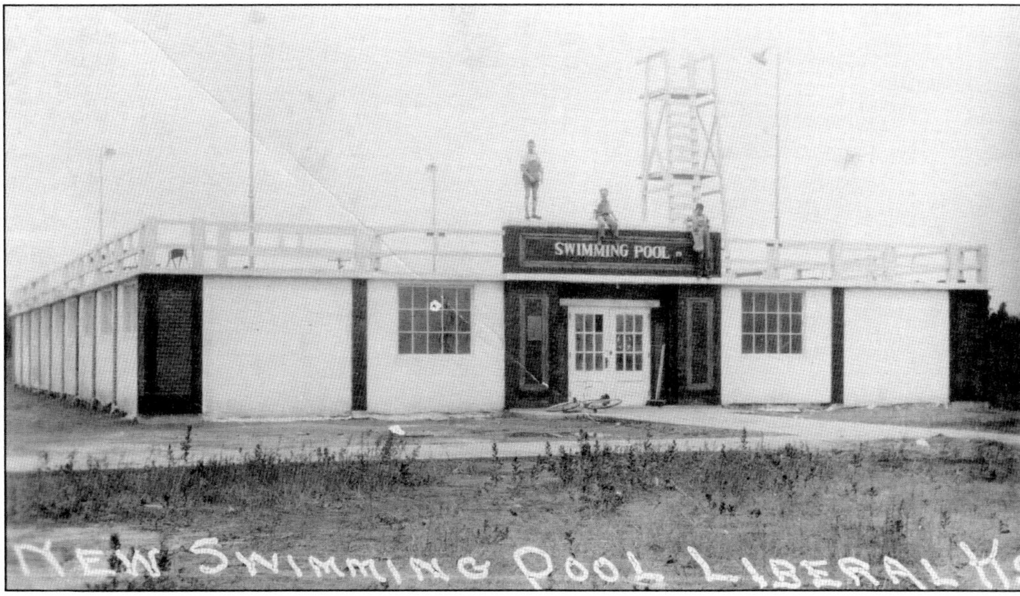

Recreation was a necessity in the growing burg of Liberal. A swimming pool was just what was needed to make Light Park a destination for Liberal youth. The city purchased a Bintz pool that measured 45 by 90 feet. Lockers and dressing rooms were around the perimeter of the aboveground pool. Rodney Horton is wearing the overalls cut off above the knee.

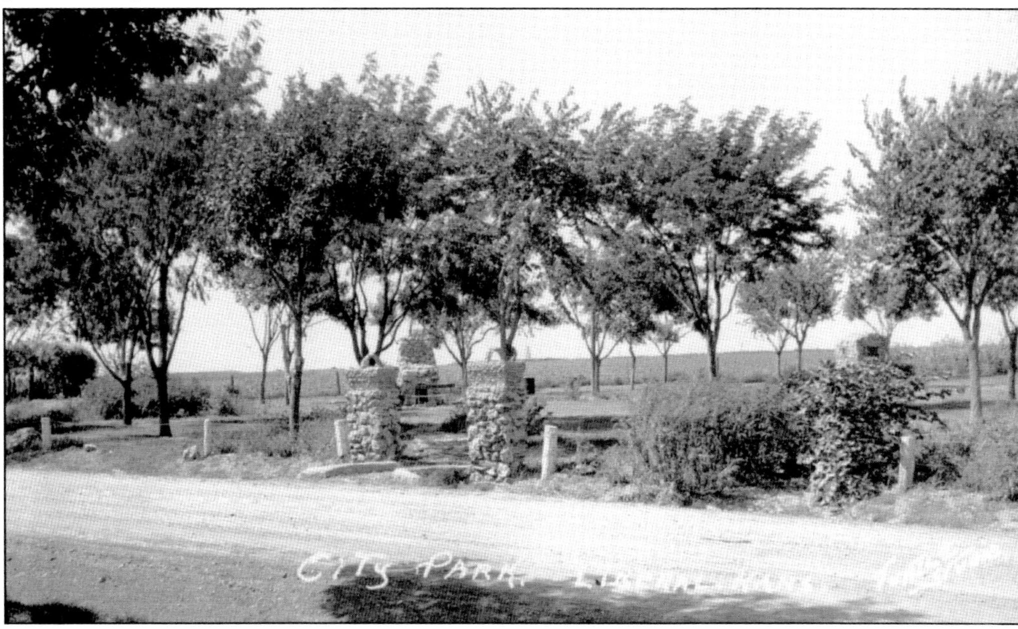

In 1927, Light Park was farm ground—until C.M. Light gave a tract of land just north of Eleventh Street and west of Kansas Avenue. Trees were planted, driveways were laid out, and the new swimming pool was built on the southeast corner. However, something was missing. Belle Vickers came to the rescue with planned flower beds, walking paths, and a rock garden with a lily pool. Rocks were brought from Sharps Creek on the Smith Ranch, Cimarron County, Oklahoma, and St. Jacobs Well in Clark County, Kansas. The rocks were used to build the pond, barbeque grills, and pillars.

In July 1932, from left to right, Billy Greenwald, "Rootin' Tootin' " Jay Wooten, Charles Hatton, and Ray Kennedy attended the Lions International Convention in Los Angeles, California. The Liberal Lions were proud to show the rest of the nation's Lions their many accomplishments.

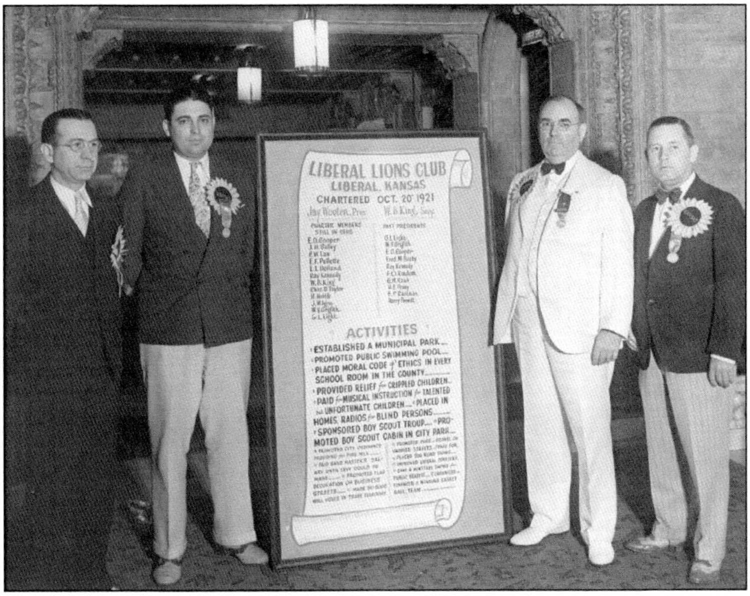

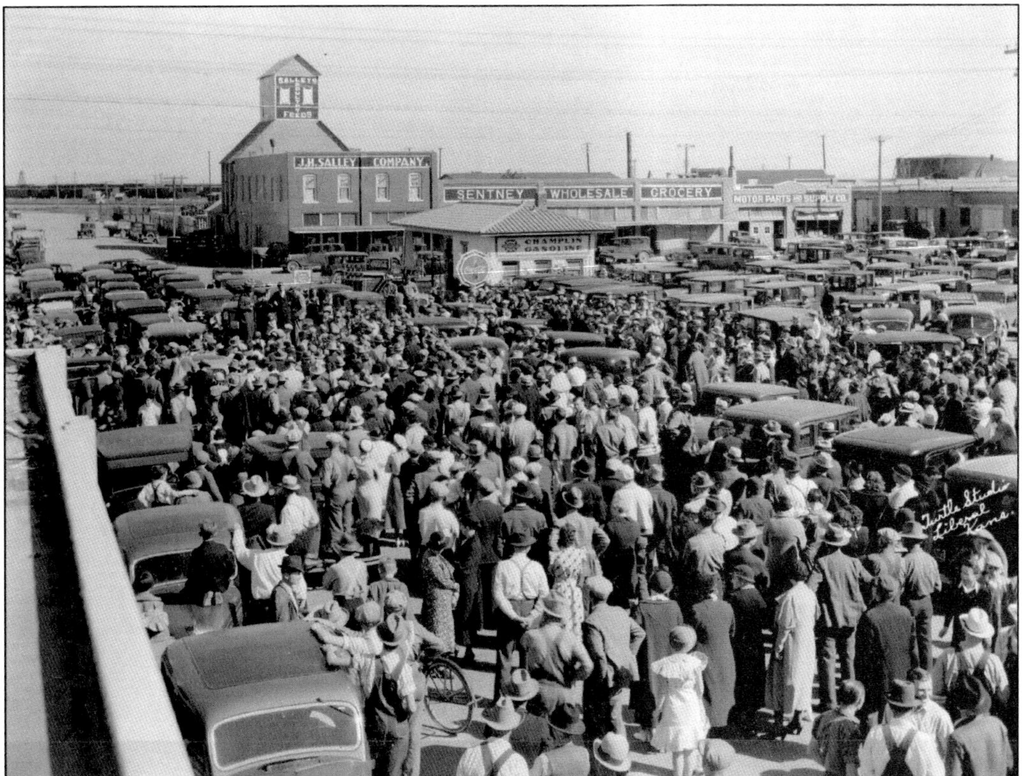

The Monthly Merchant Drawing Day always brought a crowd. Gathering on East Third Street, folks waited to hear their names drawn for cash prizes given by town retailers. Those whose names were drawn had to be present to win. Notice the J.H. Salley Company, Champlin Service Station, and Sentney Wholesale Grocery Company in the background. Neither the buildings nor the businesses exist today. (Courtesy of Seward County Historical Society.)

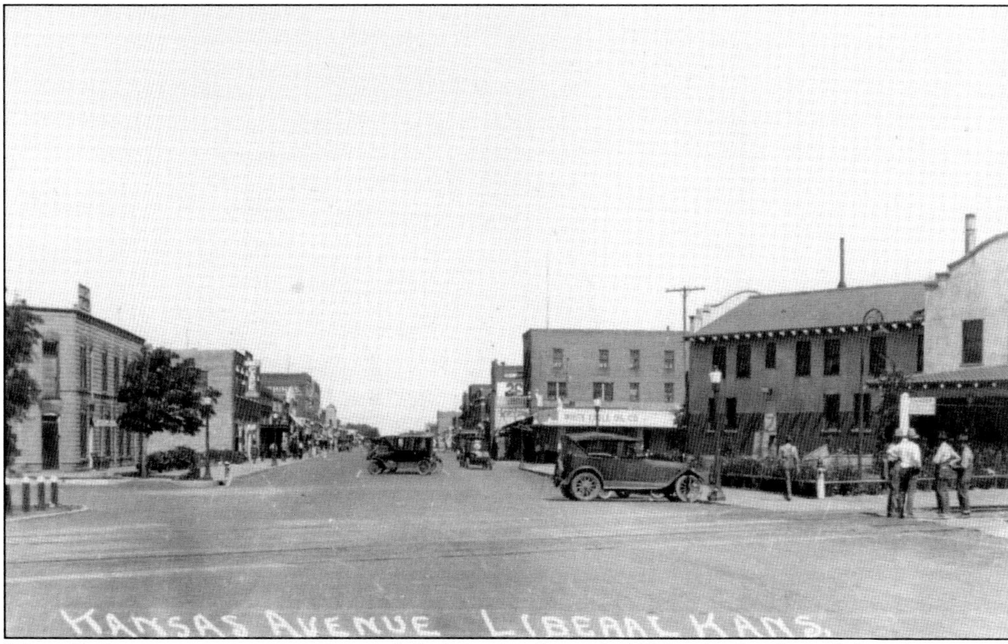

Liberal's downtown was attractive and thriving in the early 1930s. At the date of this photograph, the town seems to be insulated from the Depression. This image was taken from the railroad tracks, looking north on Kansas Avenue.

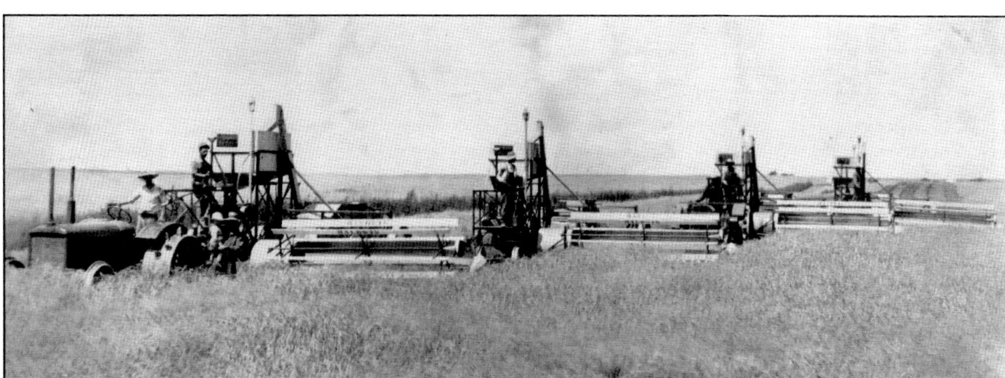
A picture of prosperity is shown with these Baldwin combines. The two tractors pull two combines—each with one man per tractor and one man per combine platform. The wheat crop for 1931 was unmatched with 12 million bushels harvested. Unfortunately, wheat was in abundance, and by July 1931, the price fell to 25¢ per bushel.

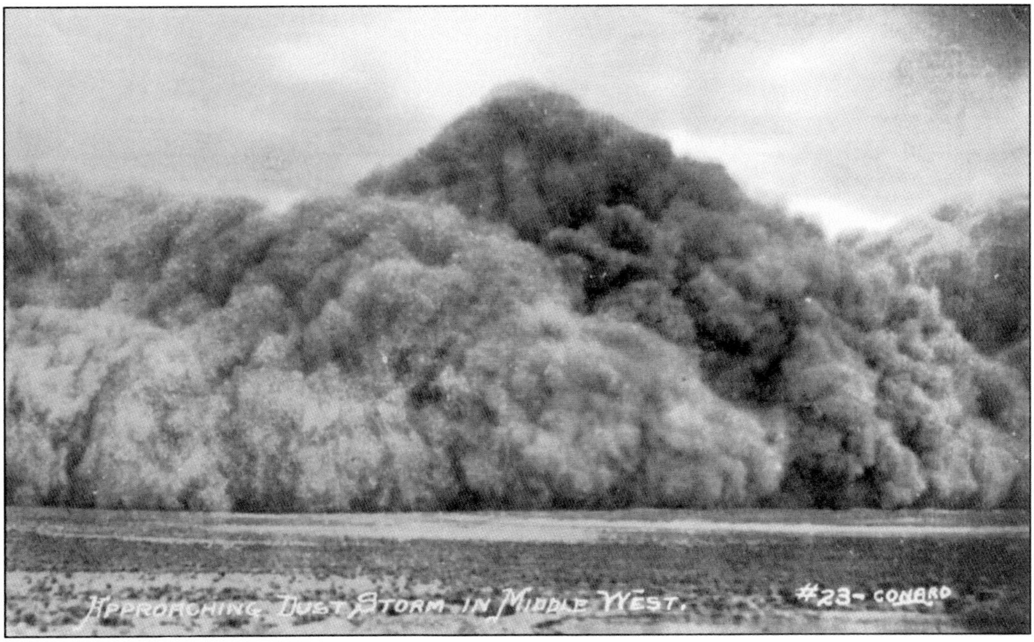

Low wheat prices, a national depression, and a record-setting drought made the high plains fields ready for liftoff. Failing crops and abandoned fields along with few soil conservation practices caused the fragile topsoil to be picked up by the ferocious winds and turned into rollers. In March 1932, there were 22 days of dirt storms; in 1933, there were 139 days of dirt.

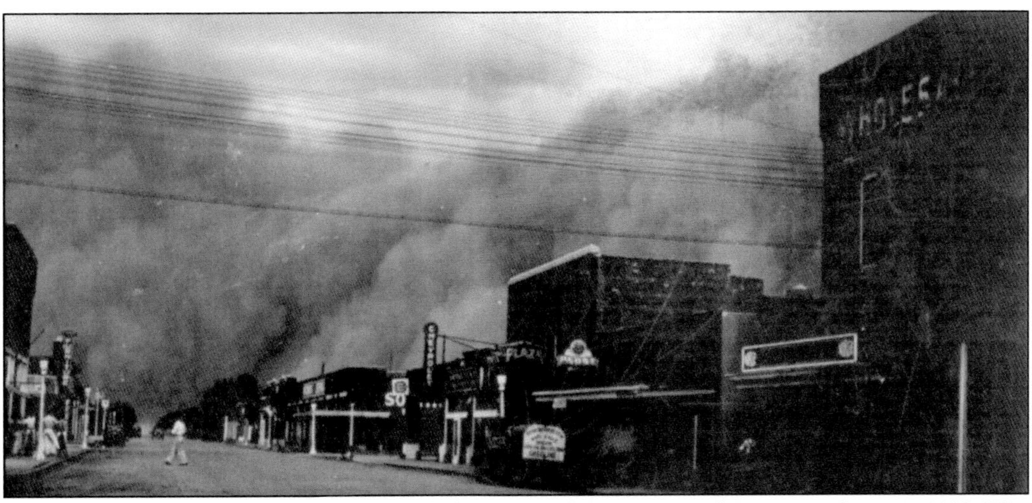

An unidentified photographer captured this view of West Second Street on June 4, 1937. The photographer's inscription on the back read, "This taken at 6:15 in the evening. Blacker than night. My first and hope my only one."

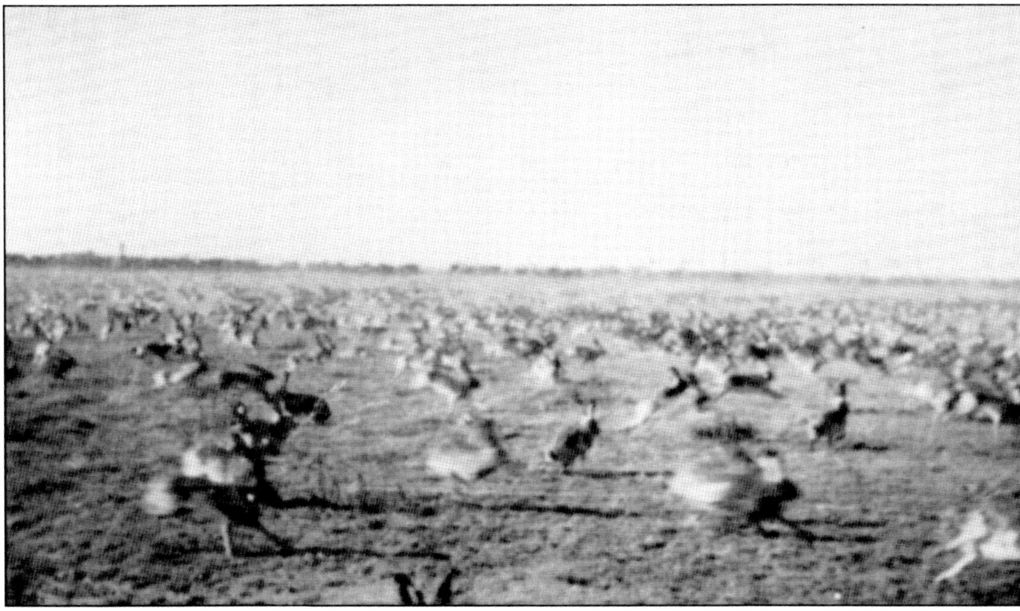

During the Dirty Thirties, Seward County, along with the rest of the Dust Bowl, was overpopulated with jackrabbits. The thirsty, hungry rabbits would eat the already-fragile wheat crops to the ground. Townsfolk and farmers would gather at a predetermined spot, spread out to cover the perimeter of a six-mile square, and walk toward each other to the middle of the square carrying clubs. The rabbits would of course run from the approaching crowd and would be forced into a catch pen where they met their demise. (Courtesy Seward County Historical Society.)

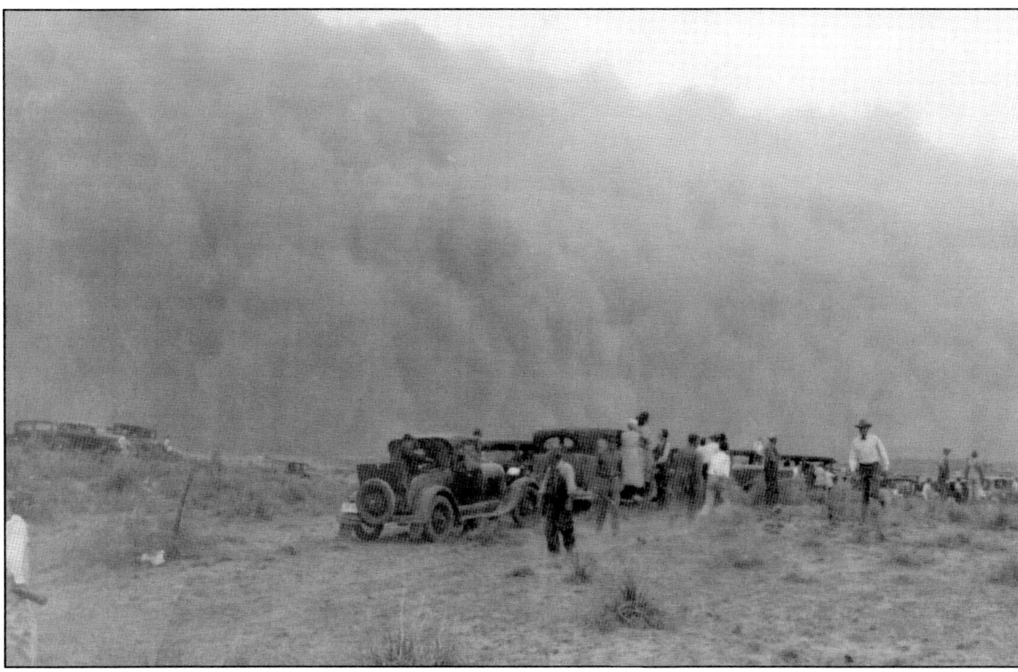

This rabbit drive ended abruptly when someone spotted a "big one" on the north horizon. The storm arrived in silence on April 14, 1935, and was considered the worst of the worst. The day has become known as Black Sunday. (Courtesy of Seward County Historical Society.)

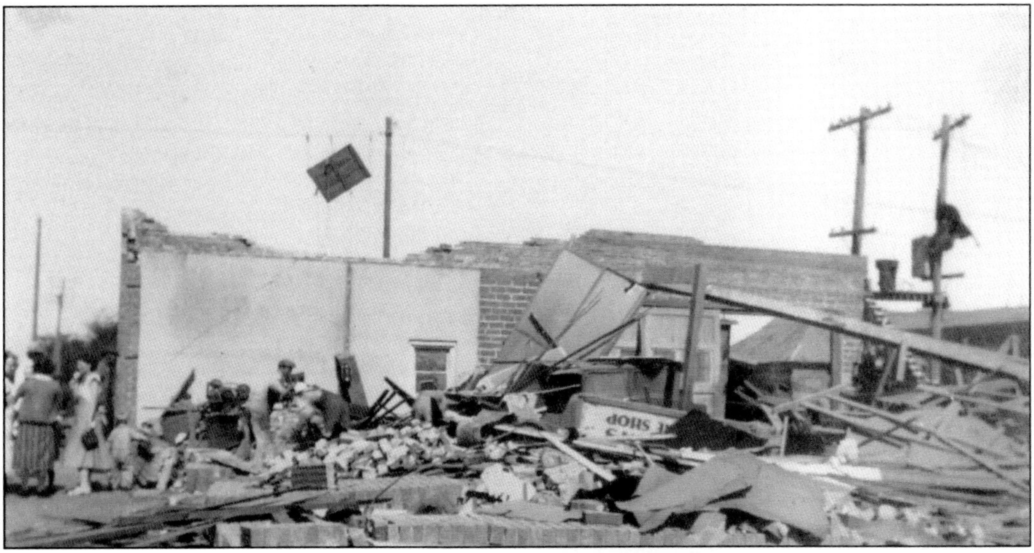

Already enshrouded by yet another dust storm, Liberal was struck by a tornado on May 23, 1933, heavily damaging the downtown area. The storm killed 4 residents and injured 141. Estimated property damage was over $900,000. The image shows what was left of the 100 block of West Second Street. Nature continued its wrath with record-high temperatures (a high of 120 degrees in Liberal) and an earthquake felt from Kenton, Oklahoma, to Liberal. (Courtesy of Seward County Historical Society.)

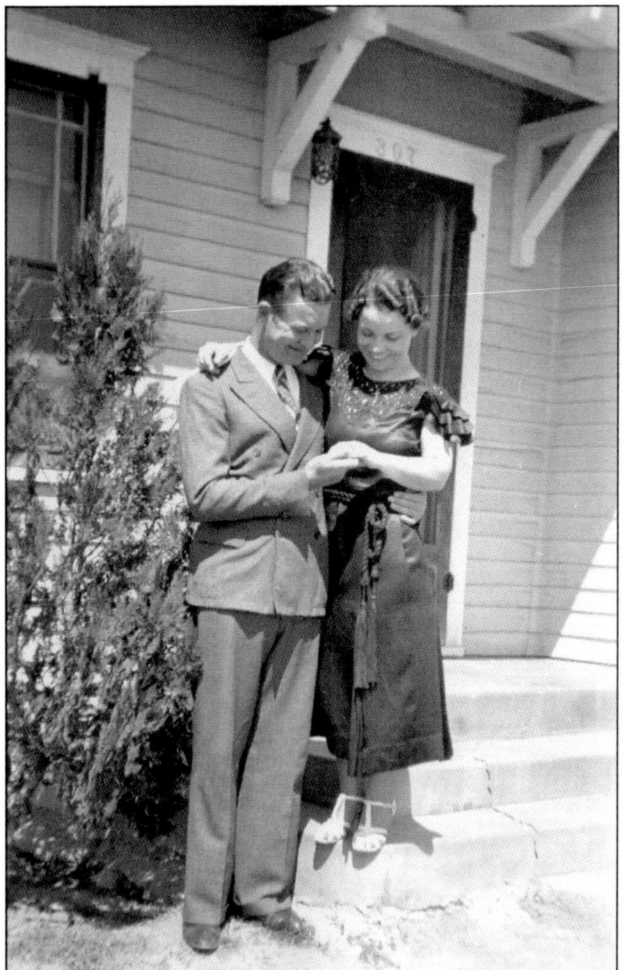

Not everything that happened in the 1930s was bad. On September 6, 1936, Rev. Forrest Wyman married Wilma Peter. Reverend Wyman was born in Liberal and Wilma Peter was from Dover, Oklahoma. The couple later moved to California. (Courtesy of Seward County Historical Society.)

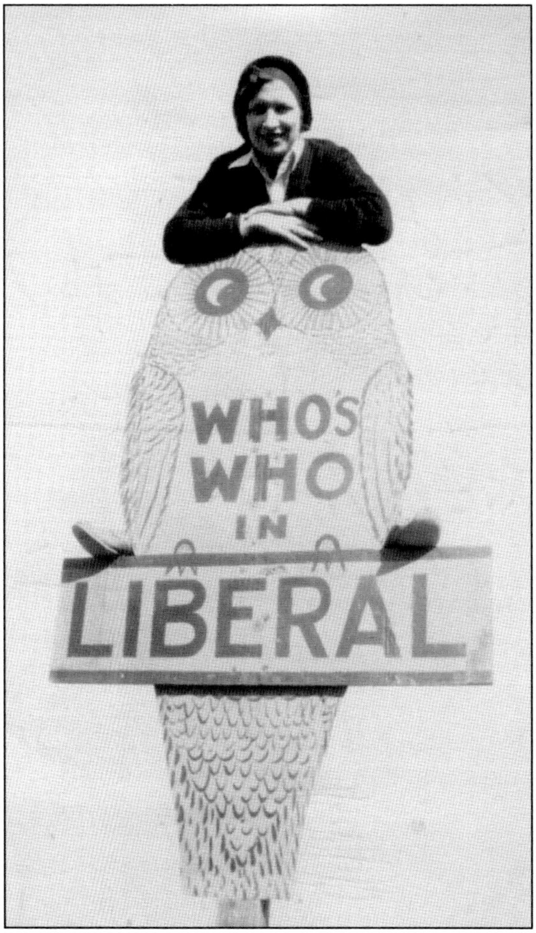

Located south of Liberal, this hoot owl sign greeted incoming visitors and made an unusual subject for photographers. The young lady is unidentified, but the caption on the back of the photograph states, "Ain't it so?"

Times were hard in Kansas during the 1930s. The Works Progress Administration (WPA) was part of Franklin Roosevelt's New Deal program to give the unemployed jobs. The agricultural building and the rock wall that surrounds the fairgrounds were constructed by the WPA in 1936. The wall and building cost $24,000. The rock for the wall was obtained 20 miles east of Liberal on the Cimarron River. This same rock was used in many country road culverts.

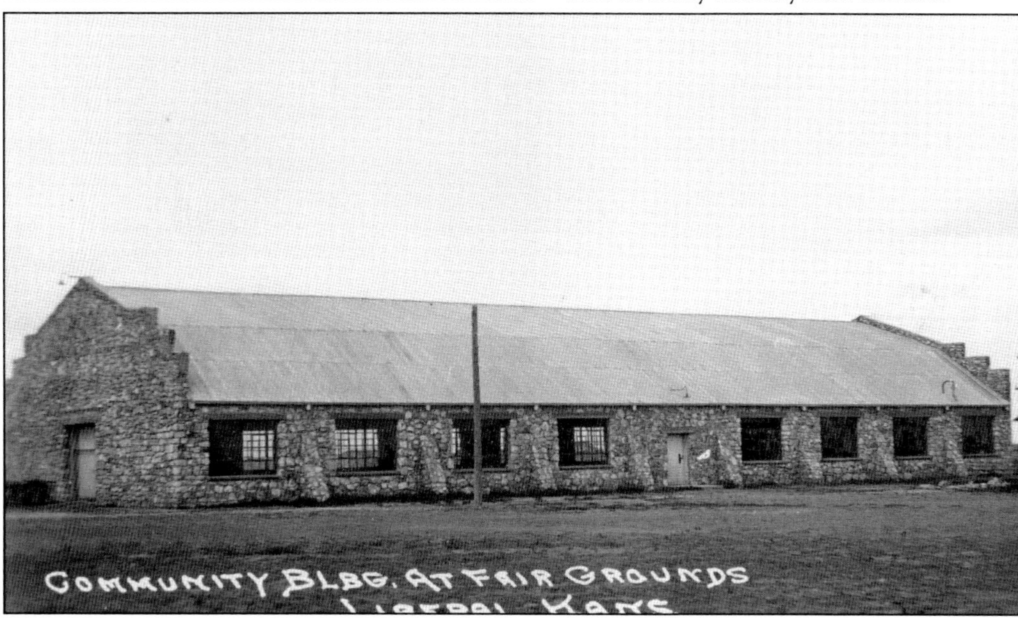

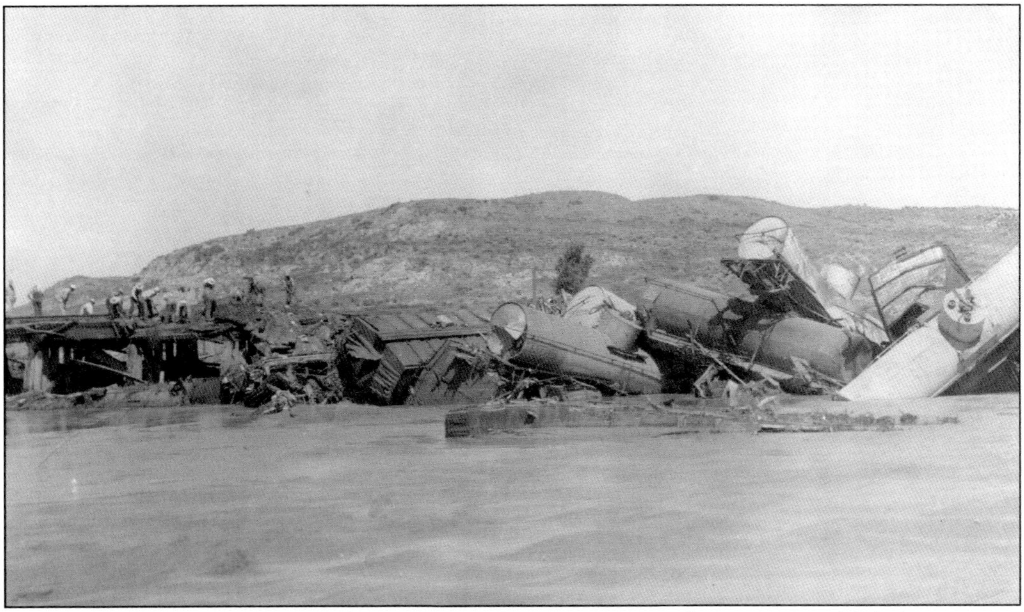

On August 18, 1938, a rain-swollen Cimarron River went on its best rampage. Unbeknownst to the early-morning crew on the Gold Ball freight train, the flooded river had taken out the pilings under the main channel railroad bridge, leaving the rail intact. The crew barreled across the series of slough bridges, and with nothing but air underneath the rails, the massive locomotive, tender, cars, and crew plunged into the river. Five men were injured, and two were killed. Turtle Studio captured this image of the wreckage and the flooding Cimarron River.

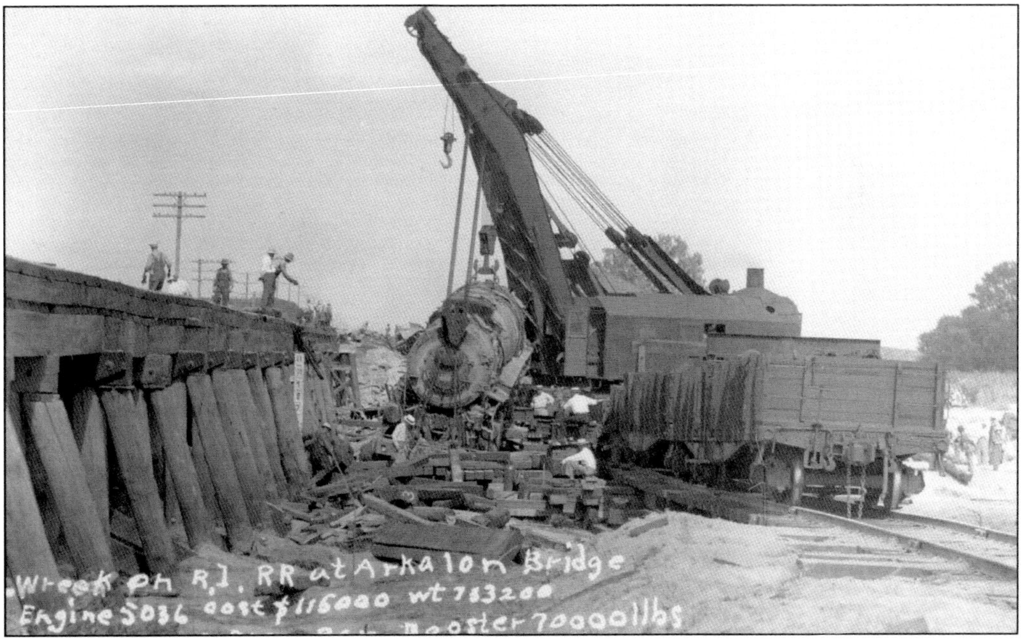

After the floodwaters of the Cimarron had subsided, Rock Island Railroad crews built a temporary track parallel to the failed bridge. The railroad's mighty steam crane was put into action pulling salvageable boxcars and flatcars from the riverbed. The most daunting pull was engine No. 5036. The locomotive weighed in at 733,200 pounds.

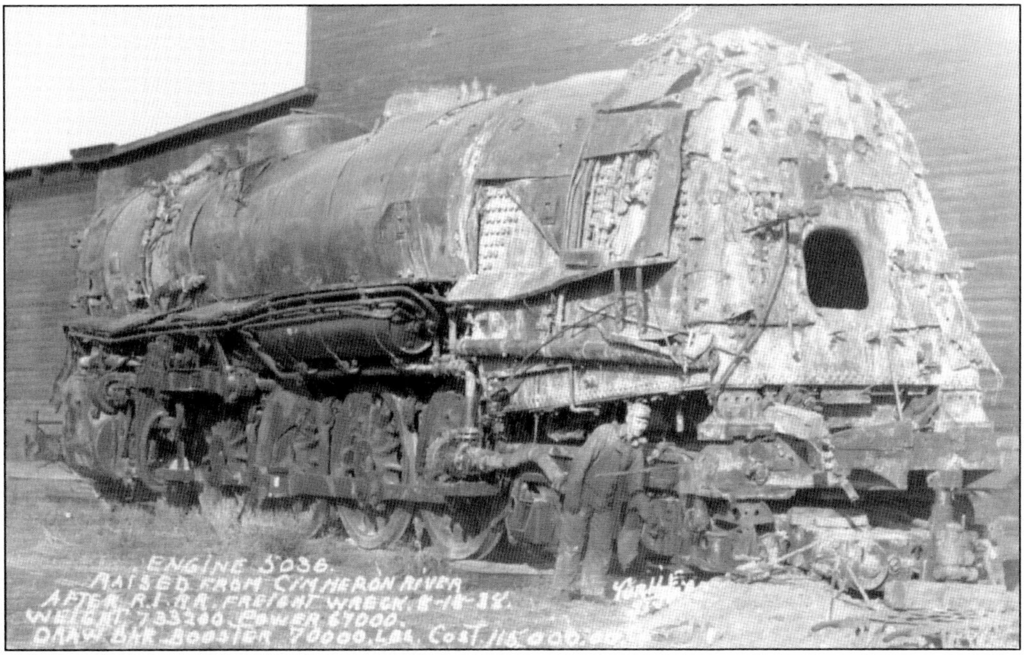

After being rescued from the Cimarron River, engine No. 5036 was pulled back to Liberal to be dried out, de-sanded, and re-oiled. The engine was then escorted to the Silvas Shops in Topeka, Kansas, where a new engine was installed and it was repainted. Old No. 5036 was put back into service for the Rock Island. Engineer Earl Walker, who also served as Liberal mayor, frequently was at the helm.

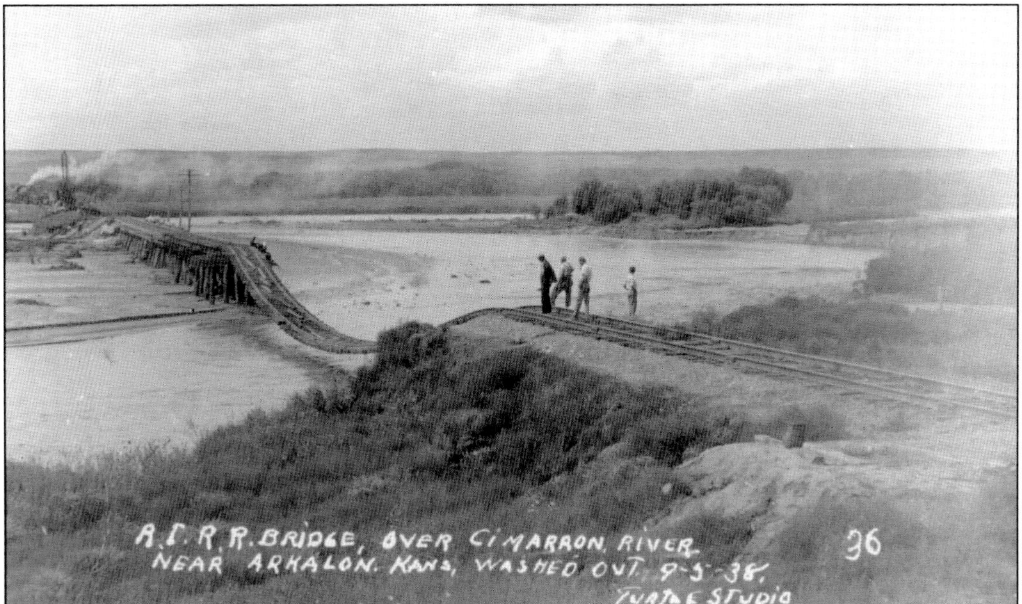

Less than a month after rebuilding the track and repairing the bridge, the Cimarron River cut a new channel, washing out the bridge and part of the approach. Once again, pilings were washed away, leaving the rails dangling in midair. This time, approaching trains were forewarned, avoiding another disaster.

On September 9, 1938, the Rock Island employed its pile driver to start repairs of the trestle bridge. Behind the pile driver was a line-up of necessary equipment, including several cars with pilings and timbers, an engine, and tender. The wreck was a major event that attracted large crowds of volunteers, workers, and the simply curious. Hamburger and soda pop stands were set up to take advantage of the crowds.

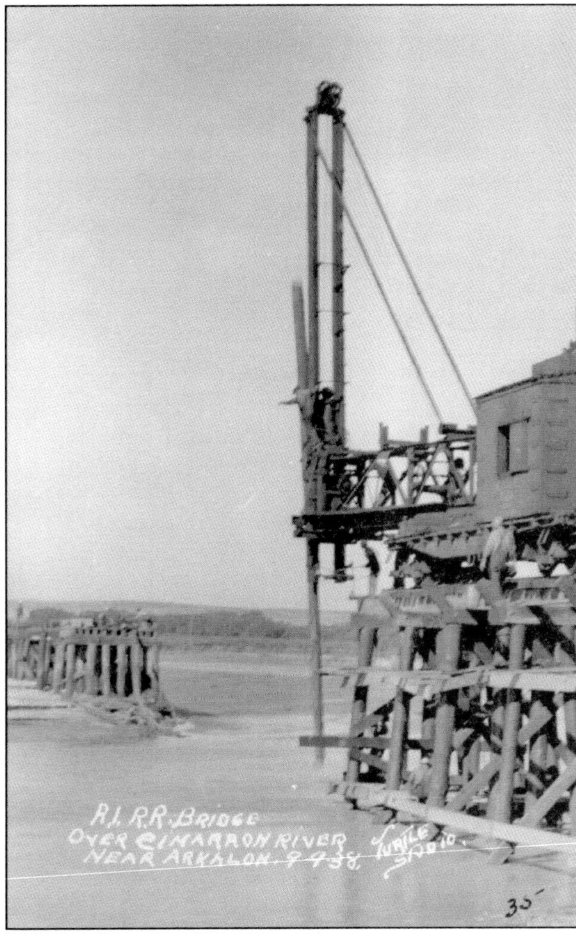

The Cimarron railroad crossing was a constant headache for the Rock Island. After the 1938 wreck and flood, chief operating officer John Farrington and other officials arrived to look at the problem. Farrington quickly decided to reroute the line and build a new bridge over the river. By early 1939, the Sampson of the Cimarron was under construction.

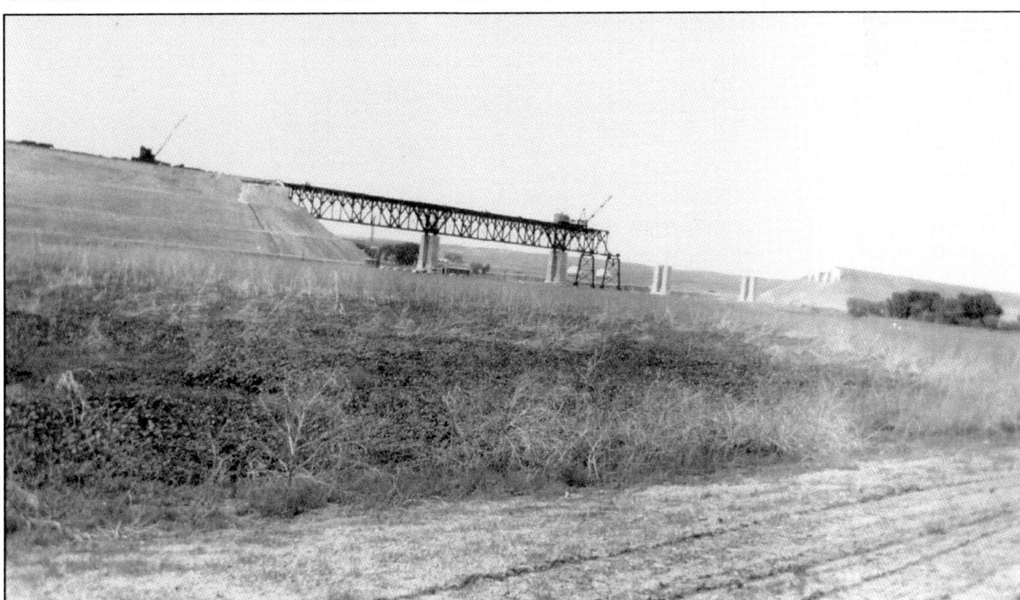

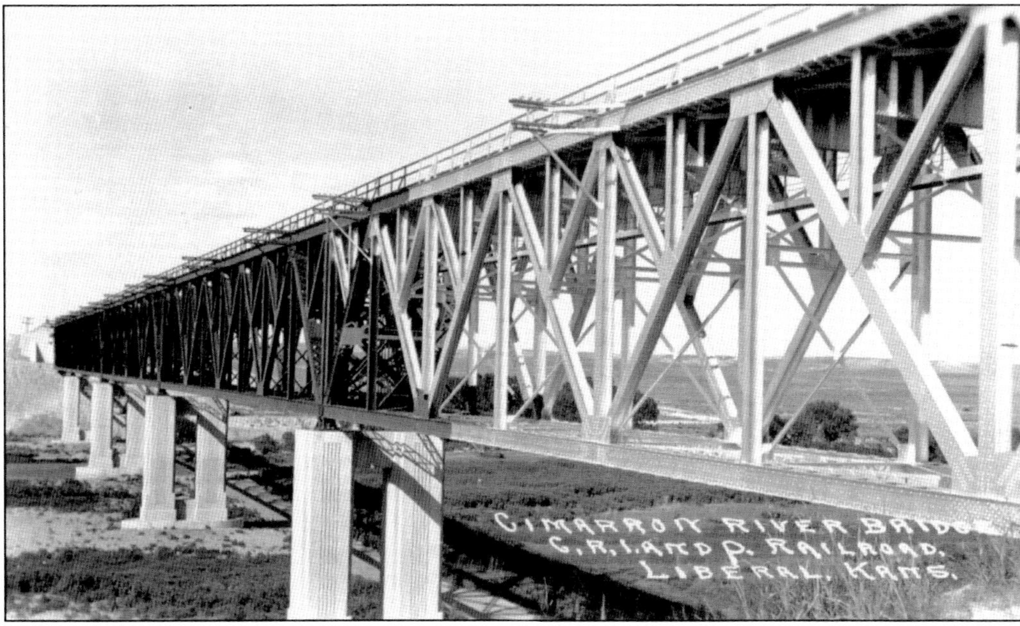

On July 8, 1939, Rock Island No. 13 crossed the brand new bridge at 2:35 p.m. Passengers included John Farrington, H. Penny, C.W. Law, Olan and T.J. Blakemore, Roy Smith, W.B. Hettic, and Ray Millman. Ironically, in the cab was C.B. Howell. Howell, a fireman, had survived the Gold Ball freight wreck earlier. The new bridge had 21,800 tons of concrete in its abutment and piers. The caisson-sunk concrete piers were placed 65 feet below riverbed with steelwork 92 feet above.

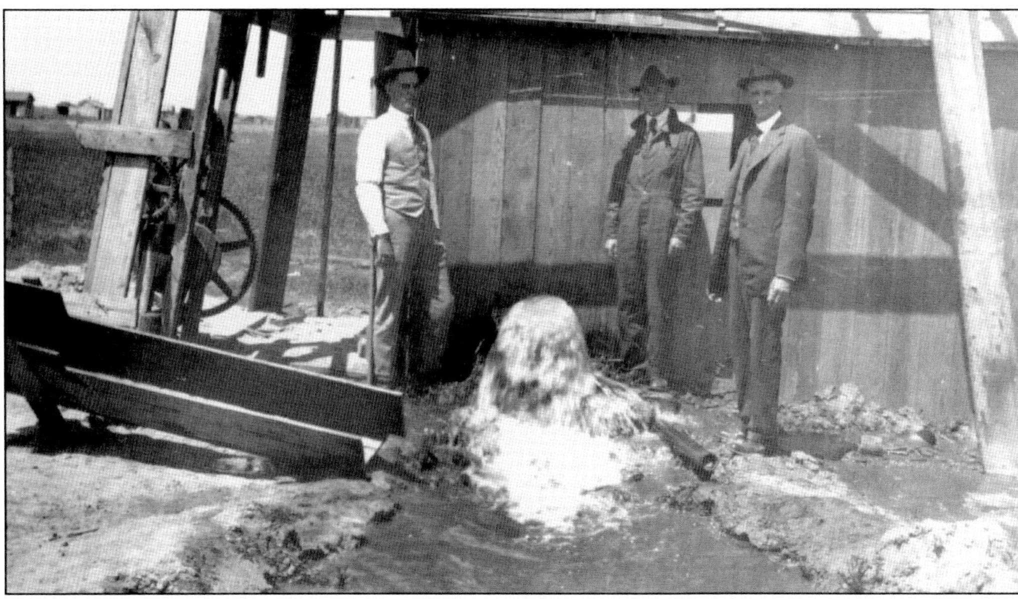

Southwest Kansas either had too much moisture, which typically came all at once, or not near enough. Long periods of drought were a constant worry for farmers. In 1937, C.M. Light, Warren Farmer, Lee Larrabee, John Baughman, Ralph Colvin, E.W. Moore, J.H. Salley, Frank Boles, Paul Light, and others financed the Liberal Deep Irrigation Well Company. The well was drilled 350 feet deep and was powered by an engine everyone called Ol' Herc. Wheat, milo, muskmelon, pumpkins, and turnips were planted with success. (Courtesy of Seward County Historical Society.)

The WPA and the Civilian Conservation Corps (CCC) introduced programs to help county residents endure the Depression. The WPA-sponsored sewing room had an open house to show off projects in the T.L. Gray Furniture Store at 312 North Kansas Avenue. Launa Dowdy supervised the making of quilts, dresses, stuffed animals, and handwork. (Courtesy of Seward County Historical Society.)

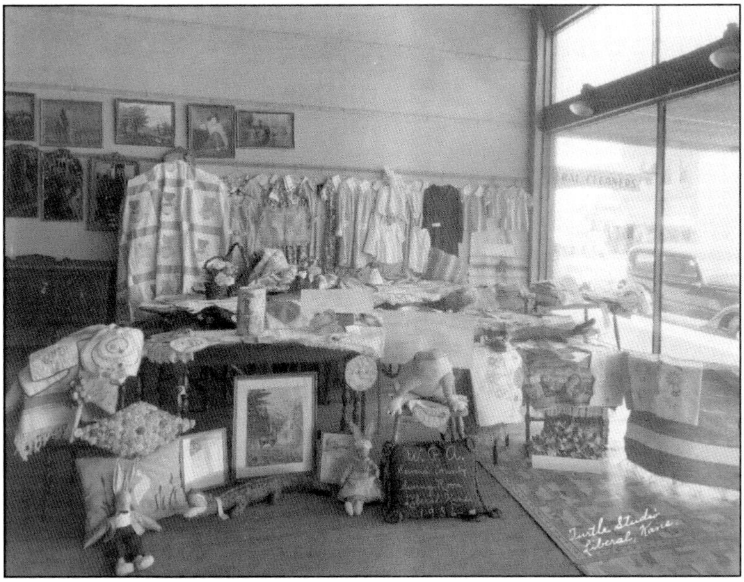

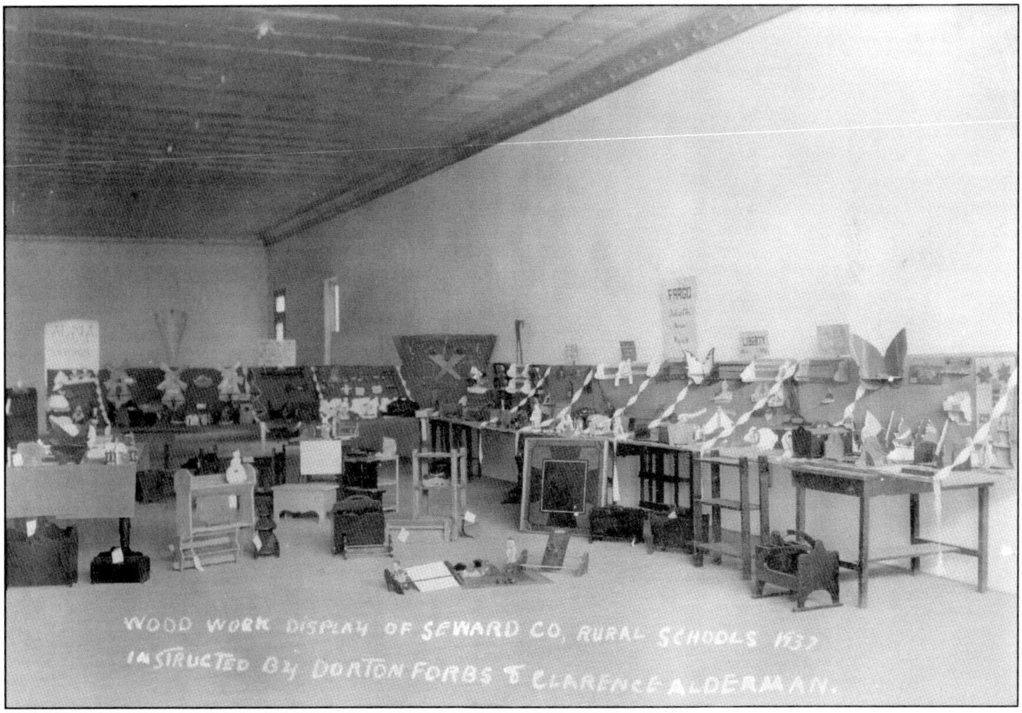

In 1937, the rural schools of Seward put on a downtown display of student woodworking talents. Magazine racks, chests, boot pullers, and shelves are featured. Classes were taught by Dorton Forbes and Clarence Alderman. Schools represented included Arkalon, Liberty, Fargo, Alma, and Hayne. (Courtesy of Seward County Historical Society.)

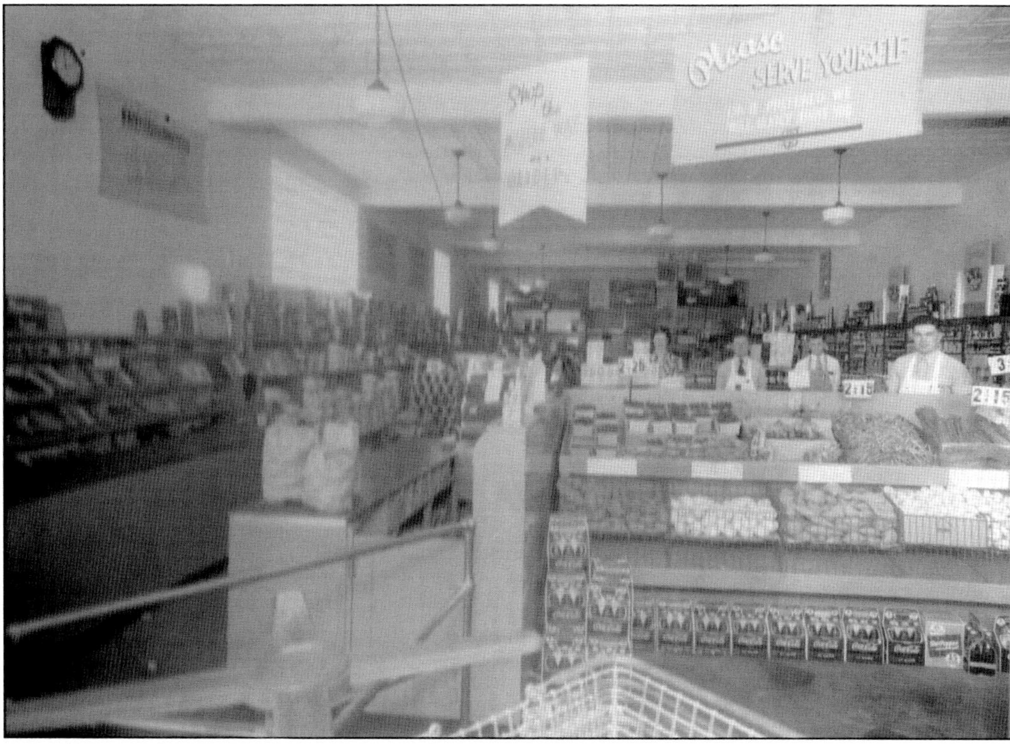

J.J. Dillons and Sons Grocery Store was located at 300 North Lincoln. Nicely displayed products included Coca-Cola, fresh green beans, berries, potatoes, and penny candy. Customers were encouraged to serve themselves and to shop the modern way with a "glider." Pictured are Bernice Bruns, Jim Clumsky, John Graham, and Delmar Riney. (Courtesy of Seward County Historical Society.)

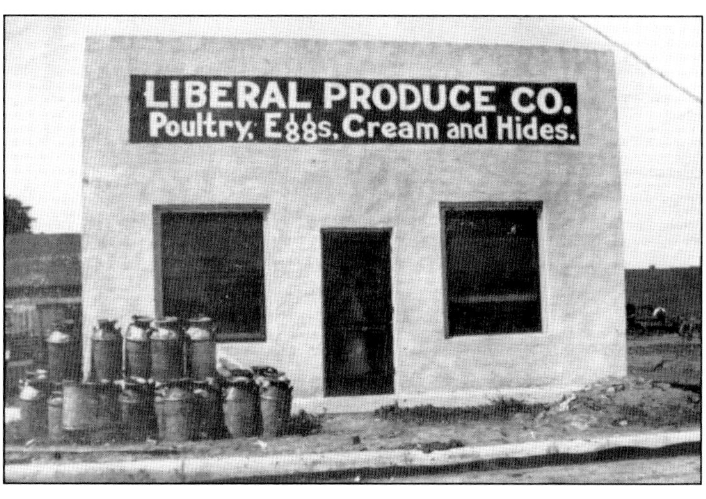

The Liberal Produce Company was important to rural Seward County. Not only did the farmers have a ready market for their produce, the local companies were ready to pay cash for the fresh eggs, cream, milk, and even hides their patrons would bring to town. The Liberal Produce Company was located on East Second Street. (Courtesy of Seward County Historical Society.)

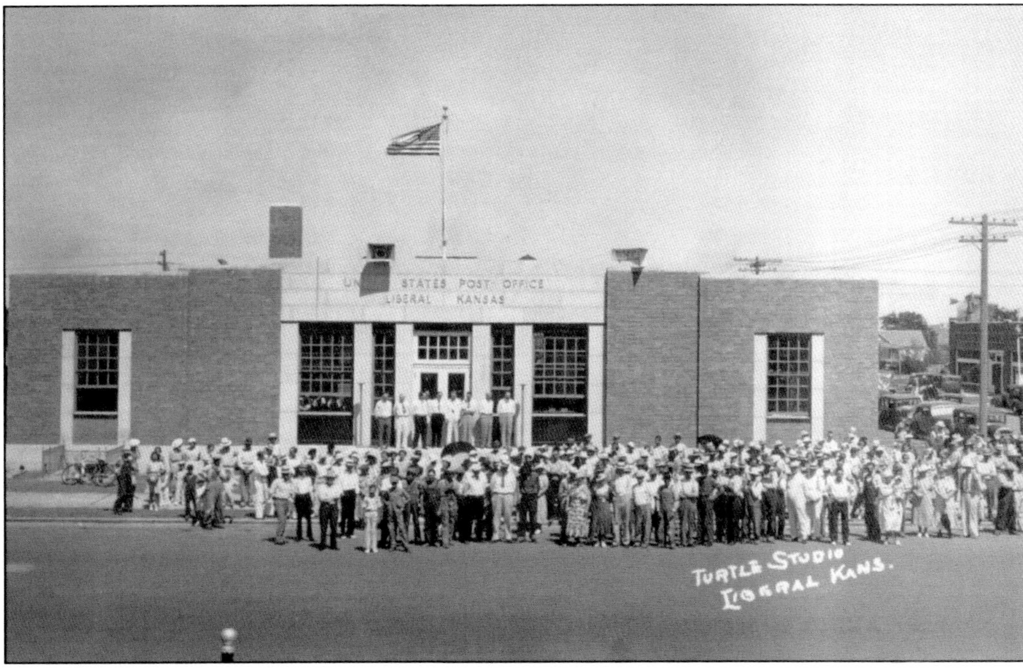

Through the years, Liberal's post office changed location at least seven times. When the post office was moved—building and all—in the late 1890s, postmaster Hurd calmly tended to his duty, delivered letters, and sold stamps, all while en route and three feet in the air. Most of the town turned out on July 18 1936, the day when the new post office was dedicated by Congressman Clifford Hope and postmaster Toby Tobias. (Courtesy of Mary Brewington.)

A Fourth of July parade in 1936 was well attended by young and old. Liberal's Boy Scout troop leads the way for the Liberal High School's summer band. Businesses along the way include First National Bank, Taylor Drugs, DuBois & Ravenscroft Clothiers, Beaty X-Ray Dentist, Stoner Jewelry, and the Tucker Theater. The feature film was *Old Corral*, starring Gene Autry.

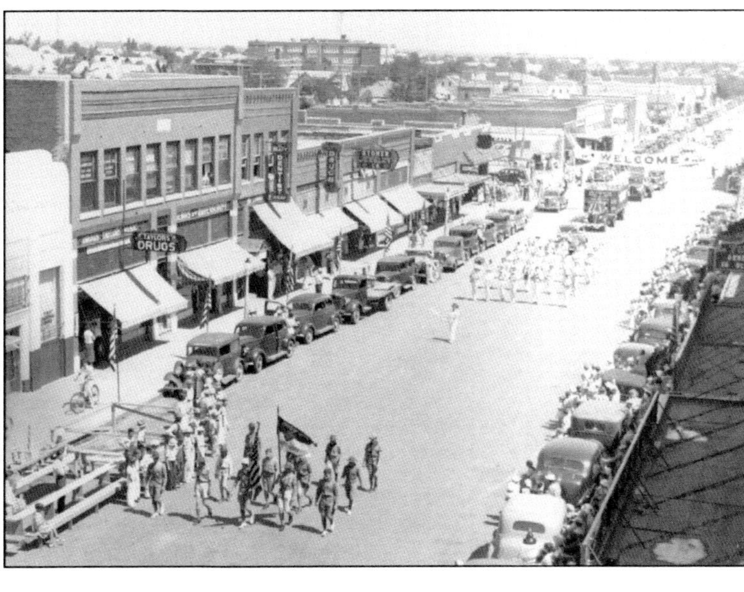

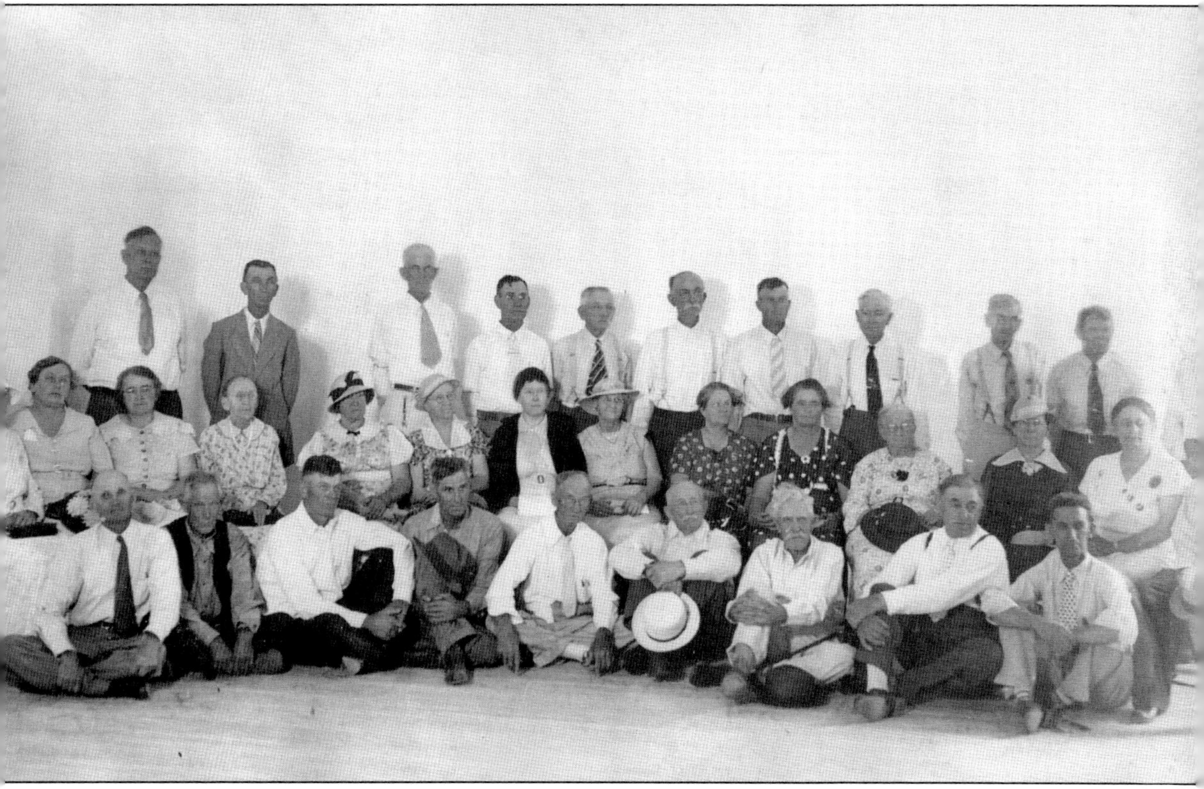

The Fourth of July celebration in 1936 brought out early pioneers of Seward County. They are, from left to right, (first row) Bernard Lemert, Maria Eldrige, Thurman Printz, Bob Smith, Warren Farmer, Joe Fuest, A.M. Ives, C.H. Rickart, and Lee Larrabee; (second row) Bettie Lemert, Mrs. Whitman, Emma Spradling, Hattie Merchant, Anise Bauersfield, Mary Fore England, Minnie Hogan, Phoebe Miller, Rosa Neill, Grace Eubank, Nancy Freeman, Anna Richart, Nettie Larrabee, and Alex McCoid; (third row) Boss Neff, John Miller, Jim England, L.L. Hogan, W.M. Miller, Frank Neill, Boston Eubank, George Smith, T.J. Smith, Guymon Wright, and Albert McLeod. (Courtesy of Seward County Historical Society.)

Five

Recovering and Prospering 1940–1950

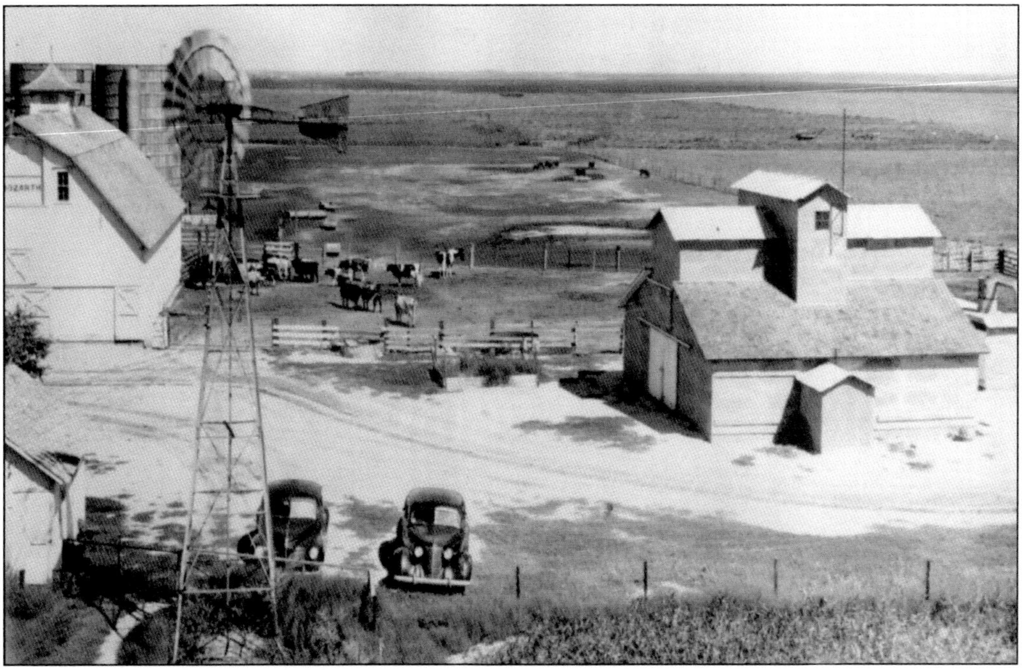

Rains returned to the land 10 years after the drought had turned Seward County into part of the Dust Bowl. Farmers were helped with diversification of crops, moisture conservation, and better equipment. This early-1940s photograph depicts the A. Bozarth farm three miles east of Liberal.

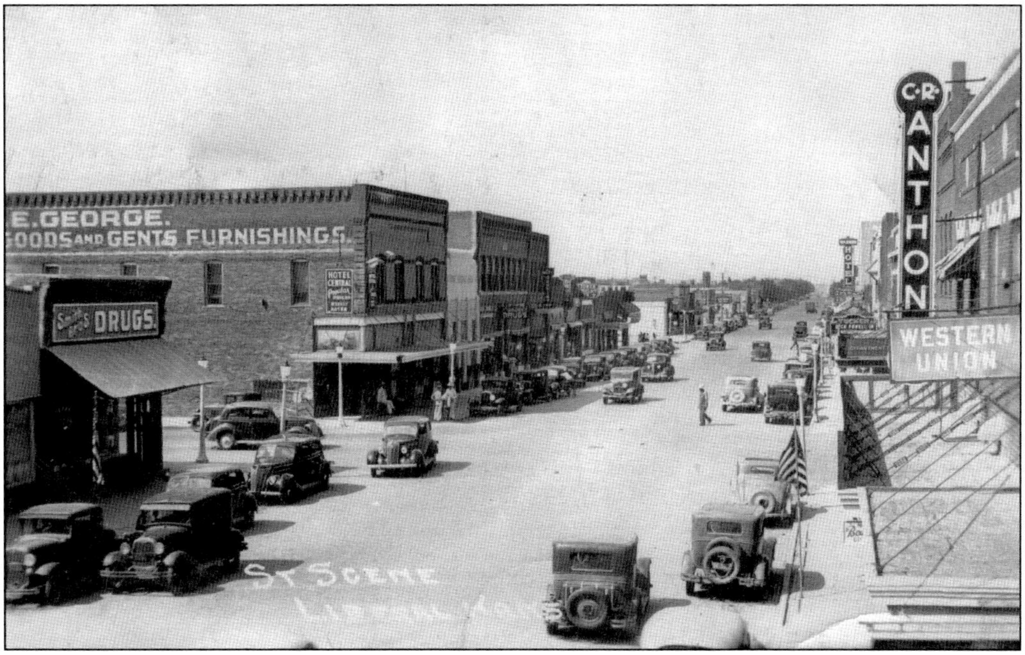

Kansas Avenue is busy with shoppers and loafers in this 1942 image. Liberal's population grew to almost 6,000 in 1940, while bank deposits rose from $1,712,000 to $10,515,000 in 1945. The Tucker Theater was showing *Model Wife*, starring Dick Powell.

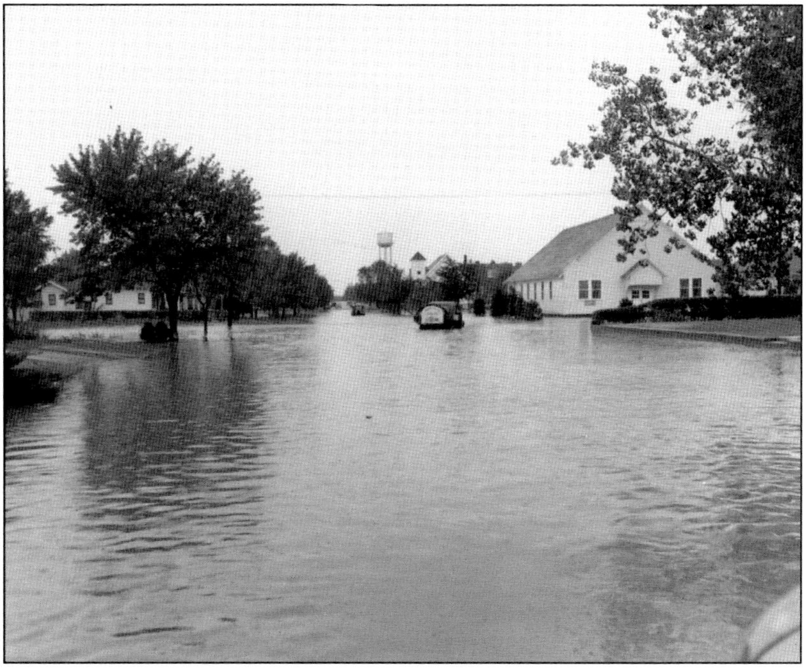

Between 1941 and 1945, the county received over 93 inches of rain. On occasion, the moisture was too abundant. Bud Kennedy took this photograph in the 300 block of North Grant Avenue. In the background is the city's water tower located on the northeast corner of Seventh Street and North Grant Avenue.

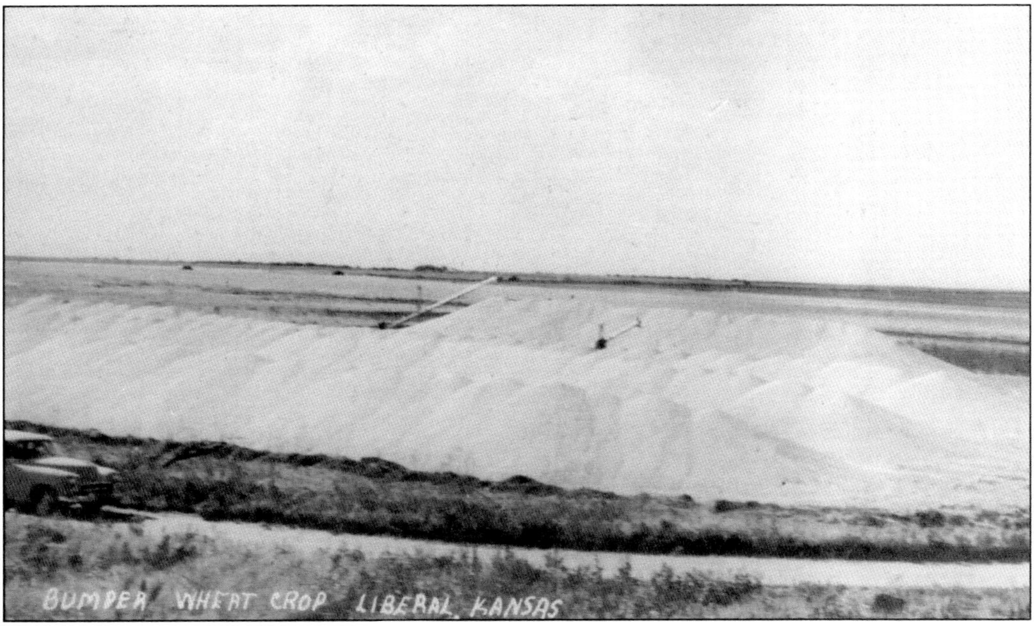

In the 1940s, production and harvesting of wheat doubled from previous years. Statistics also showed there was not any abandoned wheat compared to 1930–1934, a period that had 39,682 estimated bushels lost to drought and erosion.

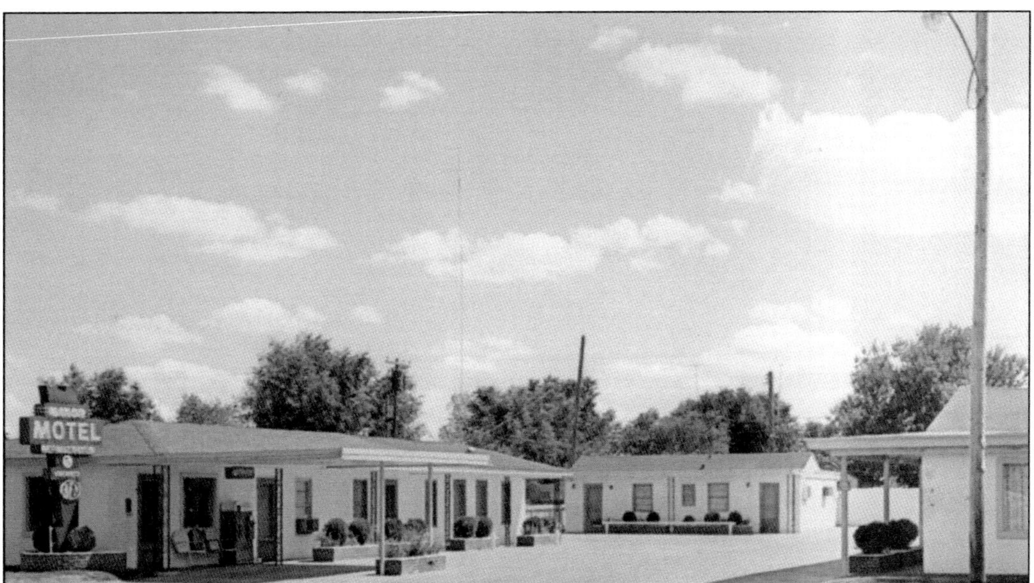

Travel courts were popular in the 1930s, but most courts converted to motels in the 1940s. The Manor Motel, located at 198 West Ash Street, featured vented heat, refrigerated air, carpeting, and kitchenettes. Ash Street became Pancake Avenue in 1952.

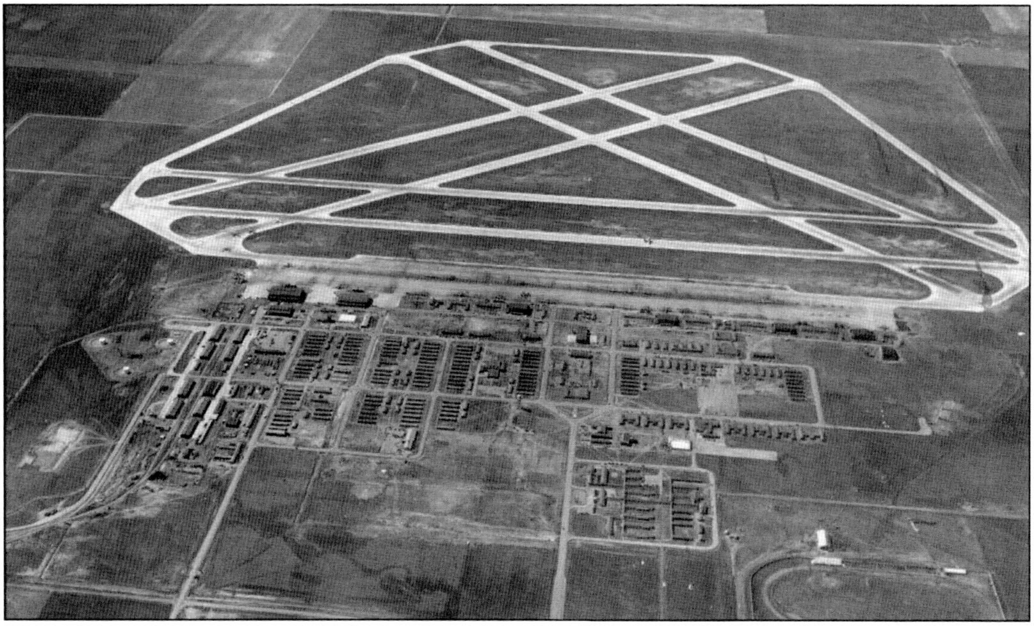

World War II brought amazing changes to Liberal. Herman Shorb, Dr. Hilbig, Paul Radke, and Charles Claybough campaigned to get a Civilian Pilot Training School located in Liberal. Instead, the US government elected to spend $8 million building an Army Air Field Base for training B-24 pilots. The facilities consisted of three concrete runways (150 by 7,000 feet), three taxiways, five hangars, three warehouses, a theater, a chapel, a gym, and an officer's club. (Courtesy of Mid-America Air Museum.)

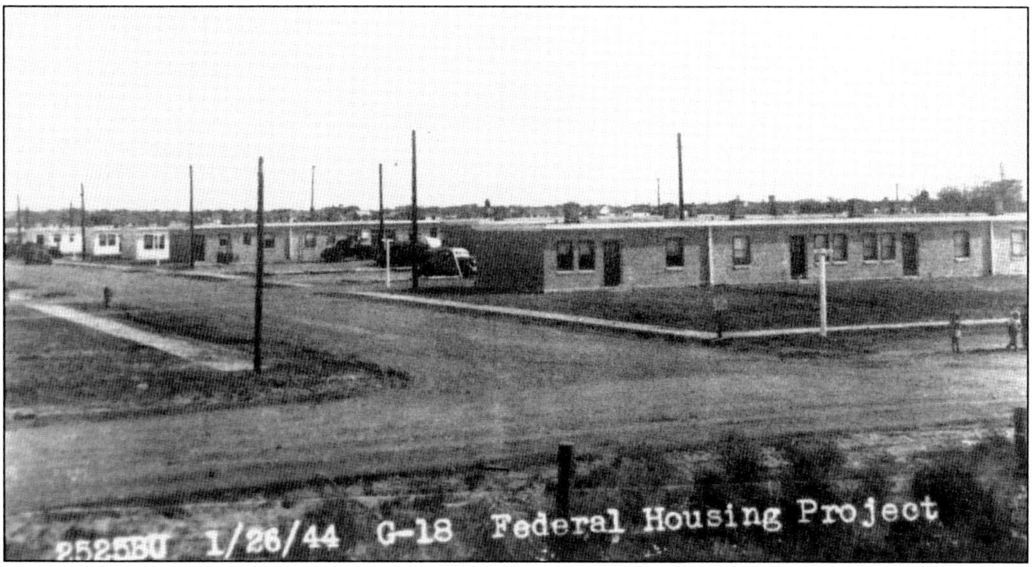

The influx of servicemen, supporting personnel, and their families almost doubled Liberal's population. Like never before, every extra room, garage, basement, and decent chicken coop was used to house the overflow. A cinder block village called Blue Bonnet Courts was erected and completed in 1944 to help house families. After the Army Air Base was deactivated, Blue Bonnet was deeded to the city of Liberal and used for rental housing. The Blue Bonnet Courts were torn down in 1969. (Courtesy of Mid-America Air Museum.)

Taken from the top of the Warren Hotel, this photograph shows that Liberal turned out in force to watch the precision marches and to support the war bond effort. From the first graduating class in 1943, to the deactivation of the field in September 1945, Liberal Army Air Base graduated 5,593 pilots.

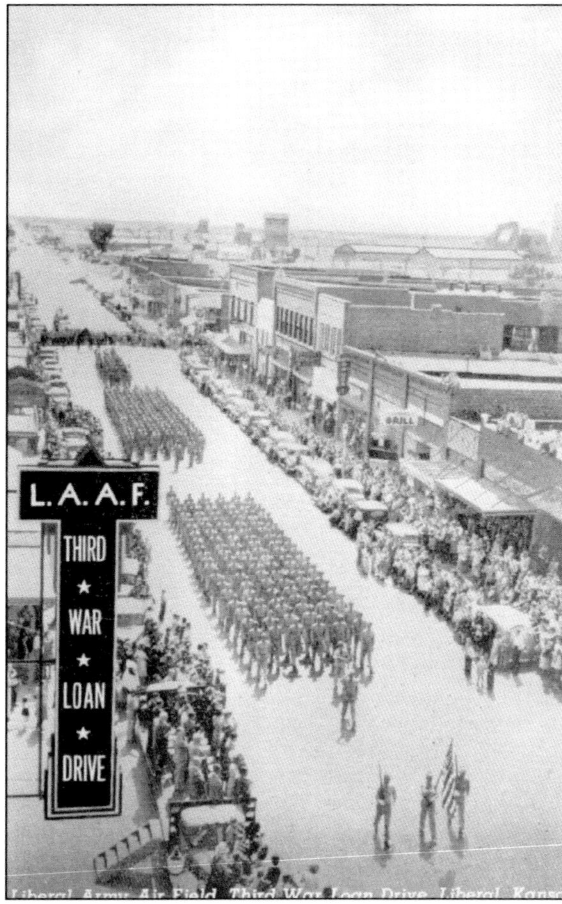

Lt. Ed Dibler sent this postcard to his hometown newspaper in Woodstock, Illinois. Lieutenant Dibler relayed to the local editor that the B-24 was what he would be flying, and he expected to take an instrument-check ride in the plant that evening, July 17, 1944.

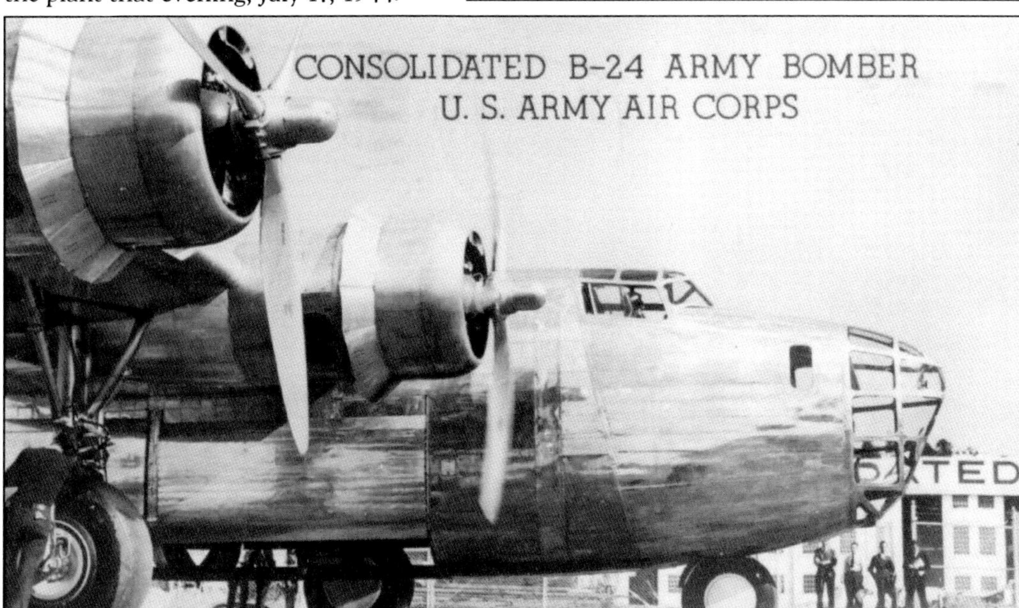

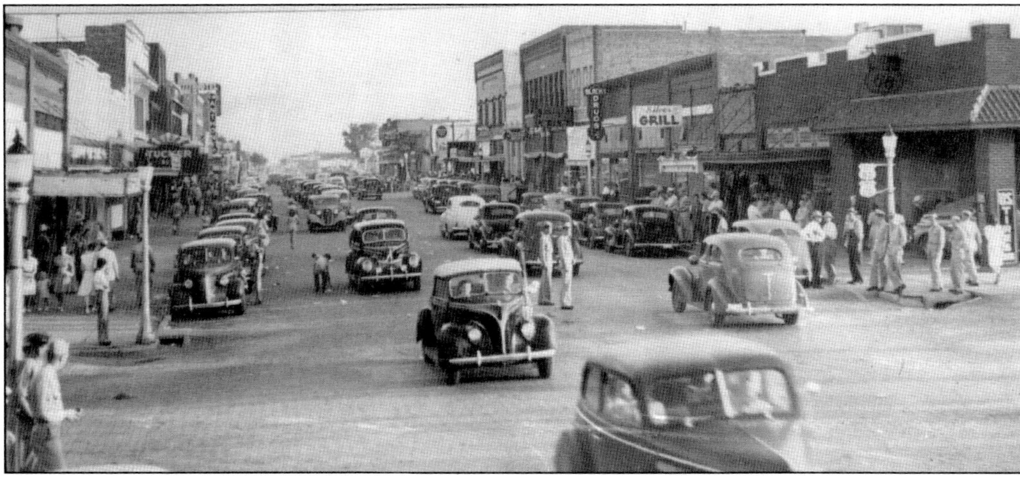

This was not a holiday nor was it a special citywide sales day, but only a normal Saturday afternoon in Liberal in 1945. The Army Air Base made an impact of Liberal's economy.

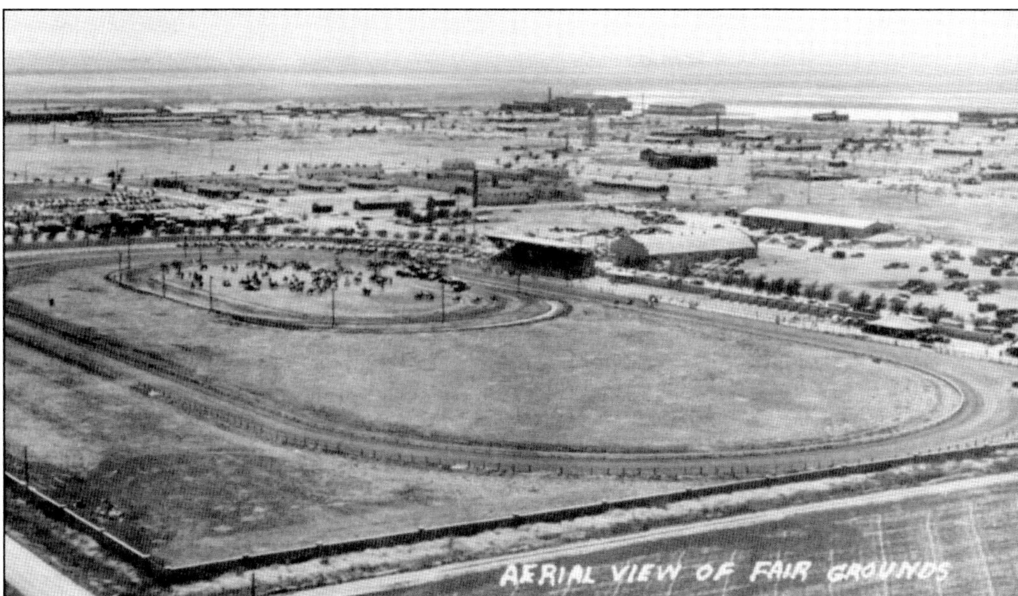

A WPA-built rock wall, the rock agricultural building, and the grandstand from the Southwest Fair Association made for a great fairground. In the background is the Army Air Base, and the infield of the racetrack is busy with horses, jockeys, and trainers.

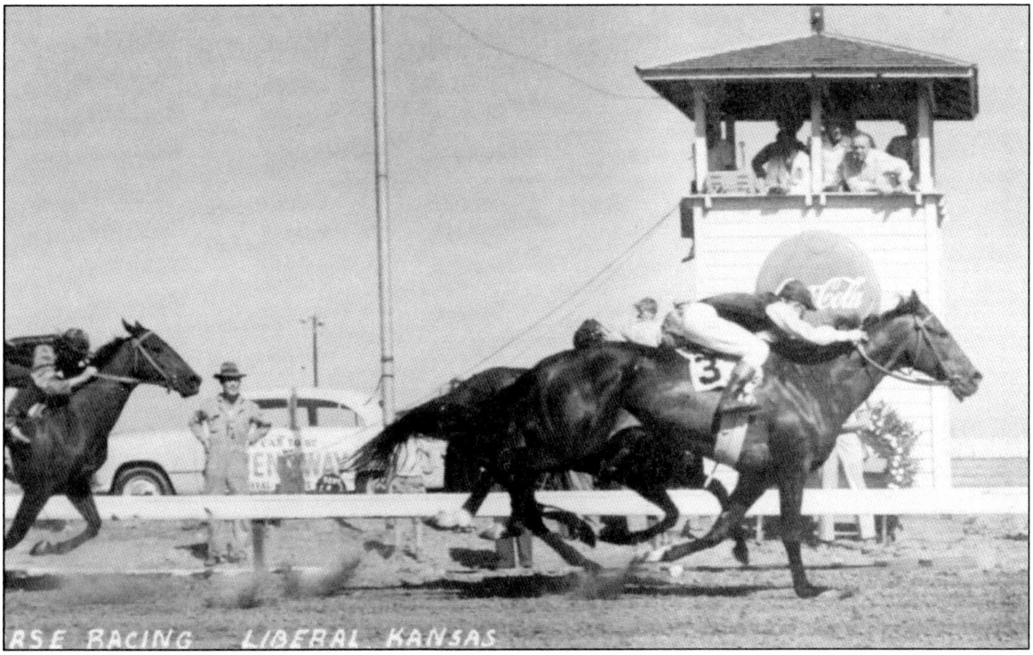

Horseracing was popular in postwar Liberal. Held at the fairgrounds, the races were run around the oval now used for automobile racing. Jockey Wantha Bangs Davis was a popular regular. In her career of over 30 years, Davis won thousands of races—even beating Johnny Longden—and was considered one of the best.

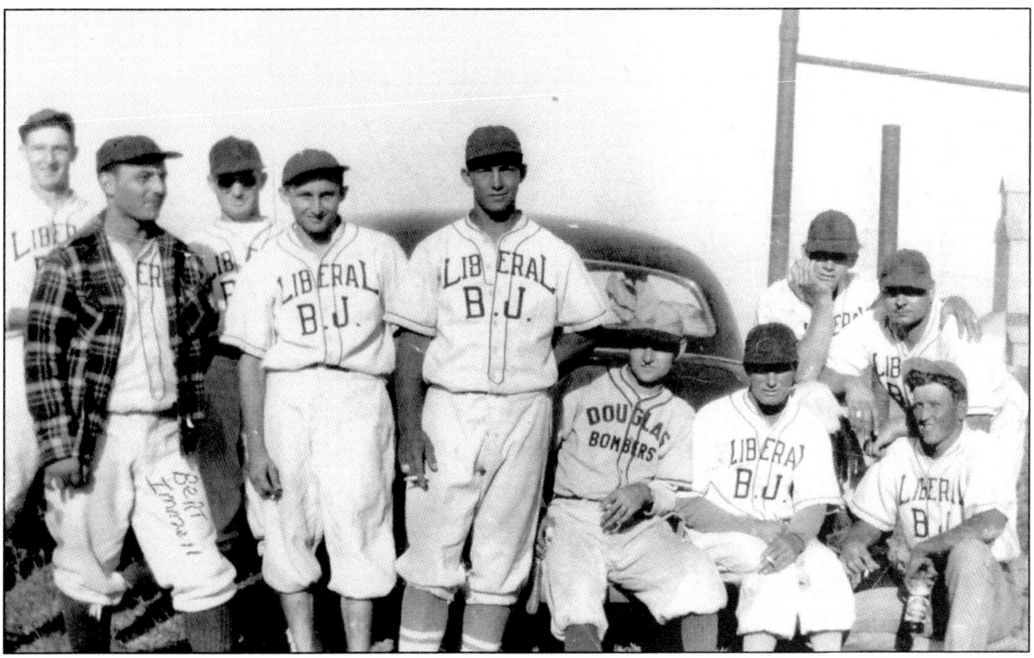

The 1948 Liberal BJs stopped playing baseball long enough for refreshment and a photograph. Players include Bob Headrick, the Wares brothers, Everett "Bert" Immell, Marvin Hoeckendorf, Ax Helm, ? Vangieson, ? Elliott, ? Johnson, and ? Schultz. The team was managed by Carl Whitmer, who also ran the concession stand. (Courtesy of Bob Immell and Kathy Immell.)

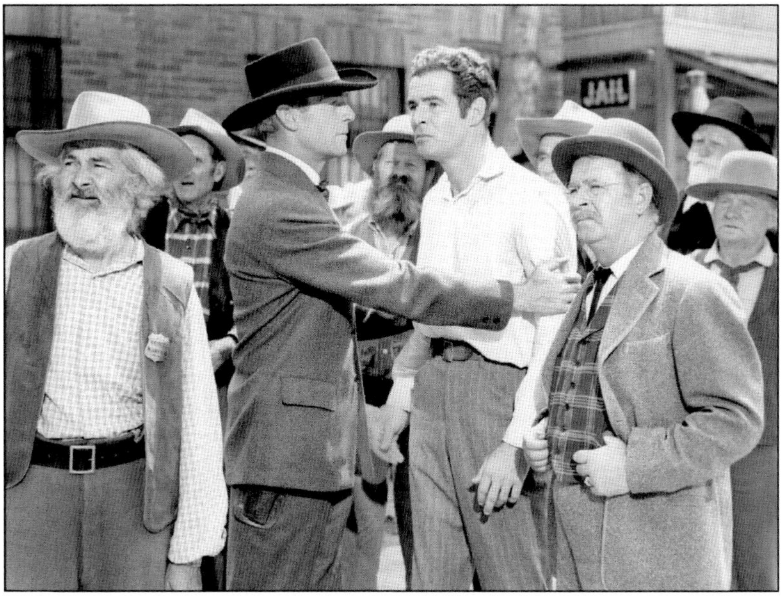

RKO Radio Pictures surprised Liberal by producing a movie called *Trail Street*. The story line was about struggling farmers and evil trail drovers being at odds over a failing spring wheat crop. Liberal, without a marshal, was losing all its farmers, but Batt Masterson (Randolph Scott) arrives to restore peace. None of the movie was filmed in Liberal.

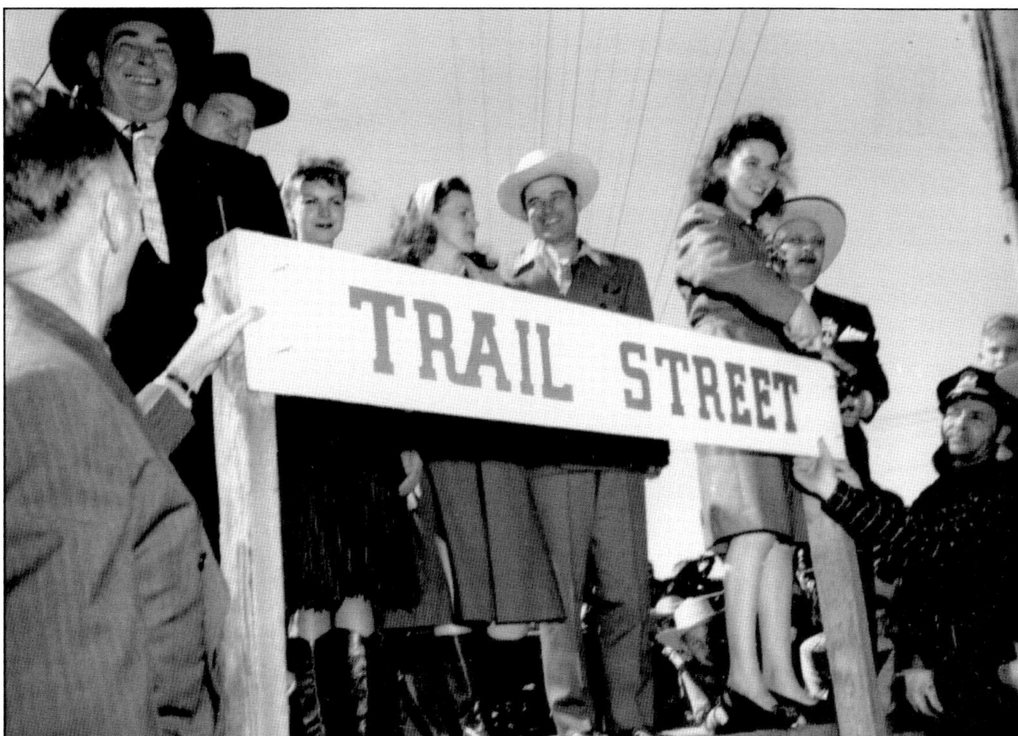

Even though Trail Street was not filmed on location, the movie premiered in Liberal on March 26, 1947. An estimated crowd of 30,000 came to take part in the parade and barbeque and to watch the movie. Hollywood stars that came for the event dedicated the street adjacent to the railroad track Trail Street. From left to right are Billie House, Charley Jones, Anne Jeffreys, Madge Meredith, Ray Whitley, and Queen for the Day Betty Phipps. (Courtesy of Bruce Jackson.)

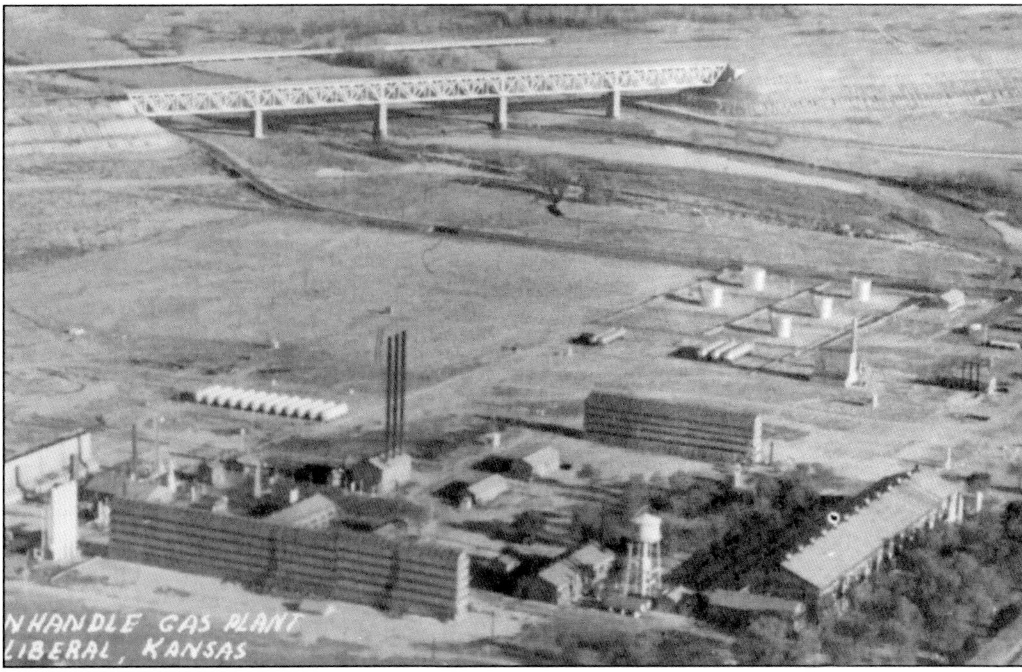

Panhandle Eastern's original compressor station, located on the banks of the Cimarron River, began operations in 1932. In 1943, the transmission station had 11,000 horsepower, and by 1947, horsepower had increased to 20,600. The plant had 17 houses available for employees.

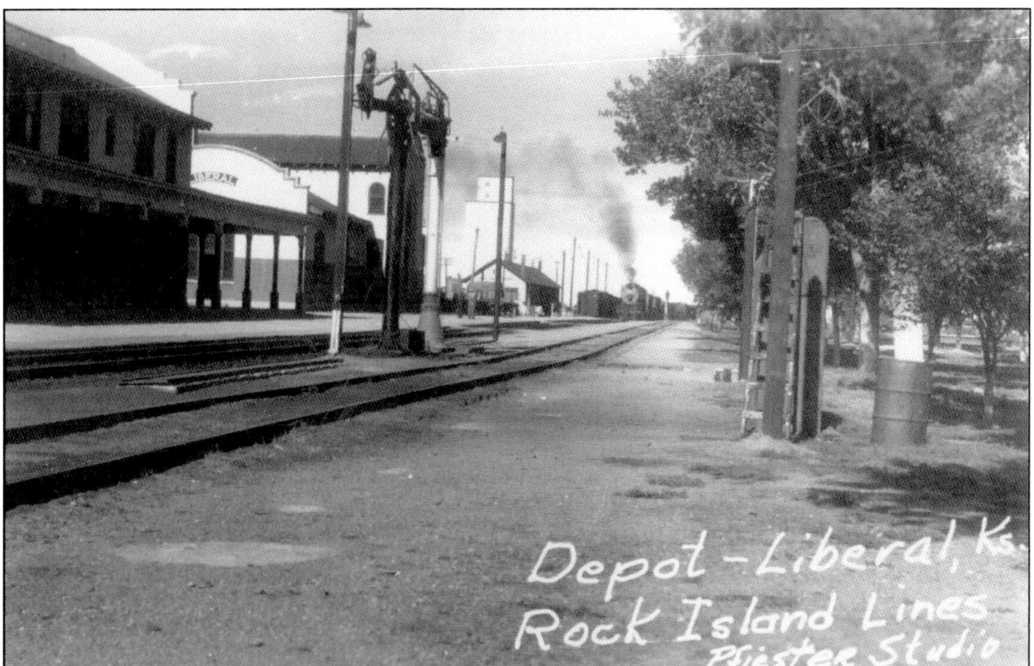

The Rock Island depot remained a busy spot in town as well as a green spot. The park across the tracks had well-tended flower beds, shady trees, and park benches that welcomed all.

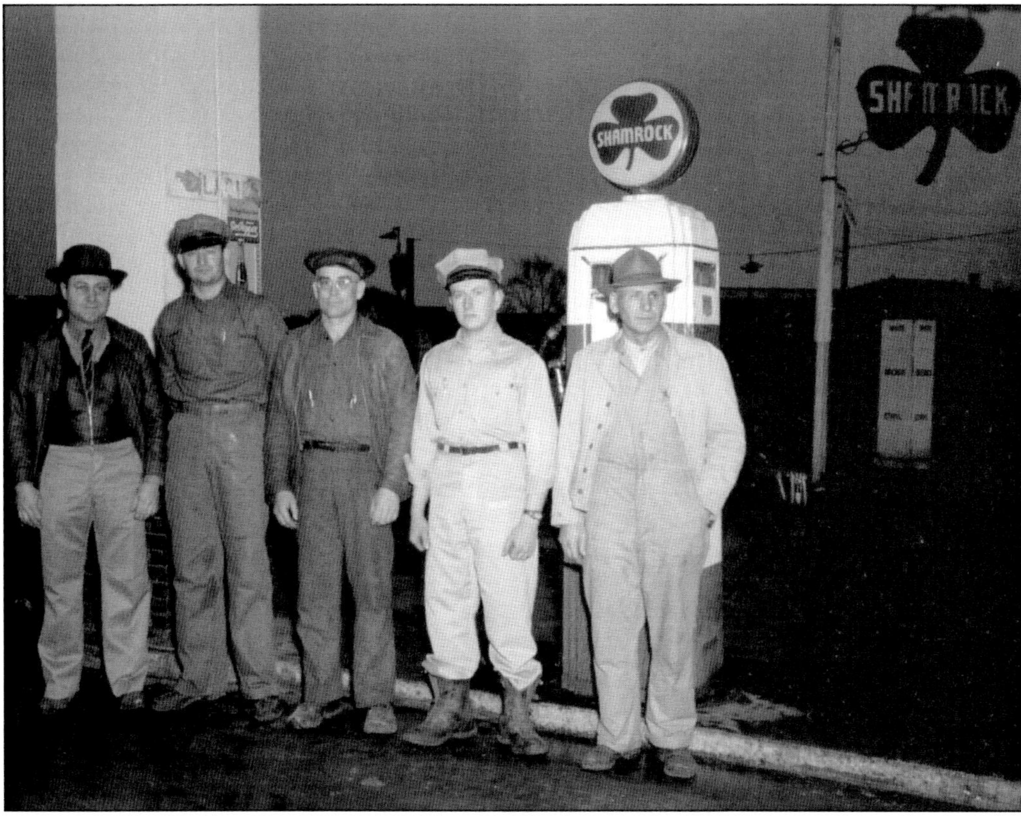

Between 1940 and 1950, Liberal grew in population from 4,400 to 7,200. Self-service was not even a thought to these men who were ready to wash windshields, check air pressure in tires, and of course to "fill 'er up," all at the sound of a bell. The Miller Service Station was located at 500 South Kansas Avenue. (Courtesy of Bruce Jackson.)

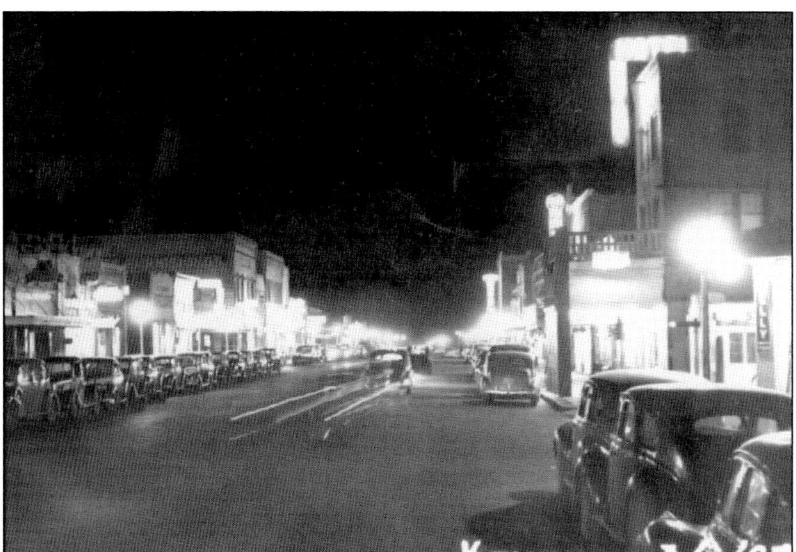

Kansas Avenue was a hopping place to be when Bud Kennedy took this nighttime shot next to the Hotel Bryant (13 South Kansas Avenue). Adjacent to the hotel was Henderson's Sandwich Shop, which was open day and night, and C.R. Anthony's, located at 3–5 South Kansas Avenue.

John W. Igou came to Liberal in 1916, moving from Guymon, Oklahoma, to serve as assistant cashier for the Citizens State Bank. He was elected president in 1942 and remained in that capacity until his death in 1957. Igou was a charter member of the Lions Club, the Southwest Shrine Club, and the Liberal Tornado Relief Association. John and his wife, Martha, had five children. Their home was at 720 West Second Street. (Courtesy of Seward County Historical Society.)

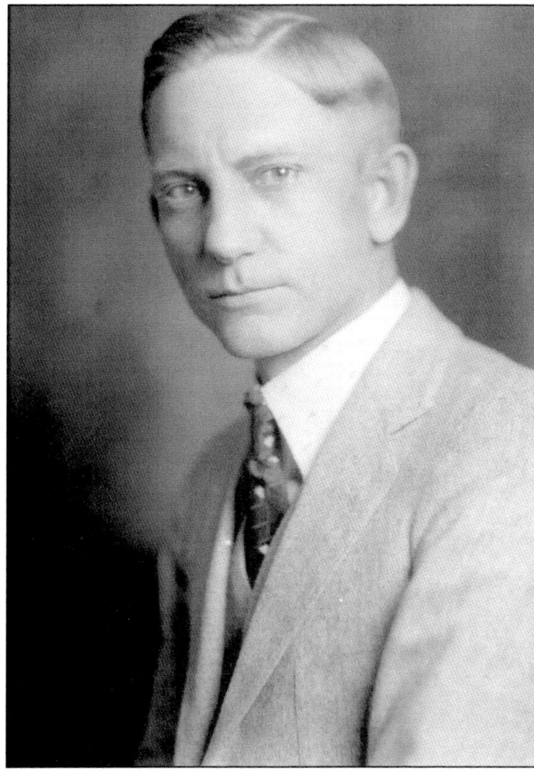

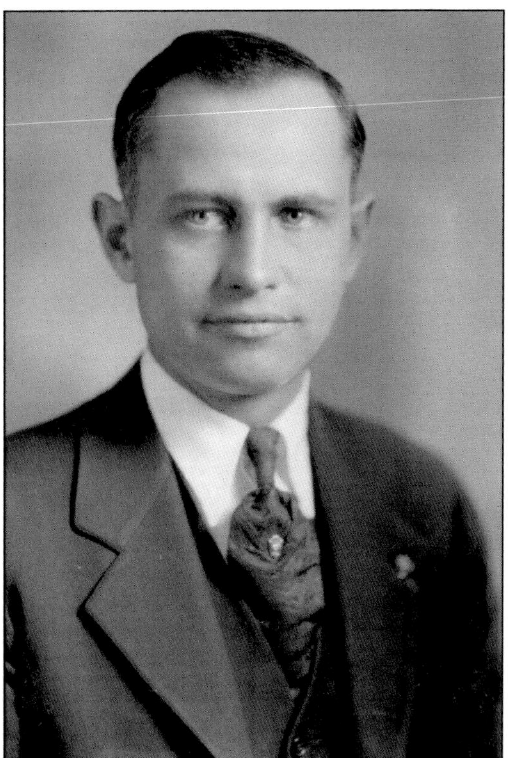

Alonza Birch Hunt was born in Missouri and came to Liberal with his wife, Leva, in 1925. They arrived in style, driving a brand new Dodge. Hunt was the Buick dealer located at 115 West Second Street. The Hunts and their three children first lived at 1007 North Pershing, but later purchased Abe Stoufer's home at 506 North Sherman Avenue. Hunt was a dedicated Lions Club member and would often provide transportation to conventions. (Courtesy of Seward County Historical Society.)

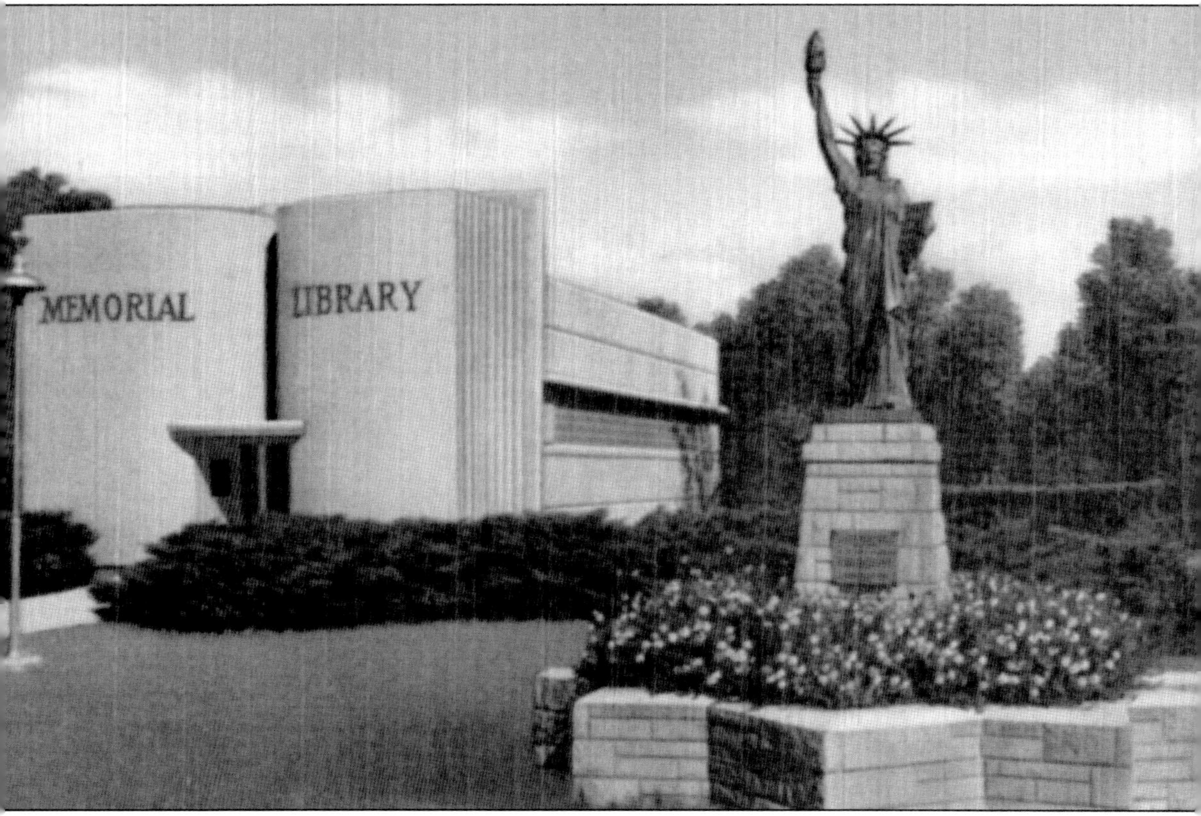

The Liberal Women's Club promoted intellectual development. In 1905, the club purchased a building on West Second Street for use as a library and to hold meetings. The clubhouse and library was sold in 1946, and the proceeds were used to begin construction of Memorial Library. The library was officially dedicated in 1955. The book front entrance was designed by local architect George Pitcher.

Ray Millman was born in 1875 in Green Castle, Indiana. Millman and his wife, Mary Alice, a Leoti native, were married in Liberal on October 10, 1900. Millman purchased the *Liberal News* (from Abe Stoufer) and the *Kismet Klipper*, changing its name to the *Southwest Tribune*. The two newspapers eventually consolidated. Millman was considered Lee Larrabee's equal in storytelling and practical joking. (Courtesy of Seward County Historical Society.)

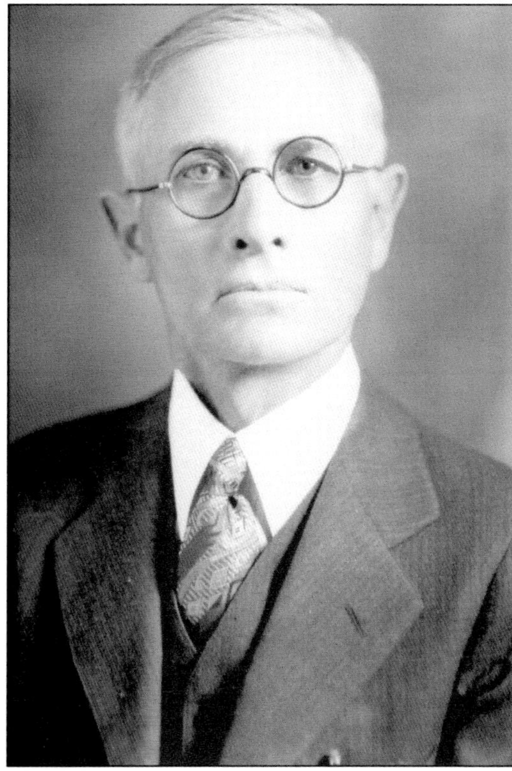

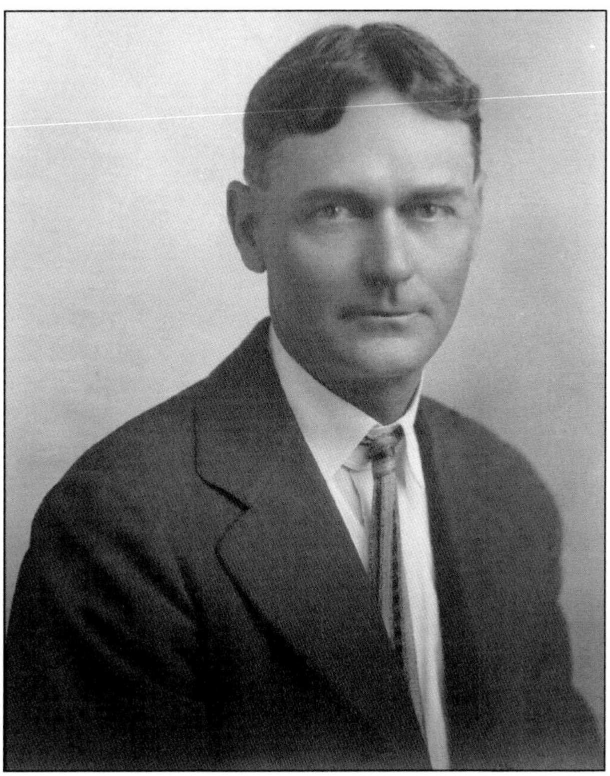

Thomas Gipson Pate was born in Little Rock, Arkansas, and first landed in Guymon with his wife, Bertha. Pate was a professional photographer for more than 50 years. His studio was located at 515 North Lincoln Street. Pate had a talent for quickly getting to a scene of a happening. His pristine photographs of the train wrecks, area buildings, and formal portraits have recorded Liberal's history throughout the years. (Courtesy of Seward County Historical Society.)

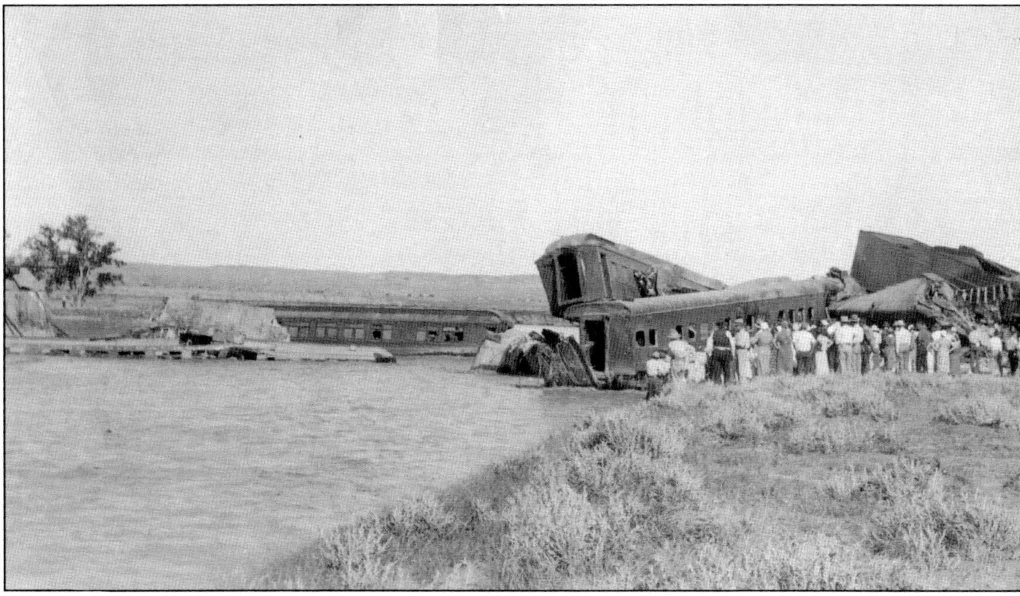

In October 1949, engineer Dave Sturdivant had left the Liberal depot headed to Chicago with 190 passengers. Just into Meade County and approaching a small chasm, the engine's headlights revealed a stretch of track hanging midair. Sturdivant applied his brakes and big-holed the engine but was unable to stop the train. The caboose and engine stayed upright, while three cars jackknifed, three cars overturned, and two cars derailed.

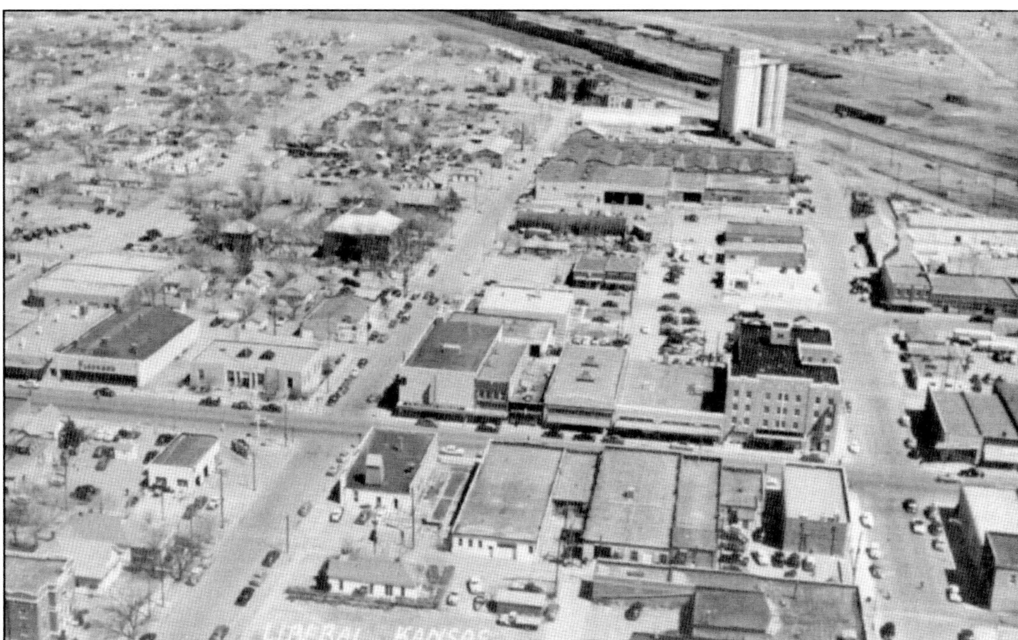

The 1940s brought changes to Liberal not thought possible. Downtown merchants were busy, streets were mostly paved, and the population by 1949 was over 7,000. In the center is Kansas Avenue and Fourth Street. The 1908 courthouse and jail are toward the upper center, and the Warren Hotel is right center.

Six

Growing and Having Fun 1950–1960

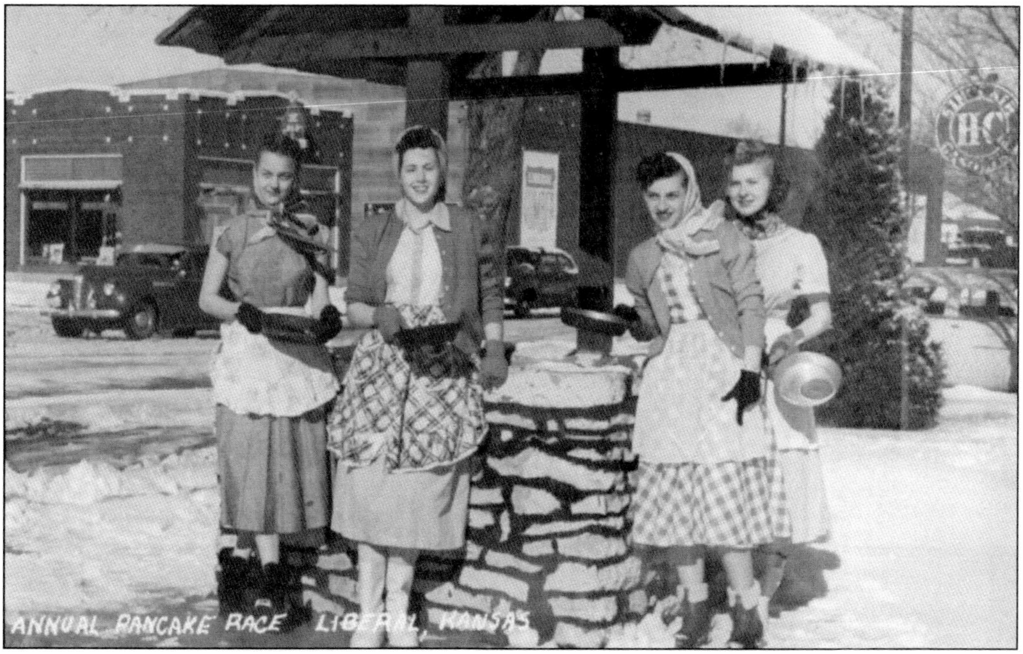

Head scarves, aprons, skillets, pancakes, and galoshes are the official wardrobe for the 1951 lineup of Pancake Day racers. From left to right are unidentified, Billie Warden, Nadine Hilyard, and Virginia Leete. Imogene Bruce won the Liberal leg of the 1951 International Pancake Race, but Olney, England, took the grand pancake.

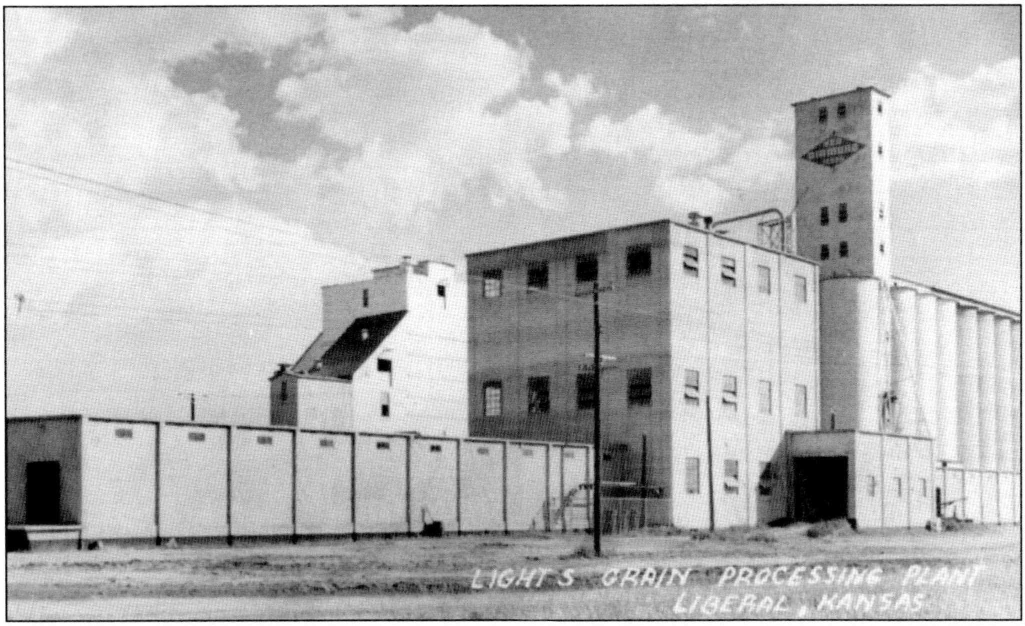

Light Grain & Milling continued to expand since its founding in 1915. The company had already perfected their self-rising blend of flour, but now also featured Lights Best, Prairie Queen, Griddle King, and Kansas Cream. The mill produced 400 carloads of flour a year, 165 carloads of mill feed, 500 carloads of formula, and 50 carloads of ground grain. The elevator's storage capacity was over 1.3 million bushels.

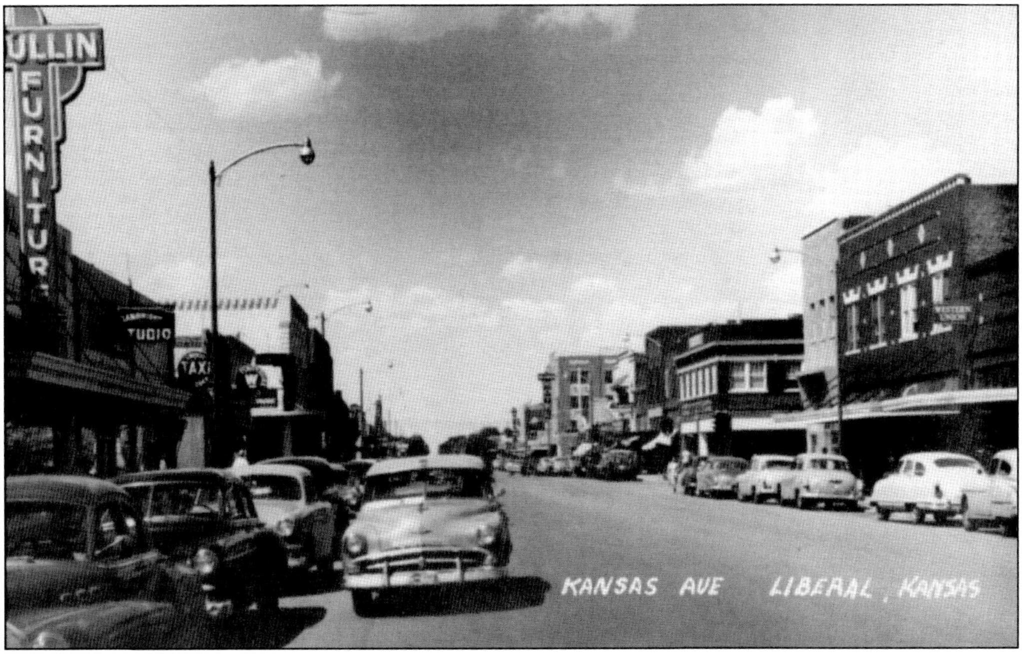

A wide variety of goods and services were available in downtown Liberal. Mullin Furniture, at 12 South Kansas Avenue; Arganbrite Studios, at 10 South Kansas Avenue; Burrs Department Store, at 201 North Kansas Avenue; Western Union, at 7 South Kansas Avenue; and City Cab are in view.

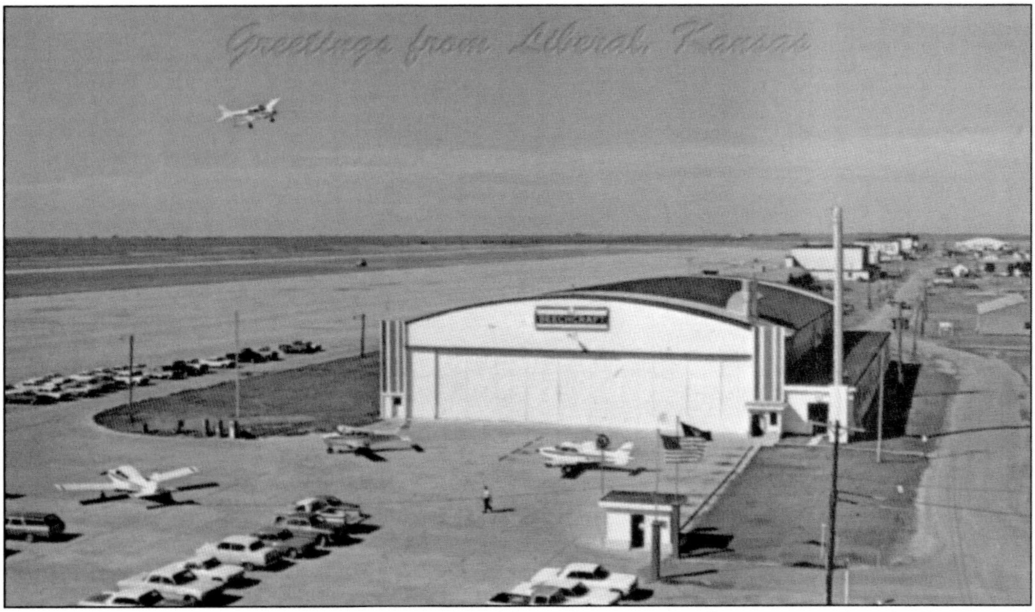

The Liberal Army Airfield left thousands of feet of runway and tarmac and eight B-24 sized hangars vacant. In 1951, Beech Aircraft seized the opportunity to increase their production using the ideal facility. The buildings were first leased to manufacture components for Lockheed, but evolved into producing single-engine planes. The Musketeer, Sundowner, Skipper, Sierra, and Duchess were proudly produced at the Liberal plant. The Model 16 was also produced, but only one was built. Olive Beech did not like the looks of the plane, so no others were manufactured. The facilities closed in 1982.

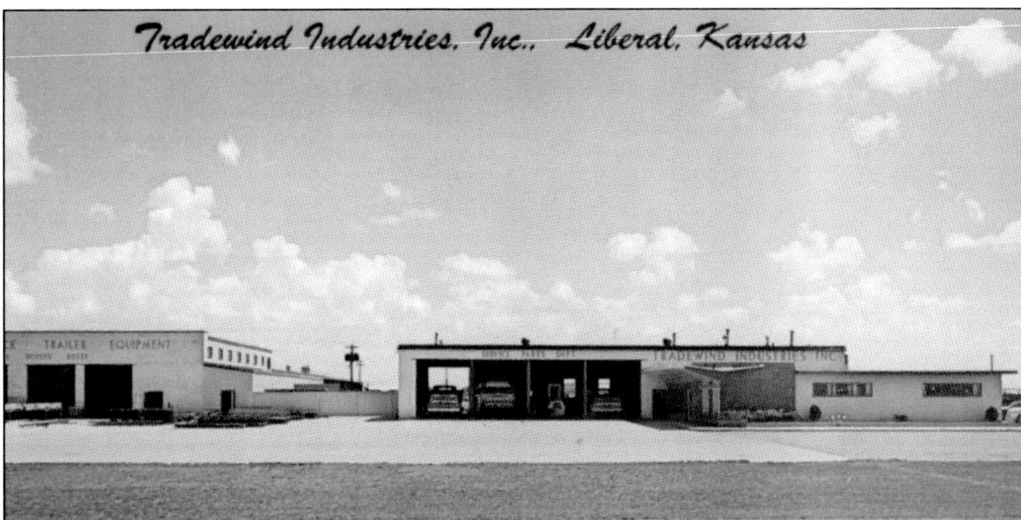

Tradewinds Industries was founded by Auburn Light, Al Shank, Carl Tedford, Charles Jones, Oliver Brown, Virgil Smith, and Bus Zook. The men wanted to bring another good industry to Liberal that could be used locally and worldwide. The Wheat King truck bed was originally built out of wood, but was later made of all steel. The company began manufacturing in a building on South Kansas, moved to the air base in 1948, and later purchased a 30-acre tract on West Highway 54.

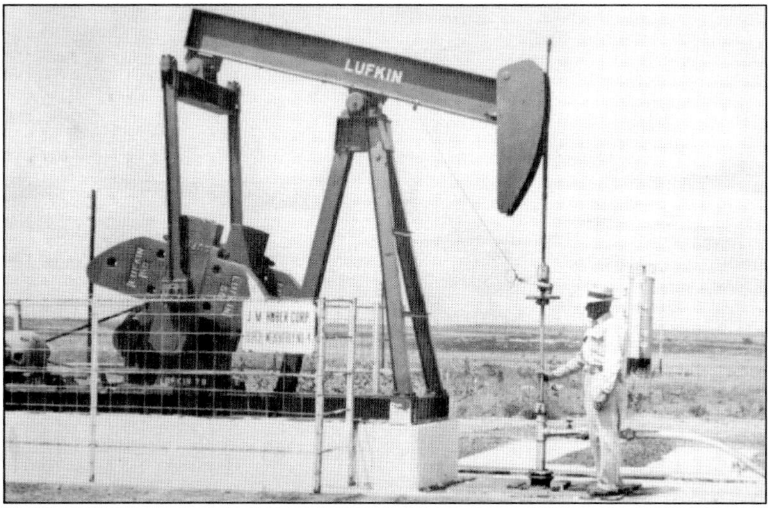

J.W. Huber Company owned this pump jack. It features a Lufkin walking beam, counter weight, and pitman arm. The pump jack mechanically lifts oil out of well if there is not enough bottom pressure. Oil and gas production continues to be a major player in Seward County's economy.

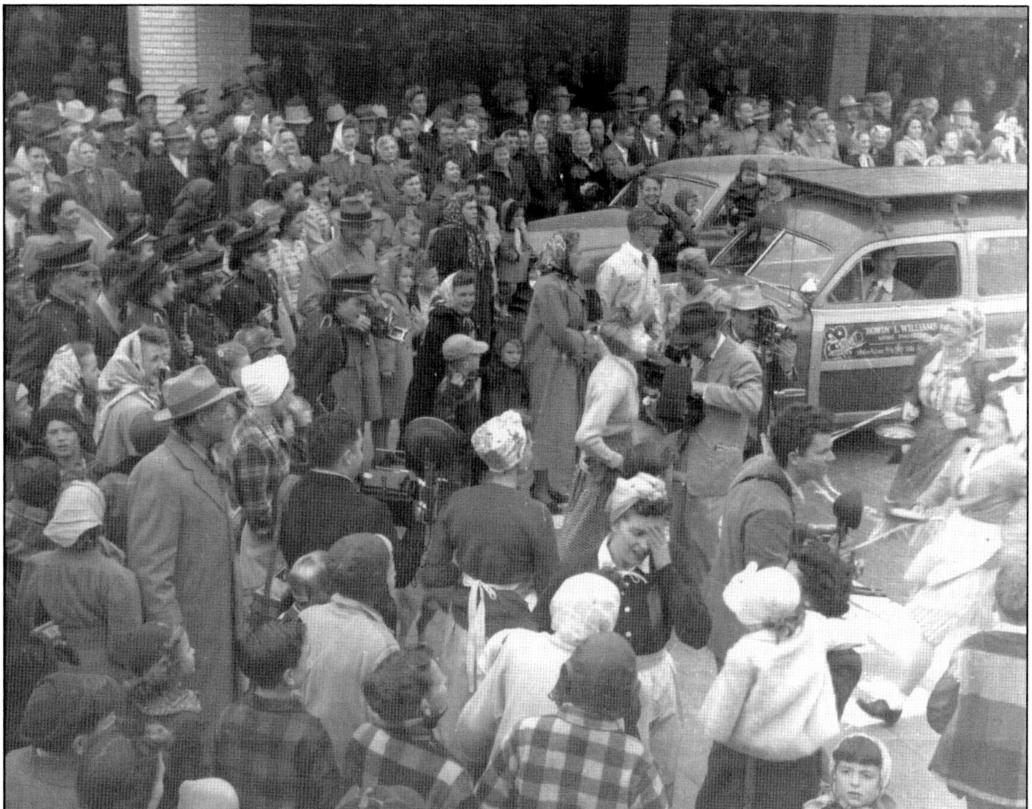

Since 1950, Liberal, Kansas, and Olney, England, have celebrated Pancake Day together. Housewives of both towns dash through their streets 415 yards with pancakes and skillets in hand, hoping to beat each other. Times are compared with a transatlantic phone call, and a winner is declared. All, of course, is done light-heartedly. Billie Warden (with her hand to face) won the first Liberal Pancake Race. Virginia Leete came in second, Mary Ulrey (in the white apron) won third place, and Betty Marquart came in fourth. Behind Betty in the station wagon was local attorney Rex Neubauer. Olney was declared the winner of the race that year.

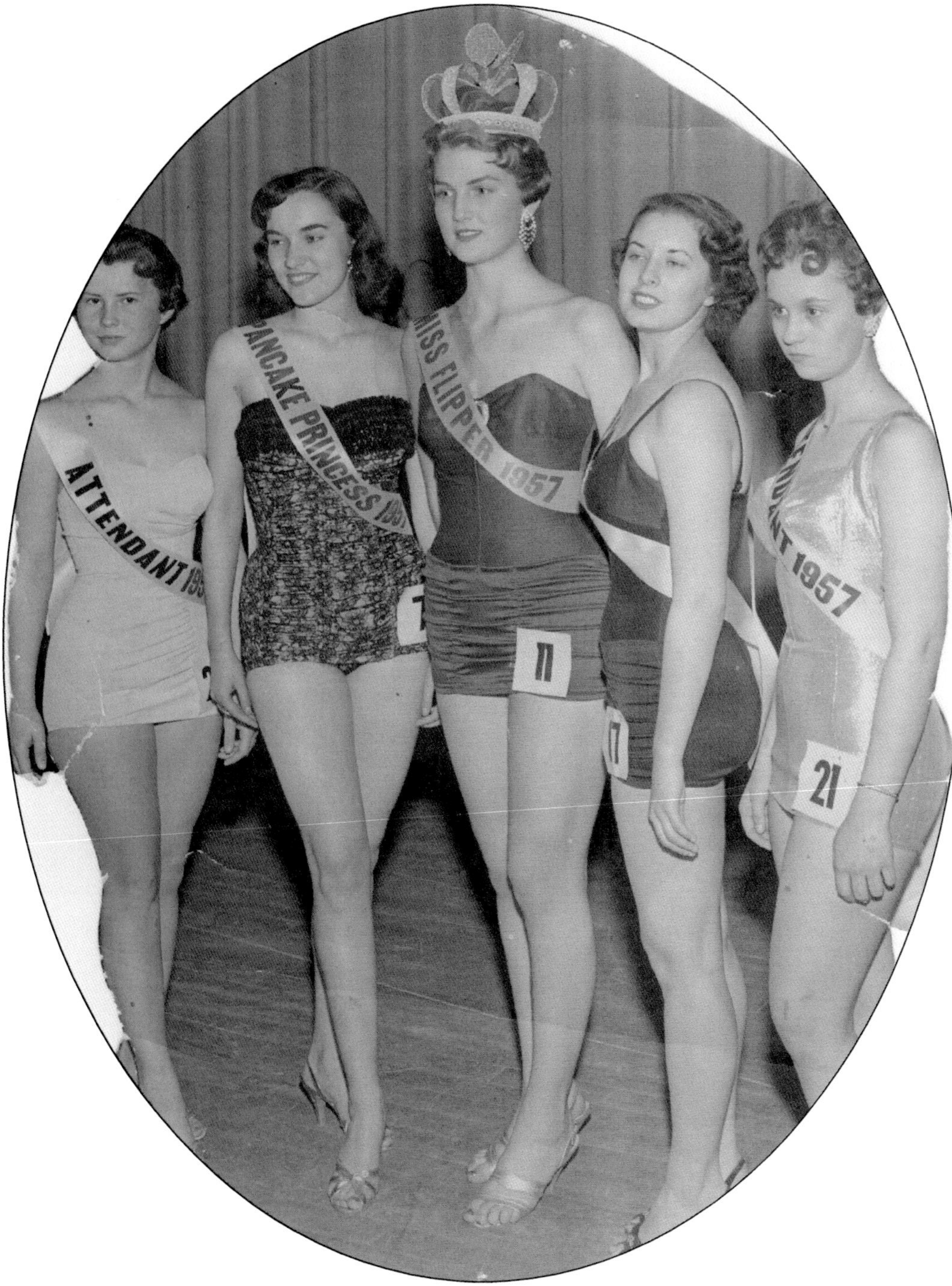

In conjunction with Liberal's Pancake Day, Miss Flipper was the title area girls vied for. Miss Flipper for 1957 was Linda Spence, of Perryton, Texas. Pancake Princess was Nola Ruspini, of Pueblo, Colorado. Attendants were, from left to right, Priscilla Taylor, Clayton, New Mexico; Becky Fowler, Guymon, Oklahoma; and Gwen Rennick, of Liberal. The pageant ran from 1952 to 1974. (Courtesy Seward County Historical Society.)

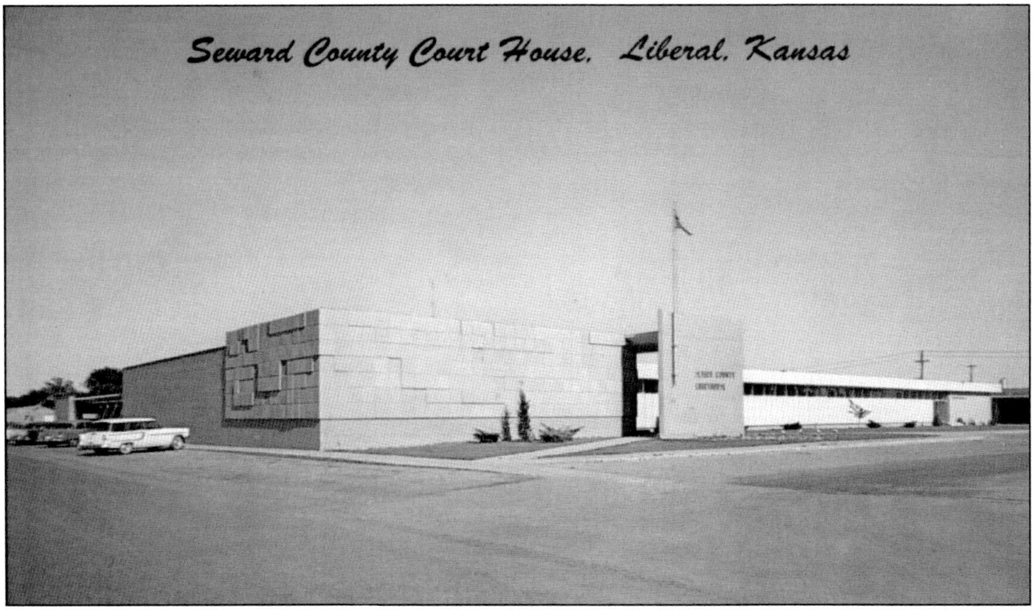

In 1954, the residents of Seward County voted to build a new courthouse to replace the two-story brick structure that had been erected in 1908. At a cost of $350,000, the new building featured fireproof vaults, central heat and air, and an escape-proof jail.

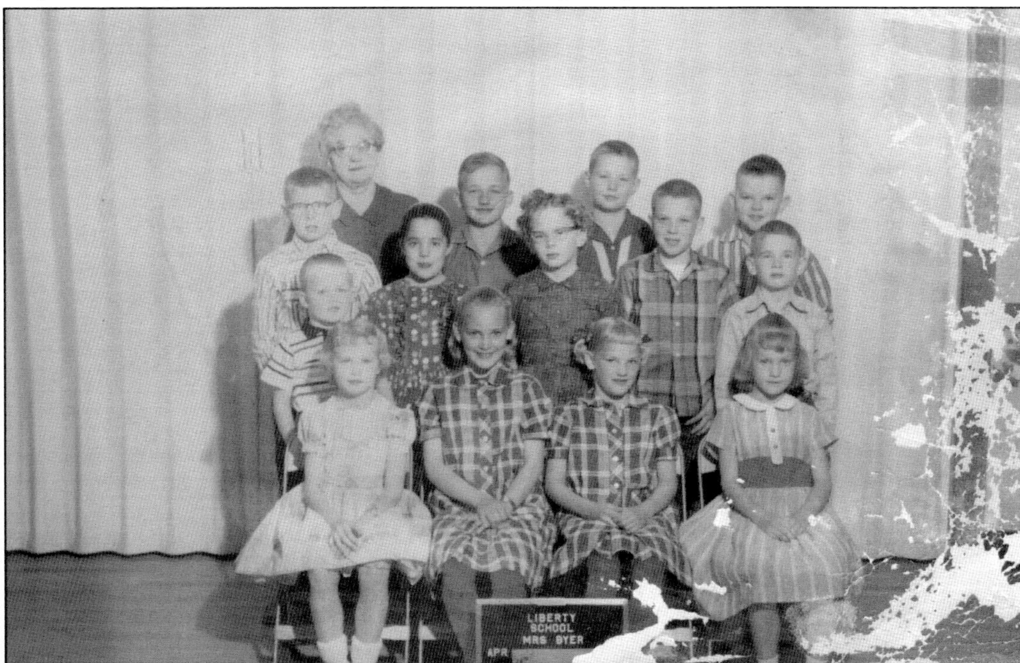

The Liberty School District was established in 1909 and was still educating children in 1957. Grace Byers's pupils were, from left to right, (first row) Nancy Jo Harnden, Martha Fitzgerald, Elizabeth Fitzgerald, and Laverne Patterson; (second row) Dale Patterson, unidentified, Nancy Lynn Bozarth, John Fitzgerald, and Steve Bozarth; (third row) John Bozarth, Darrell Webb, Dean Brown, and Jerry Rice. (Courtesy of Seward County Historical Society.)

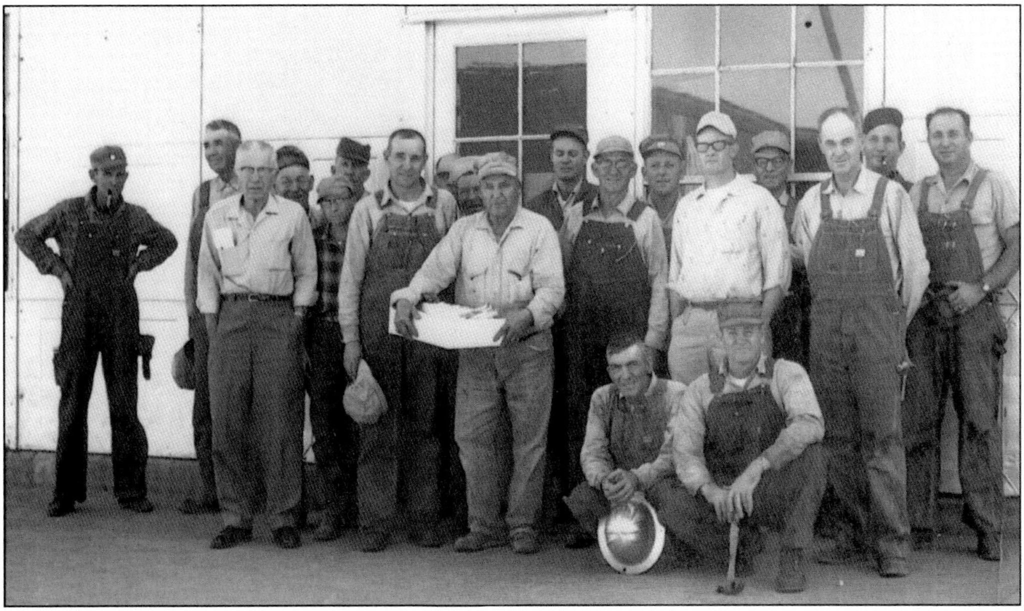

Stopped in the midst of their various Rock Island Railroad duties, these employees posed for a photograph in 1957. In front of the freight office are, from left to right, Dean Vernon, Bill Williams, W.E. Downing, Vern Applebee, Charles (Peanut) Franke, Joe Garcia, J.P. Keeter, Rod Donham, Ed Reilman, Alvin Coonce, Harry Raymer, Charles Drake, Bob Sheppard, Roy Lamon, Raymond Wilson, Darvin Weard, Jack Ekart, Nick Gaona, Punk Gibbons, and Clayton Gibbons. (Courtesy of Charles Franke.)

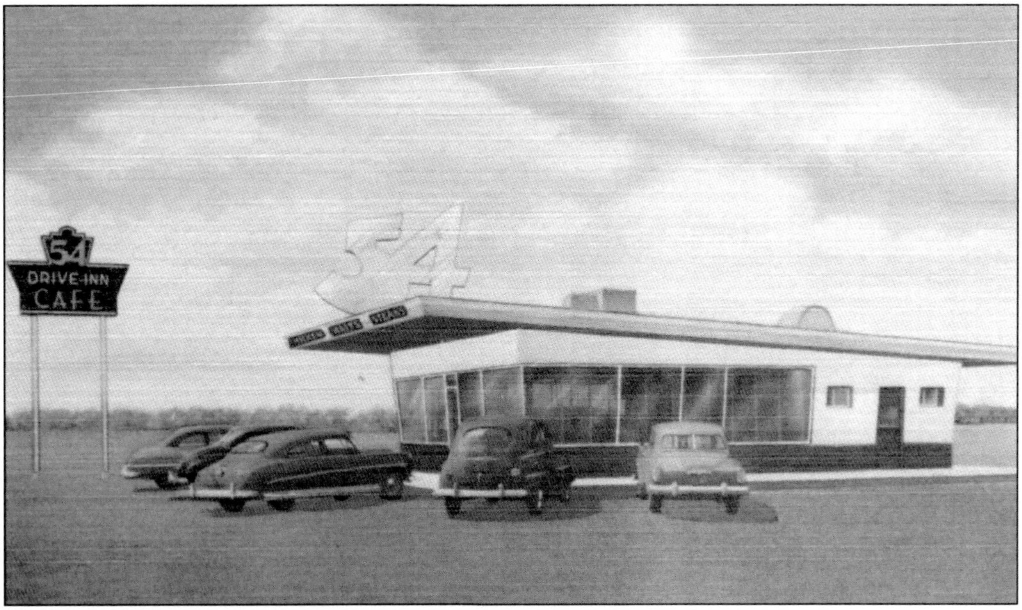

Jess, Mike, and Lucadia Andrade purchased this popular restaurant from George Nelson in 1954. Henry Andrade was overall manager for both the 54 Café and the El Patio Club. The El Patio actually started out as a walled corral with a fence around it. The restaurant also employed Donnie McNabb as morning chef, Henry Vargas as evening chef, and Dora Jiminez as Mexican food chef. Wait staff included Lois McMullin, Betty Starnes, and Juanita Irwin.

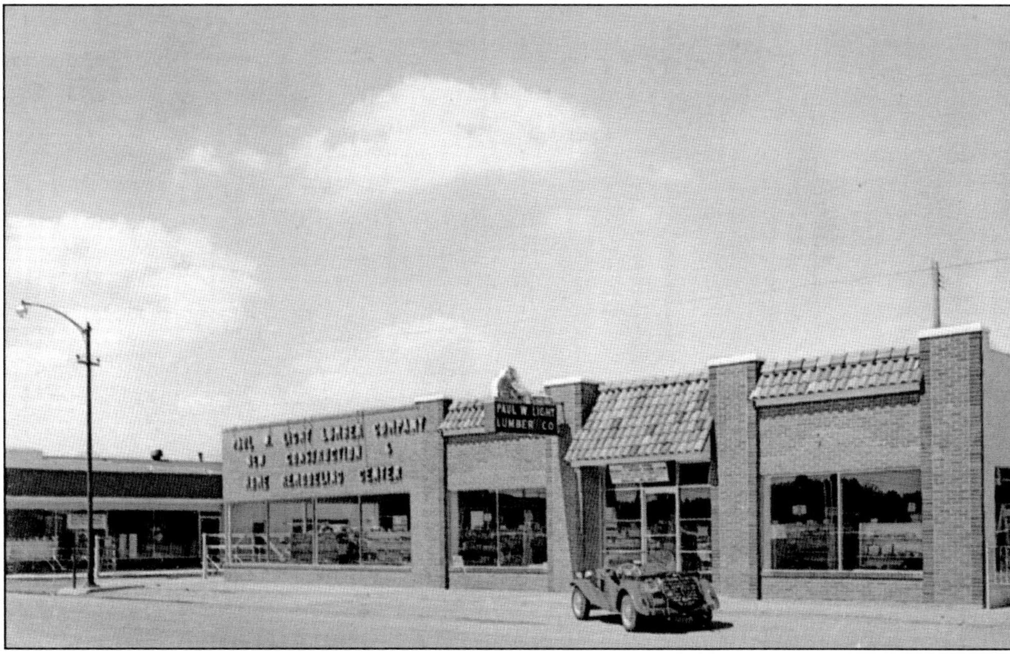

The Paul Light Lumber Company was founded in 1907 as the J.E. George Lumber Company. Paul Light was manager, but after three months, he bought into the business and eventually changed the name. Paul Radke became manager in 1948, later becoming a partner with Light and bringing about another name change to Radke-Light Lumber. The business was known for assisting homeowners with interior and exterior ideas. The retail building itself was noted for its hammering carpenter neon sign that graced the front door for years.

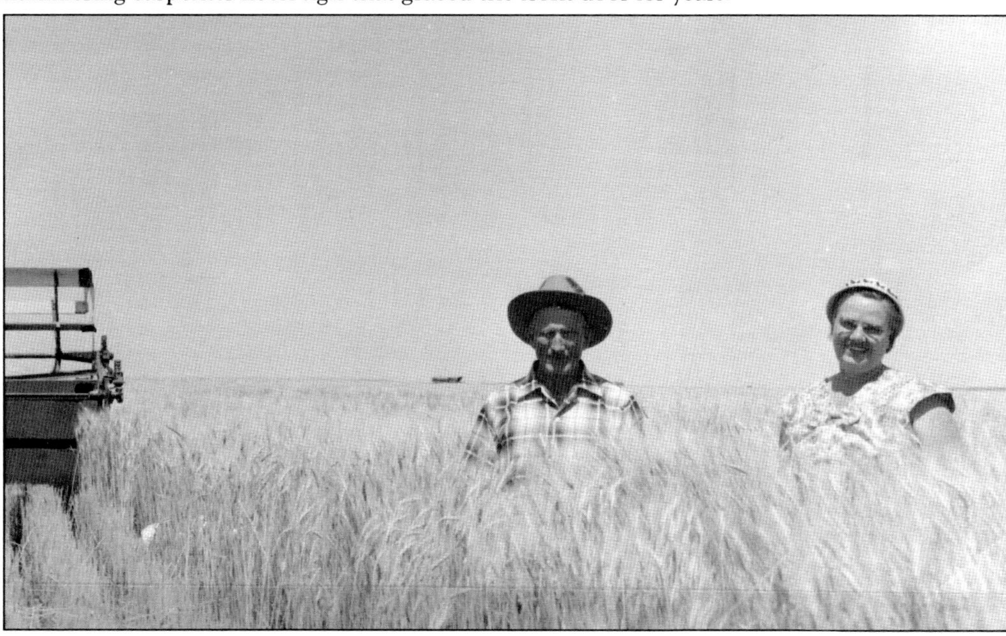

Frank and Gladys Bookless set their combine reels high to be able to harvest their outstanding wheat crop of 1958. With plenty of rain and no hail, farmers and custom harvesters in the State of Kansas brought in over a billion dollars in cash receipts for the year.

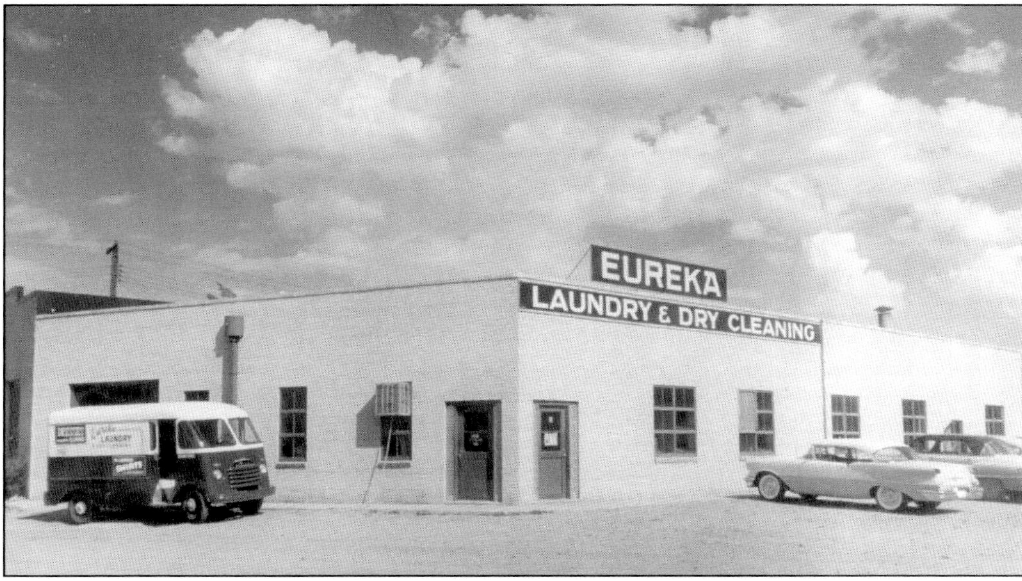

Charles and Arletta Leete founded the Eureka Laundry in 1906 in a 30-by-50-foot covered metal building. In the early days, Arletta kept track of her four children while operating a chest-type flatwork ironer. (The ironer measured 100 inches wide.) In the 1950s, with son Rod at the helm, Eureka Laundry had grown to employ 35 operators. Services included linen, industrial towel and mop, uniform, and dry cleaning. The laundry helped Liberal keep clean until closing in 1969. (Courtesy of Seward County Historical Society.)

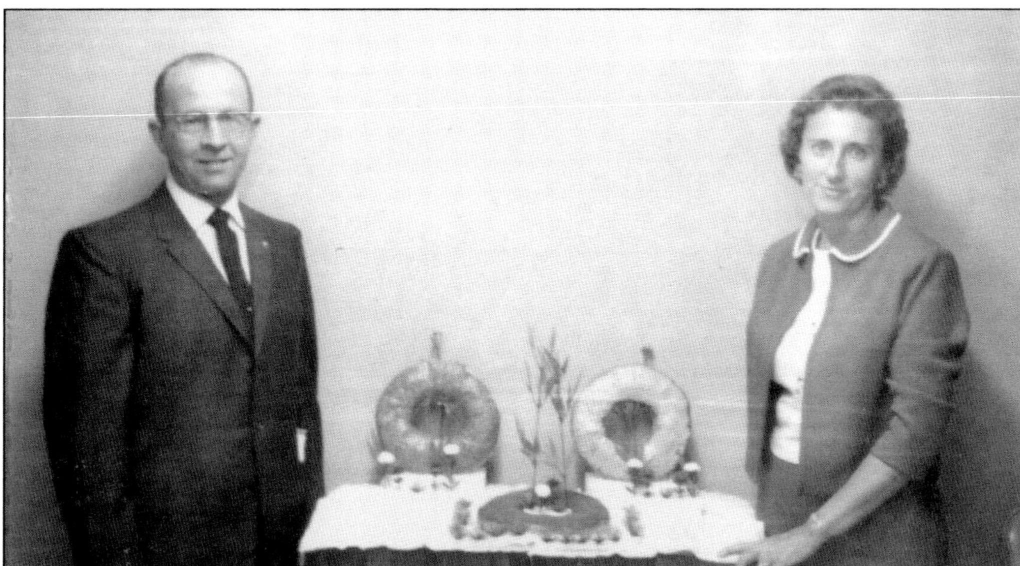

Claude and Cleo Meisenheimer described their first year in the Spudnut business an experimental, cautious undertaking. The Meisenheimers established the Spudnut Shop in 1957, at 317 South Kansas; they worked it completely themselves. By 1961, they expanded to two locations, six employees, and sold 300 dozen Spudnuts per day. Claude and Cleo received many awards for their delectable treats. One in particular was given by Spudnut's founders, the Pelton brothers, who awarded the Meisenheimers the distinction of being seventh highest producer out of 300 Spudnut shops nationwide. (Courtesy of Marlin and Dorothy Meisenheimer.)

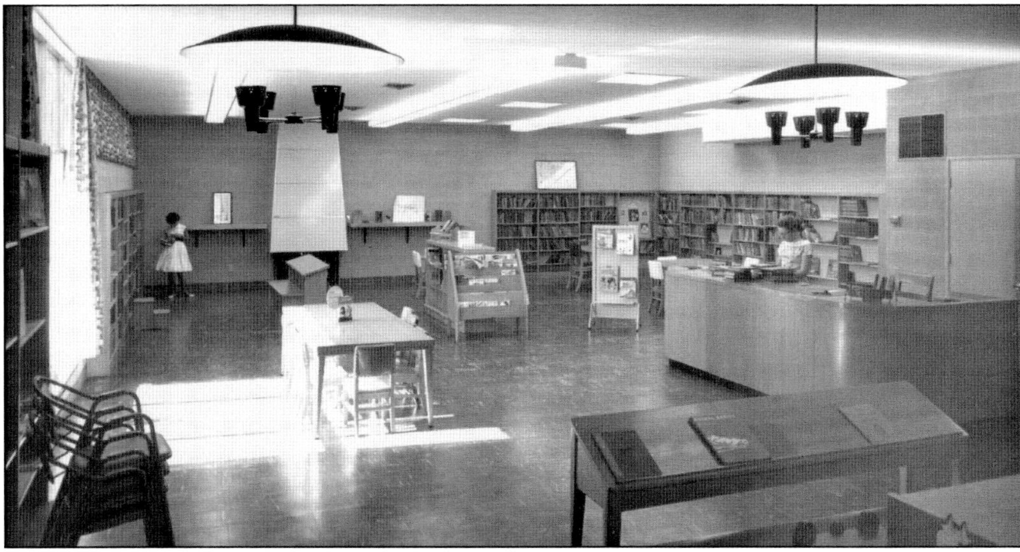

Gertrude Mahan was named head librarian for the new Memorial Library in 1955. A local gift of $15,000 and a $60,000 bond provided for a children's and adult's wing, but furniture was lacking. A call went out to the residents of Liberal, and library patrons were soon browsing through books and reading newspapers while enjoying the white birch furniture and shelving provided by the community. (Courtesy of Seward County Historical Society.)

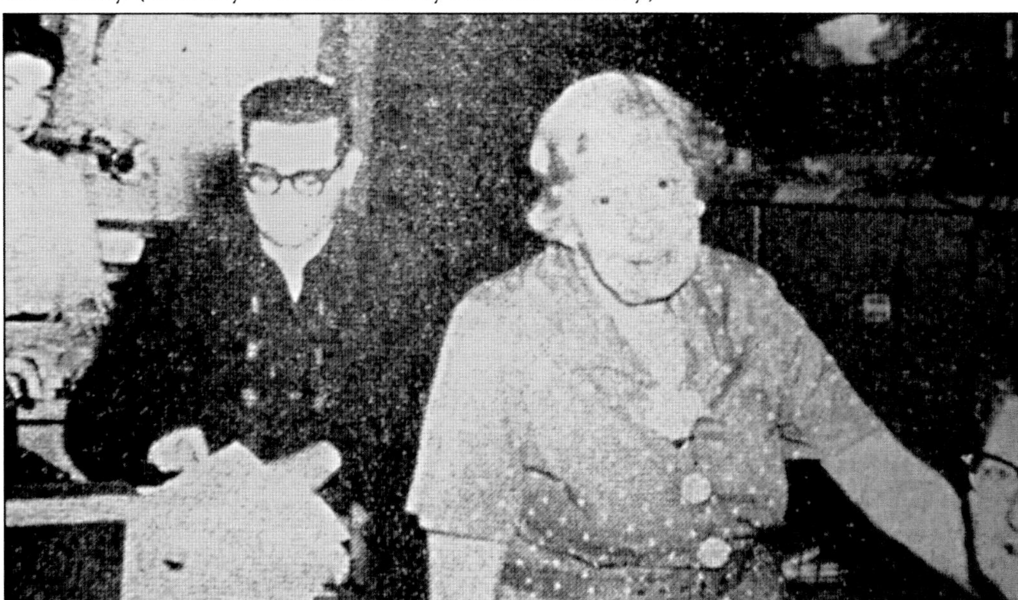

Maurine Long Tate moved to Liberal with her parents, Bert and Lillian, in 1910. She graduated from high school at the Liberal Opera House in May 1912. Maurine began work in 1918 as a typesetter and roving reporter for her uncle Warren Zimmerman at the *Liberal News*. Long was well known for her popular Scratch Pad column. Her journalistic career spanned 52 years before her retirement in 1970. In the 1920s, Maurine and her good friend Emma Jacquins both had cabins built in Cuchara, Colorado, where they and their families enjoyed vacations. She married Crompton Tate in Cuchara in 1938. Maurine passed away in 1985, but her Scratch Pad is still talked of today.

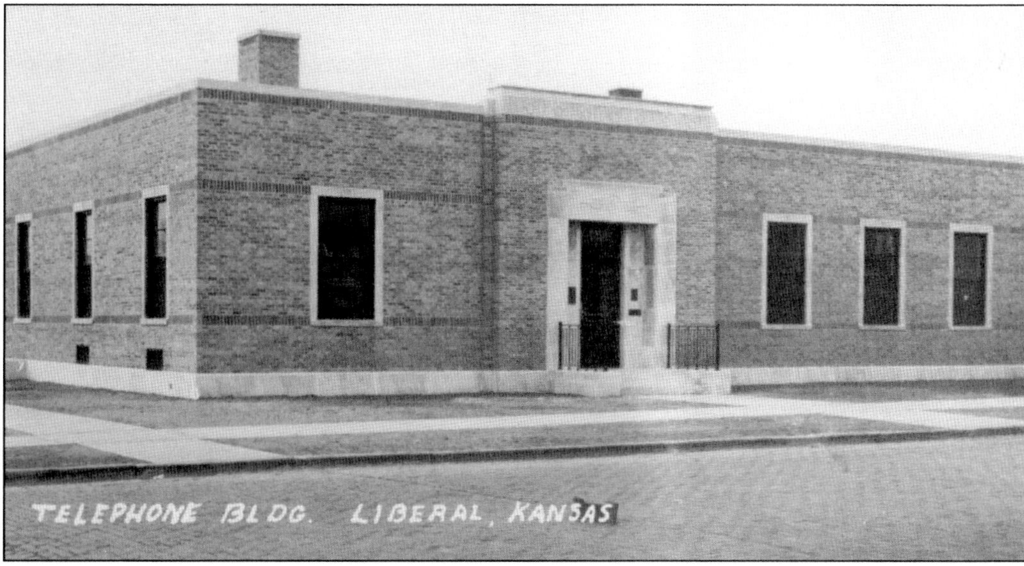

The familiar encircled blue bell logo had not been installed on the new 1956 expansion of the Southwest Bell building at Fourth Street and Washington Avenue. Southwestern Telephone was absorbed by Southwestern Bell in 1952. The building housed equipment, supplies, and 26 long-distance operators, who were always ready to assist.

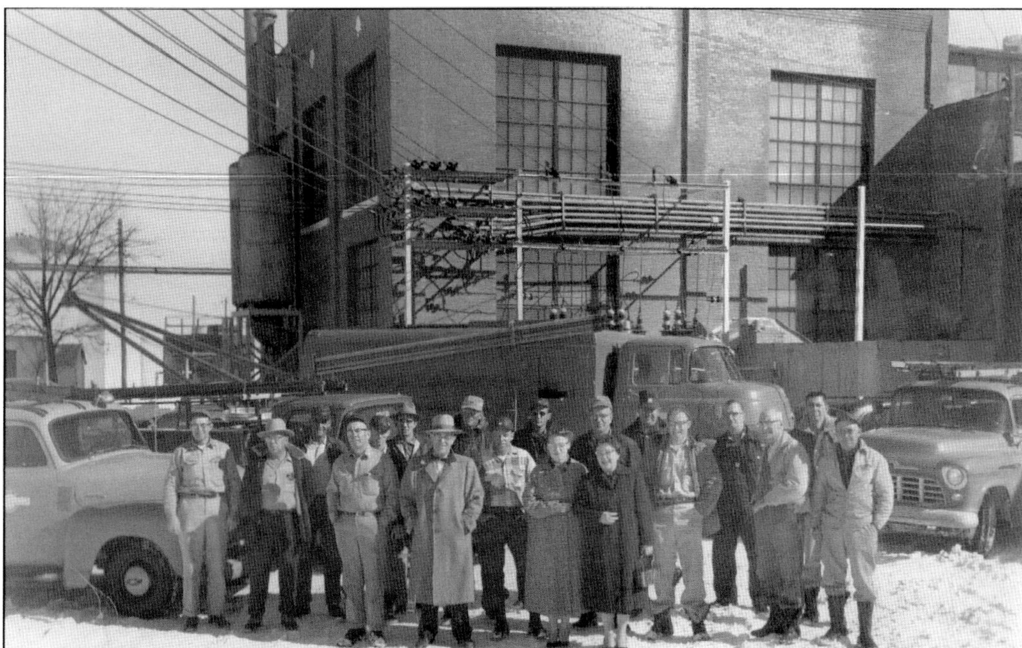

Keeping Liberal bright and light was this brick building on East Fourth Street. In 1955, four generators kept things and these employees busy. They are, from left to right, Tom Miller, L.B. Kirk, Merle Grovers, Bill Helm, J.D. Mollenhaur, Everett Mead, Fred Moffet, Pete Hickey, Joe Brown, Jerry Neese, Mearl Killingsworth, Leta Brown, Willie Bagshaw, Bob Autland, Sonny Brooks, Ed Winters, Dewey Frame, Kenney Mason, and Dorton Forbes. The power plant was torn down in the 1970s after becoming obsolete. (Courtesy of Bob Killingsworth.)

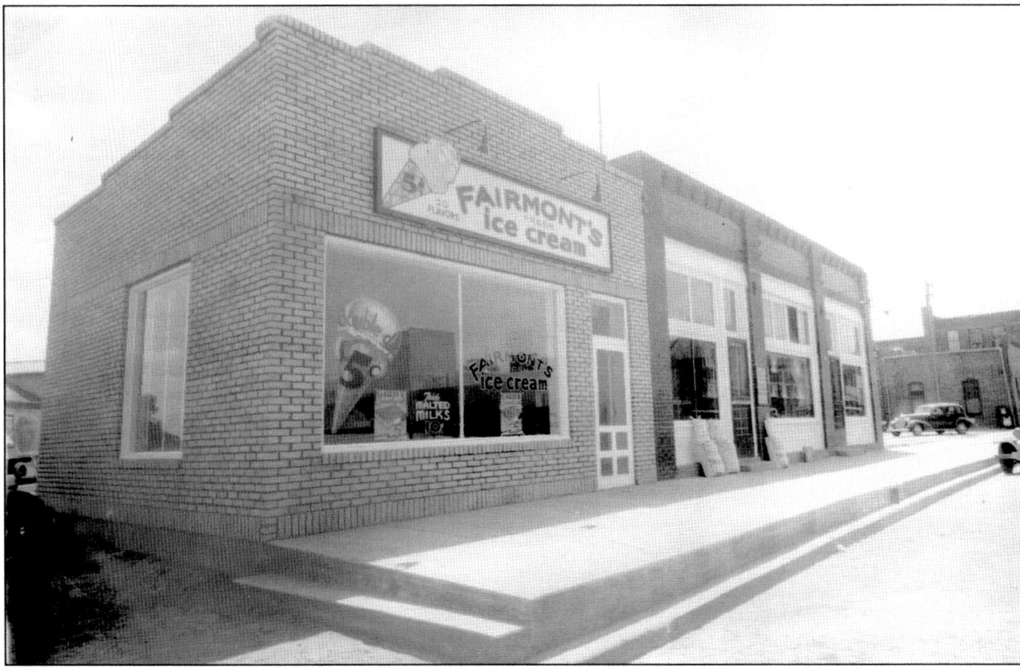

The Fairmont Ice Cream Parlor, located at 18 East Second Street, was the place locals frequented during hot Kansas summers. Maud Bruner and her daughters Mary Lou and Sue Ann kept all 20 flavors ready to be served. Next door was the Fairmont Creamery. Owen Keen delivered milk door to door to Liberal residents with his faithful horse and wagon for years. (Courtesy of Bob Killingsworth.)

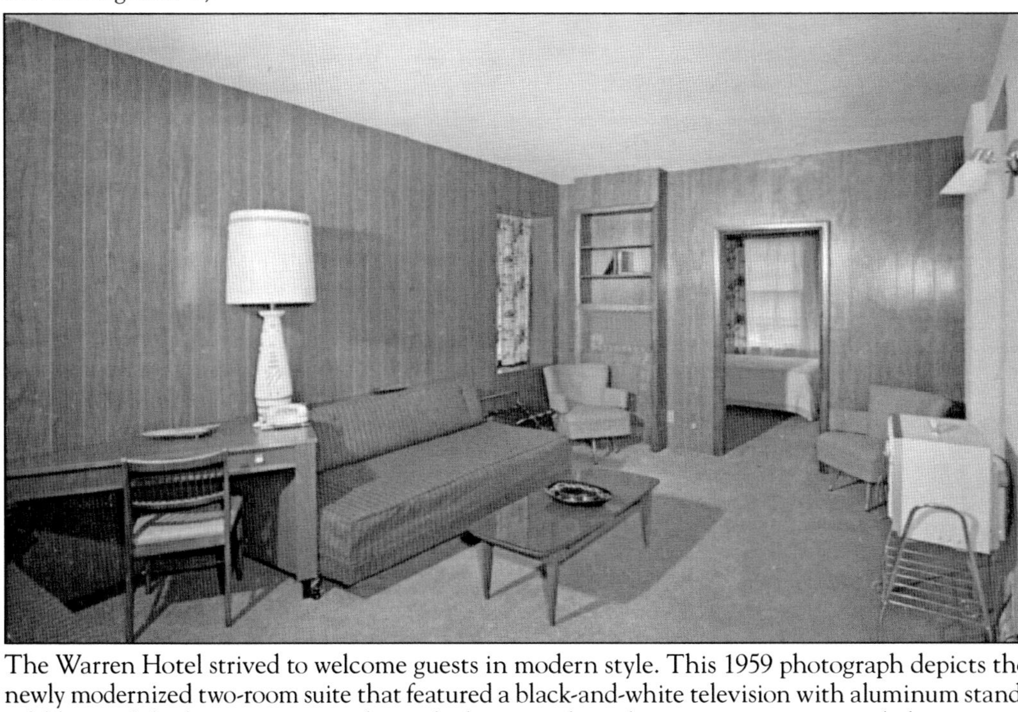

The Warren Hotel strived to welcome guests in modern style. This 1959 photograph depicts the newly modernized two-room suite that featured a black-and-white television with aluminum stand, a foldout sofa bed, a new princess-line telephone, and two burnt orange occasional chairs.

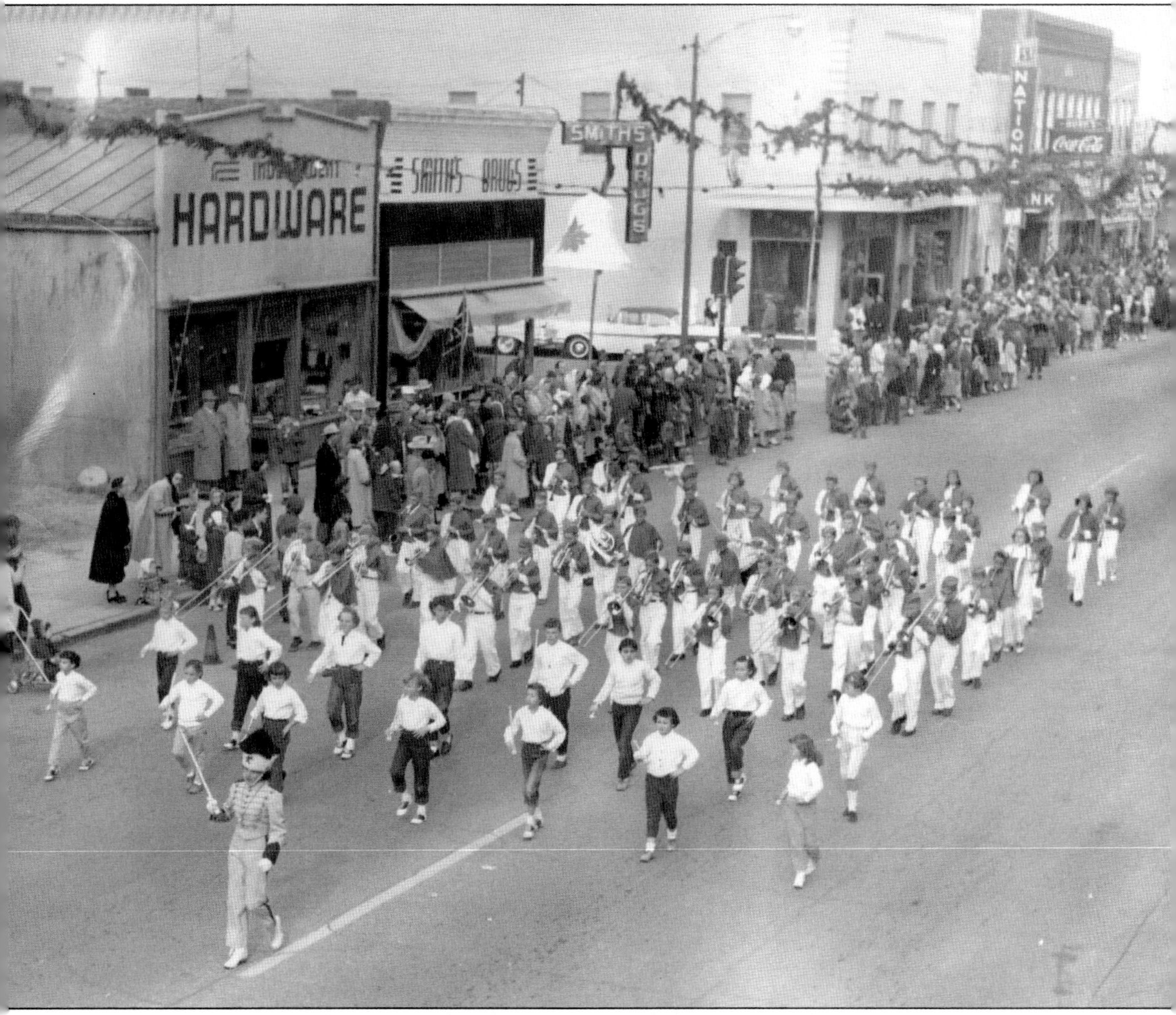

Downtown Liberal was decked out for the holidays and the annual Christmas parade in 1959. The crowd gathered to watch the floats and to listen to Liberal's Junior High Band. Independent Hardware, Smith Brothers Drug Store, Woods Dress Shop, Central Hotel, First National Bank, Burks Drug, and Black Drugs are visible in this photograph by Bud Kennedy.

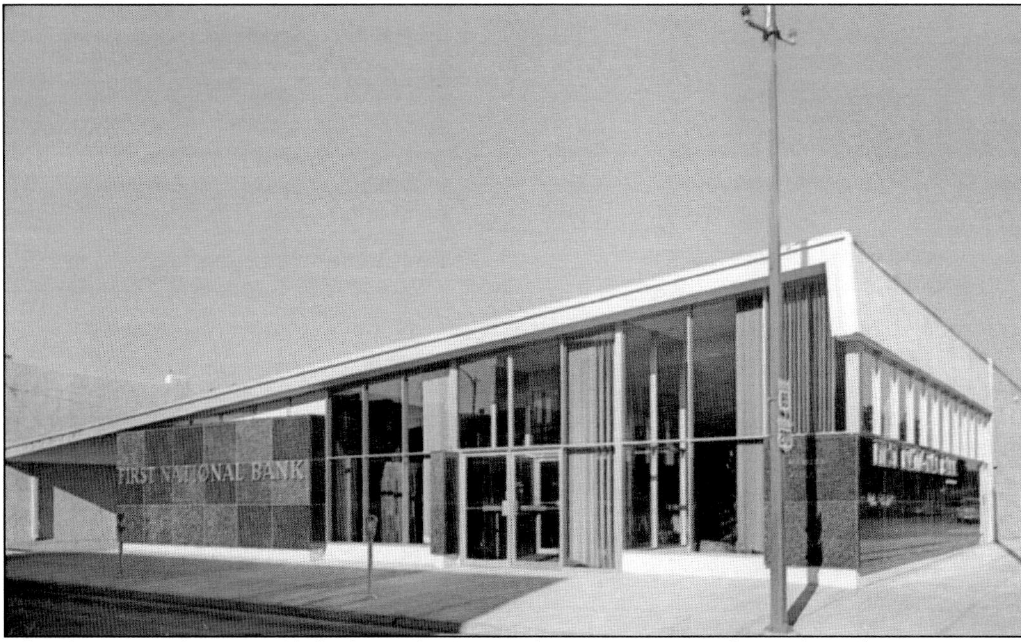

Liberal State Bank was established on July 13, 1900, by J.E. George, Paul Woods, and J.W. Berryman. The first location was at 220 North Kansas Avenue. The bank changed its name to First National Bank in 1903 and moved to 206 North Kansas Avenue, but after a customer fell through the floor, the bank began construction at 324 North Kansas Avenue in 1959. The new building created such a stir that bank director C.W. Law issued "sidewalk superintendent" licenses to the most ardent observers.

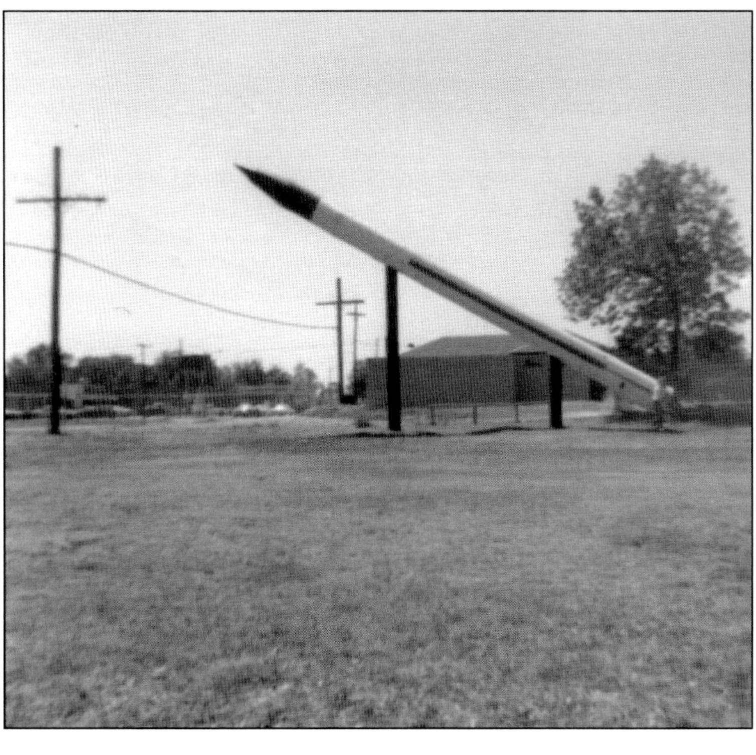

Located adjacent to the city swimming pool in Light Park, this Korean surplus rocket provided a place for children to explore and imagine. The rocket was completely hollow inside, except on summer days when there was usually a kid inside. The rocket disappeared without fanfare sometime in the mid-1970s.

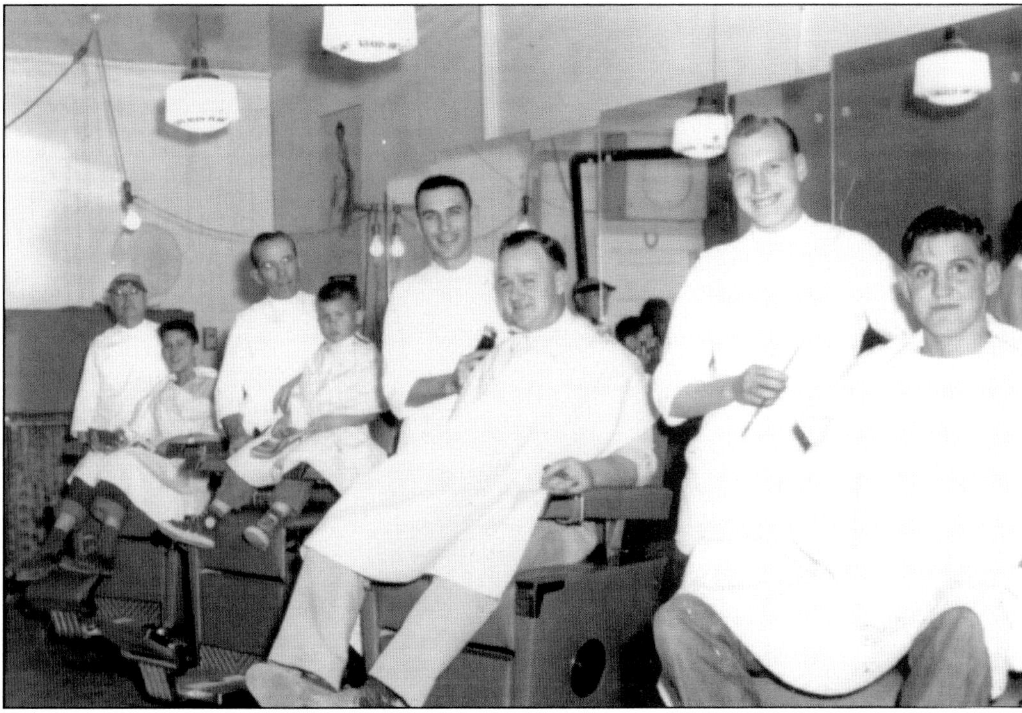

The barbershop was the place to catch up on the latest gossip while having a little taken off the top. Barbers are, from right to left, Charles Warden, Coy Miller, Ted Hanlin, and Forrest Warden. Customers are, from left to right, two unidentified, Bill Pittman, and Doug Pomeroy. The photograph was taken in 1953 at an unknown location. (Courtesy Seward County Historical Society.)

A 390-pound Graphotype machine and a Sensimatic bookkeeping machine help furnish the well-equipped city hall in 1955. Moving from cramped quarters at 324 North Kansas Avenue, the police station, city hall, and fire station were conveniently combined at 325 North Washington Avenue. (Courtesy of Seward County Historical Society.)

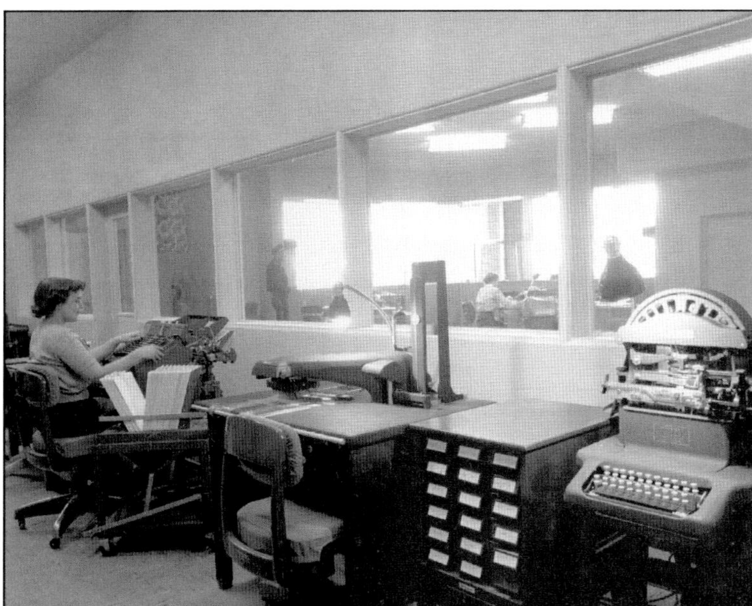

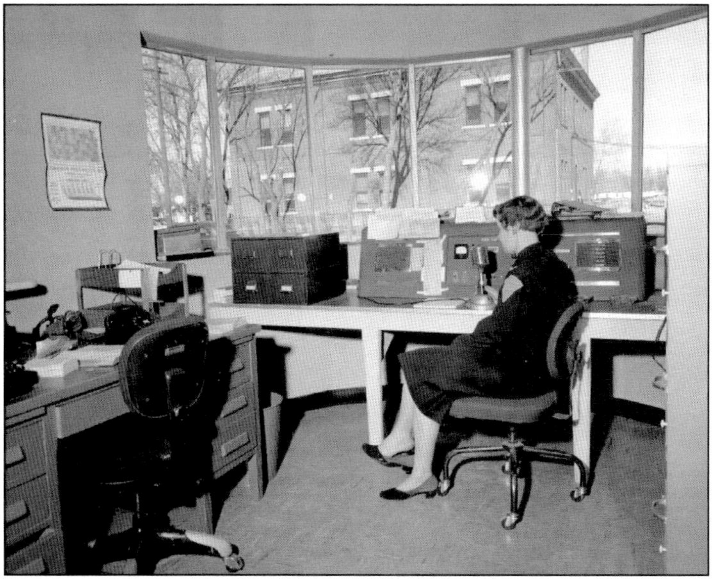

Working from her post at the Liberal Police Department, this policewoman handles the dispatching over her Motorola equipment. The police department had a bay window for good visibility and was just across the street from the two-story Seward County Courthouse. (Courtesy Seward County Historical Society.)

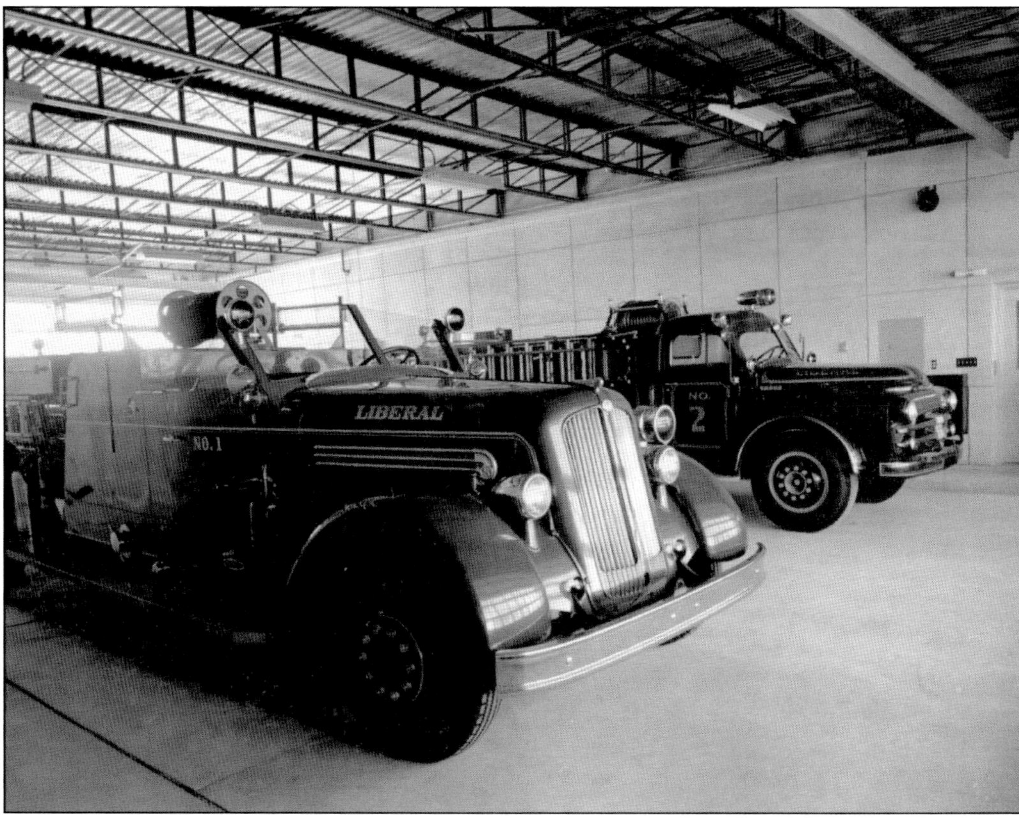

At the time of this 1955 image, the Liberal Fire Department was located adjacent to the police department, at 325 North Washington Avenue. A double-bay door flew open at the sound of the alarm so firemen and No. 1 and No. 2 fire trucks could respond immediately. The fire department moved to their new station at Fifteenth and Kansas in 1981. (Courtesy Seward County Historical Society.)

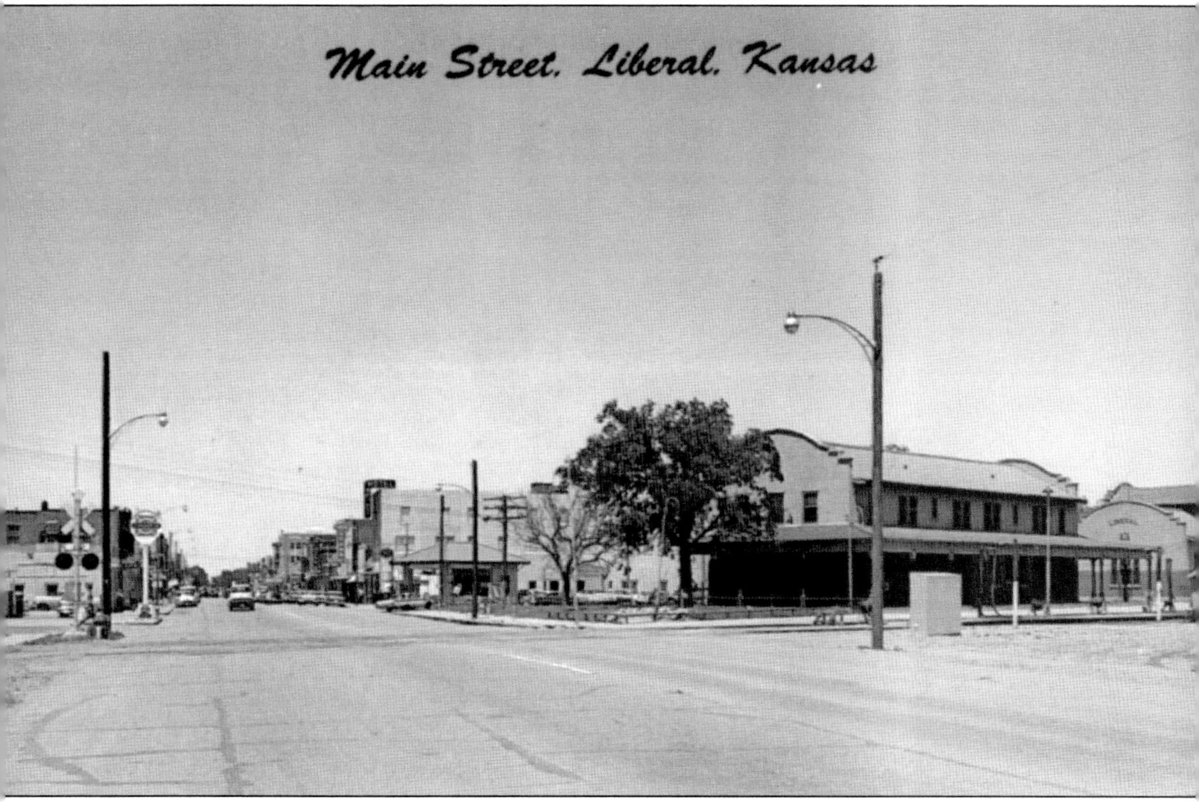

Kansas Avenue witnessed many changes since that beginning day in April 1888. Buildings have been erected, remodeled, torn down, and rebuilt again. Only the hardy, friendly, and determined people who made the decision to call Seward County home have remained the same.

www.arcadiapublishing.com

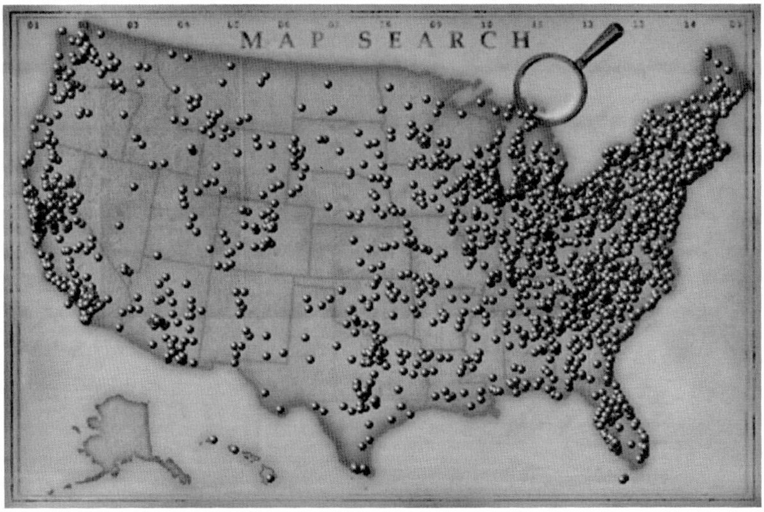

Discover books about the town where you grew up, the cities where your friends and families live, the town where your parents met, or even that retirement spot you've been dreaming about. Our Web site provides history lovers with exclusive deals, advanced notification about new titles, e-mail alerts of author events, and much more.

MADE IN THE USA

Arcadia Publishing, the leading local history publisher in the United States, is committed to making history accessible and meaningful through publishing books that celebrate and preserve the heritage of America's people and places. Consistent with our mission to preserve history on a local level, this book was printed in South Carolina on American-made paper and manufactured entirely in the United States.

This book carries the accredited Forest Stewardship Council (FSC) label and is printed on 100 percent FSC-certified paper. Products carrying the FSC label are independently certified to assure consumers that they come from forests that are managed to meet the social, economic, and ecological needs of present and future generations.

FSC
Mixed Sources
Product group from well-managed forests and other controlled sources

Cert no. SW-COC-001530
www.fsc.org
© 1996 Forest Stewardship Council

Find Your Place in History.